'Helen Pitt's exceptional book *The House* captures this saga in forensic detail. Pitt dovetails historical and political records with the social mores of Australia at the time. *The House* streams with material dug from old records and 10 years of research and interviews, meticulously recounting the battle over a building that, when heritage-listed in 2007, was described as a masterpiece in the history of humankind.'
Judges' comments 2018 Walkley Book Award

'It will fascinate its readers, even those not fortunate enough to be part of Generation Jørn.'
Sydney Morning Herald

'This is the closest you'll get to the Opera House walls talking.'
AU Review

'Thoroughly researched, colourful and shocking.'
Australian Book Review

'By breathing life into the assortment of characters cast by destiny to play a role in the construction of the Sydney Opera House, Helen Pitt has turned a history lesson into a drama-filled page-turner.'
Ita Buttrose AO OBE

'Australia in the seventies—mullets, platform shoes and, miraculously, the Opera House. At least we got one of them right. A great read.'
Amanda Keller, WSFm breakfast presenter

'Helen Pitt tells us so much about the building of the Sydney Opera House we've never heard before: even those of us who have worked for the NSW government. Like a piece of investigative reporting into our state's past, it's an absolutely fascinating account.'
Bob Carr, former Premier of NSW

'A Shakespearean drama of intrigue, misunderstanding, deception, the human failure enacted by Goossens the music visionary, Utzon the architect, Arup the engineer, NSW Government and the replacement architect Hall. All were losers except the people of Australia who gained the Sydney Opera House.'
Professor Philip Cox AO, COX Architects

'As gripping as Scandi-noir but set in Sydney.'
Ole Søndberg, Danish producer of The Girl with the Dragon Tattoo

'The gripping tale of our legendary Opera House, written with great eloquence by Helen Pitt.'
Marta Dusseldorp, actor

Helen Pitt is a *Sydney Morning Herald* journalist who has worked as the opinion and letters editor at Australia's oldest daily metropolitan newspaper where she began her career in 1986. She has worked as a writer for *The Bulletin* magazine, in California for *New York Times Digital*, and as a television reporter at *Euronews* in France. In 1992 she was selected to take part in the Journalists in Europe program in Paris. Her feature writing has won the Austcare Media award and been highly commended in the UN Media Peace prize.

The House

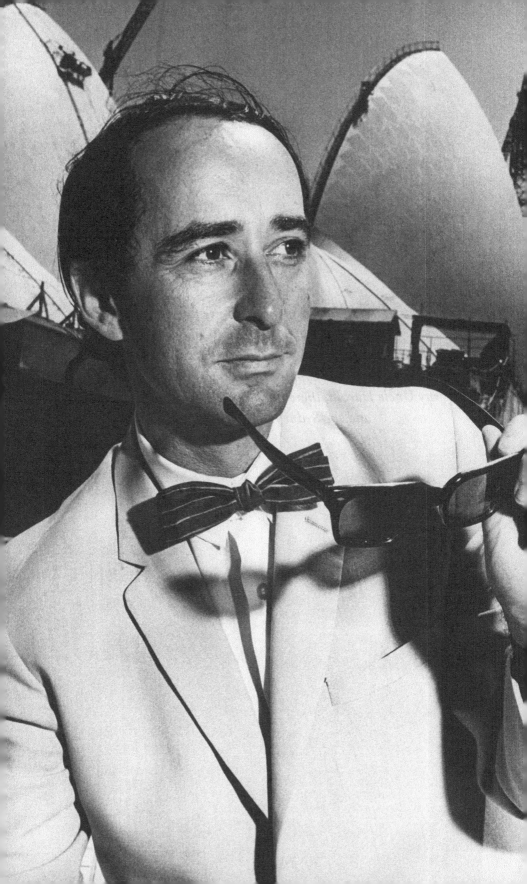

In loving memory of my family:
my father Allan, the analytical engineer;
my mother Grace, the pianist with perfect pitch;
my opera- and symphony-loving Aunty Margaret;
my Uncle Harold, there the day De Groot cut the ribbon;
and the Sydney of my childhood . . .

The House

The dramatic story of the Sydney Opera House and the people who made it

Helen Pitt

ALLEN&UNWIN

SYDNEY · MELBOURNE · AUCKLAND · LONDON

First published in 2018

Allen & Unwin
83 Alexander Street
Crows Nest NSW 2065
Australia
Phone: (61 2) 8425 0100
Email: info@allenandunwin.com
Web: www.allenandunwin.com

 A catalogue record for this book is available from the National Library of Australia

ISBN 978 1 76029 546 2

Internal design by Philip Campbell Design
Set in Sabon 11.25/15.75pt by Midland Typesetters, Australia
Printed and bound in Australia by Pegasus Media and Logistics

10 9

Contents

Prelude

Why we love the Sydney Opera House

I was driving across San Francisco's Golden Gate Bridge listening to the BBC World Service on the car radio when I heard that Danish architect Jørn Utzon had died. It was 29 November 2008. I felt an instant stab in my heart. We Sydneysiders born in 'Generation Jørn' all knew the great gift he gave our city: the Sydney Opera House. 'One of the indisputable masterpieces of human creativity, not only in the 20th century but in the history of humankind', as UNESCO described it in 2007 when it joined the World Heritage list.

I glanced to the right as I drove across the Golden Gate that day, almost expecting to see the magnificent white sails of the Opera House. I'd lived in San Francisco for nearly a decade at that point but was overcome with a wave of nostalgia for the city of my birth. As I listened to Utzon's obituary on the radio, instead of the San Francisco Bay, I saw a sparkling Sydney

Harbour and was transported back to Bennelong Point on a windy spring day in 1973.

I was an eight-year-old girl on 20 October, the day Australia's most famous building was officially opened by Queen Elizabeth II. With my family on a chartered ferry, I was perched in a prime position to catch a glimpse of the newly completed Sydney Opera House.

Like most Sydneysiders, we were eager to see the opening of our city's much-talked-about building. The harbour was packed with people on pleasure craft bobbing up and down in the swell. Out on the harbour there were more bikinis than mink furs. The white tiles of the sails glistened, slinky and smooth like the skin of a reptile sunning itself beneath a brilliant blue sky.

I got a little seasick, but my dad took me out on deck for a better view. 'Keep your eyes on the horizon,' he told me, as he looked through his binoculars to view proceedings at the Opera House up close. Listening to his 'tranny' radio through an earpiece, he pointed skyward and uttered words I still remember to this day: 'There's a black fella on top of the big white shell.' My uncle, who had watched the opening of the Sydney Harbour Bridge from atop its arch, thought it might have been a prank, just as Francis De Groot had galloped on horseback and 'opened' the bridge before state premier Jack Lang could cut the ribbon.

Aboriginal actor Ben Blakeney, wearing skin-coloured briefs—'a sort of black jock-strap' as he called it—stood on the top of the biggest shell. 'I am Bennelong—and my spirit and the spirit of my people lives: and their dance and their music and their drama and their laughter also remains,' he pronounced in the prologue to the opening ceremonies.

● ● ●

Decades after the ribbons were cut and the balloons and pigeons were let loose, Ben Blakeney's words have a resonance that I little understood as an eight year old. The spirit of the Aboriginal people who called this place Dubbagullee still inhabits the Opera House, as does the music and laughter of the many people from all over the world who built it. Its creation was the backdrop of my Sydney childhood—and the leitmotif of my parent's love story.

My parents became engaged in 1957, the year Utzon won the competition to design the Sydney Opera House. My dad, an engineer, had taken my mum, a pianist with perfect pitch, on a date earlier that year to see the entries at the Art Gallery. When they married in 1958, they planned to build a house on my grandparents' farm in Sydney's sprawling suburbs, very much along the lines of Jørn Utzon's Danish home—a simple rectangle with ceiling-to-floor glass letting in the sunlight. In March 1959, while having lunch in the Royal Botanic Gardens, my mother saw the 400 or so people gathered there for the sod turning that marked the official start of building. She followed the building from empty shell to final form in the way others followed the British royal family. After she died, I found a clipping from *Woman's Day* in her dressing table. It was headlined 'The Perfect Home' and told the story of the Utzon's Danish house 'with all the mod cons' and carried the simple sketch Utzon had drawn of his home. My parents were committed modernists— down to the Arne Jacobsen egg chairs. Like most Sydneysiders, we loved the Opera House.

Every Christmas and birthday in the 1960s and 70s we gave rice-paper thin Opera House Lottery tickets to family and friends. We had a jade plant by the door for luck, in the hope of winning an Opera House lottery, just like our neighbours who had splashed out on a swimming pool with their winnings.

We lined up like many eager Sydneysiders to take a tour inside 'the House' before the 1973 opening, and I can still see the colours of the Coburn curtains of the sun and moon hanging majestically in the Drama and Opera halls. I thought they were beautiful. I was transported to a magical place.

During the sixteen or so years I lived outside Australia, the Opera House was the only thing anyone ever knew about my home town. Sydney was a town, before the Opera House. After the Opera House, it became an international city. It remains the city's greatest urban story.

And every time I've flown into Sydney, often after long absences, it's the white tiles of the Opera House that tell me I've arrived. I don't see the Sydney Opera House, I see *my* Sydney Opera House. And my heart soars. I *am* home. It's such a part of the fabric of the city it's hard to imagine a time without it.

I wasn't the only one moved the day Utzon died, according to the then premier of NSW, Nathan Rees. At the 25 March 2009 state memorial for Utzon, held at the Opera House, he said: 'Utzon had a unique place in the affections of the Australian people. For many, his passing was like a personal bereavement. It is difficult to think of another foreign national whose death has meant more to Australians.'

• • •

In my more than thirty years as a journalist, I've covered more stories about the Opera House than I care to count. I have often wondered if the media should be blamed for the downfall and poor treatment of not just Jørn Utzon but also the conductor Eugene Goossens, who first championed the Opera House, and Australian architect Peter Hall, who completed it.

So, a bit like an archaeologist, I went on a dig into the past to find out. Reading the library files was like taking a time machine back to a different Sydney. I was stunned to see the column inches devoted to Jørn Utzon. When he died, it was front page news and the *Sydney Morning Herald* devoted more that two broadsheet pages to his obituary. Yet Peter Hall barely got a mention. His obituary was barely four paragraphs long. I had no idea how pivotal Hall was to completing the building, despite him working on the Opera House project for eight years, just one year short of the nine years Utzon toiled at it.

In Sydney, when it comes to the Opera House there are two kinds of people: those who believe its interiors and acoustics are imperfect and would have been much better if Utzon had completed it; and those who celebrate the fact it was completed at all, against the odds, and wonder if Utzon could have finished it anyway.

I've tried not to take sides. I am not an architect or an engineer, an opera singer or an acoustics expert. But I am a Sydneysider, so naturally I have my own relationship with this building.

Like all great works, the Sydney Opera House arouses great passions, and the retelling of the story may open some unhealed wounds and unresolved arguments. The drama lingers still like the backwash from a Manly ferry as it ripples across Sydney Harbour.

Chapter one

A phone call from half a world away

A tall man is walking in the woods with his wife in the middle of a deep Danish winter. Skinny beech trees surround them like giant silver stick figures, their dead brown leaves rattling in the January wind. Large larch trees, once sought as masts for sailing vessels, and ancient oaks majestic with moss, creak in the breeze. There is no snow on the ground, but it is coming. From afar the sinewy man, clearly a descendant from Vikings, and his almost white-haired Norse wife blend into the backdrop. Tall and slender like the trees.

They are not far from the Øresund, the stretch of water that separates Denmark from Sweden. The woodlands of Hellebæk, which means 'holy stream', are filled with trickling creeks that wind their way into lakes that glisten in the distance.

The pair venture out on their daily walk in the direction of the train line. They are savouring the soothing sounds of nature; relishing the outdoors. Think Nordic *noir*, but starring Gary Cooper and Ingrid Bergman.

The village of Hellebæk is around 40 kilometres north of Copenhagen. The train line runs right by the property, but their house is hard to find, hidden as it is at the end of one of the many woody unmarked trails. If the couple keep walking the five hundred metres or so to the end of the path they are on, it will dead end in the long white sandy coast of the island of Zealand. Scandinavians race skiffs on this shallow sea during the summer, when the beech trees are great green canopies of shade. Five hundred metres in another direction from their house is an old watermill, built in 1600, known as Hammermøllen. The thatched white building is perched on the edge of an idyllic lake in a forest clearing, reminiscent of the woodcutter's cottage in the *Hansel and Gretel* fairy tale. The water wheel was originally used to power a weapons factory that for centuries produced armaments to keep Danes safe from invading marauders. Then it fuelled Hellebæk's textile industry, which made this hamlet one of Denmark's first industrial centres. Workers arrived to populate the village's yellow row houses.

But this couple live in a modern yellow brick house in a forest clearing. The flat-roofed spartan structure they built in 1952 couldn't be more different from the nearby traditional village houses, which date to the 1740s. It is Denmark's first open-plan home, inspired by the vision of American architect Frank Lloyd Wright. Facing south to make the most of the northern hemisphere sunlight, it was built without plans other than paying attention to the laws of nature. Inside on this day, 29 January 1957, their newborn boy Kim is sleeping. Their daughter Lin, who is aged ten, is at home too. The baby—just four weeks old—was born on New Year's Day. It's an unremarkable domestic scene until the phone rings.

'Hello,' she says in the confident tone that only a little girl can muster when she's tasked with being the sole guardian of her baby brother.

Hellebæk is a tight-knit community, a small village of about two hundred people. Everyone knows everybody's business; but none more so than the local telephone operator, who is on the end of the line when the little girl answers.

'Lin, is your father home?' she asks in Danish. 'No' is the reply.

'Is your mother home?'

'No,' Lin tells her, 'they're out walking.'

The operator can't contain her excitement. 'Quick. Go find your father, he has won a prize. It's someone from the newspaper in Sydney, Australia—go tell him to come quick.'

Without hesitation Lin drops the phone, with the operator still on the other end of the line. She rushes out the door to her bike leaning against a brick wall, knowing this will be the fastest way to reach her parents to deliver the good news. Like a telegram boy.

She hops on and starts pedalling, without thinking about her clothing. She's lightly dressed for the Danish winter, so pedals as fast as she can to beat the cold. Her little legs pump the pedals like pistons as she races down the track.

She's like a comet streak. Her hair as white as snow is blowing in the breeze behind her. Fortunately, she knows exactly the route her parents have taken, though the trails around their home confound many outsiders.

She starts yelling, breaking the solemn silence of the forest. She screams, but from afar they can't hear her.

Lin has no clue about the significance of the message she is delivering. Only the fact that it is good news. And what little golden-haired girl doesn't want to deliver a piece of news like a prize win to her parents?

But, like most catastrophising parents, the thoughts of the couple walking in the woods turn to their children when they finally hear Lin's cries. The pair exchange worried glances and start running towards her. Has something happened to their baby? Has there been some accident? Perhaps it was a bad idea to leave her at home with a newborn?

'Sydney, Sydney,' she is chanting in breathless anticipation. But from afar they can't hear her.

It is bad news they are expecting as she slams on her back brakes when she reaches them and throws her bike into the nearby ditch.

Her wide smile comes as a pleasant surprise. 'You've won a prize, you've won something in Sydney, someone is on the phone and they want to talk to you,' she tells her father. Before she can help it, she blurts: 'Now you can buy me that white horse you have always promised me.'

The white horse is a storybook-inspired *Black Beauty* pre-adolescent fantasy. But it's another white fantasy—a building as daring as India's Taj Mahal—that is her father's preoccupation now. As it has been for the past six months. She can tell from his instant smile he's happy. He hugs her. Then he runs back to the house.

As he races back through the woods to take that phone call he is no doubt in shock. In disbelief. Could it be true that the sketches he submitted to the world-wide competition have really won? Has there been some mistake? Or would it be like the countless competitions he's entered before—where even a win quite often did not lead to a commission.

It has been a particularly bleak January, with the average temperature hovering around 0 to 1 degree Celsius. But suddenly the winter's day loses its dour complexion. As he runs toward his house, a shard of mother-of-pearl-coloured light pokes through the forest, like a 'finger of God' as if pointing to the 'chosen one'.

When he gets to the house, his heart is beating fast and he's out of breath. He steps onto the wooden floor warmed by its underground heating. He'd wanted to create a cosy home, something the Danes call *hyggelig*. He'd designed the simple chairs and tables in the living room himself. Until now, this house—complete with its ceiling-to-floor windows, skylight and interior courtyard—has been his proudest accomplishment. He zooms past the stone fireplace, hooded with gold-leaf aluminium, the hub of his family life, straight to the phone dangling off its cradle.

His hands are shaking, and he can barely speak as he picks up the receiver and hears the familiar voice of the Hellebæk phone operator congratulating him. Then come the words that will alter the course of not just his life, but also that of his family's and an entire nation on the other side of the world.

• • •

It's a sunny summer day in Sydney, 1957, as a reporter races down the eight sandstone steps of the city's art gallery. The winner of the Sydney Opera House design competition has just been announced at the National Art Gallery of New South Wales ('National' will be removed from its title a year later).

Inside the classical Greek temple–style building, the NSW Premier Joe Cahill and the competition judges are besieged by the press. The flash bulbs of cameras explode, and a frenzy of newsmen circle them. But one reporter, Martin Long, has slipped from the huddle and into a company car. The driver has been waiting patiently on Art Gallery Road for some time to whisk him back to the office.

They make their way through The Domain, the large tract of parkland in the heart of the city. Past the Moreton Bay fig trees, beneath whose shade speakers gather on Sundays to preach their soapbox oratory.

They skirt the edge of Hyde Park, its Archibald Fountain sprouting cool water into the hot afternoon summer sun, and finally speed past the imposing sandstone edifice of Sydney's Central Station. The company driver pulls up in front of the *Sydney Morning Herald*'s Broadway office at 235 Jones Street, a fourteen-storey drab grey building—a sort of skyscraper, by Sydney's standards at least. An information factory that looks like Superman's *Daily Planet* office. At the time, the tallest structure in the city is the fourteen-storey AWA Tower.

Long, a general reporter with an interest in classical music, steps out of the car and hurriedly makes his way to the elevator to rush to the *Herald*'s fifth-floor newsroom. As he walks into the building, the headquarters of the John Fairfax & Sons media empire, his mind is racing. How will he contact the winning entrant, number 218—whose name the premier pronounced as 'Yawn Ootzon'? In Denmark? Hopefully the operator can patch him through on the radio telephone. As he makes his way down the corridor to the newsroom, a smoke-filled cacophony of characters punching Olympia typewriters, he hears the unmistakable sound of journalists busy on their afternoon deadline. The announcement had been made at 3.32 p.m. Now it's well after 4 p.m. The Fairfax presses have been kept open for a special edition of *The Sun* newspaper—the company's afternoon tabloid—to announce the winner. The building is shaking as the presses roar into action. The smell of the hot metal and newsprint wafts into the air, mixing with the yeasty fumes from the nearby Kent Brewery. But the readers of next morning's *Herald* are expecting a little more information than the winner's name by the time their newspapers arrive.

As Long makes his way to the chief-of-staff's desk to brief

him, editors are yelling instructions at headline writers; reporters scream 'copy' once they have filed stories on duplicate pages of butcher's paper, typing 'MTC' (more to come) in the bottom right corner until they triumphantly type 'END' at its conclusion. Copy boys collect the small bundles of copy paper and dispatch them via vacuumed chutes to the typesetters and compositors downstairs, who wait to create hot metal pages for the printing presses. The telex machines are working overtime as they clatter out the news of the winning entrant to the waiting world.

This is going to be the *Herald*'s front-page lead. It's a big news day for Sydney. The city, the country and other parts of the world wait with bated breath for word of the winner. Across the city, Sydneysiders have gathered around their wirelesses to hear the news broadcast live on ABC Radio. Long knows the newspaper is sweating on him to talk to the competition winner in time for their first evening edition deadline of 10.50 p.m. He's filling in for Lindsey Browne, the regular opera critic.

He sits down at his desk in the newsroom, which the *Herald* shares with *The Sun*. As is his wont in stressful situations, Long runs one hand through his mane of thick black hair. He picks up the black Bakelite phone in his other.

• • •

From the very beginning the Opera House was conceived as an ornament for Sydney—like a pendant to adorn the neck of this beautiful city. And the *Herald*, Australia's oldest daily broadsheet newspaper, was one of the building's most ardent advocates, having first mooted the idea to construct an opera house in its pages in the early 1940s. Readers had been begging for something like it for years.

The paper's writers, editors and cartoonists had become influential in shaping the architectural fabric of the city. Its publishers, the Fairfax family, had not long ago moved the paper from its former headquarters on the corner of Pitt and Hunter streets (known affectionately as *Herald* Corner). The newspaper had outgrown its offices in the city's financial district, hence the move closer to Central Station, where trucks and trains could more efficiently deliver the country editions to regional NSW. It was all part of a bigger movement—a city expanding as it became more aware of its potential.

A team of reporters, photographers and illustrators had been selected to work on this breaking story. Martin Long, the second-in-charge of the opera and music round, had been chosen to rush back to the office and attempt to contact the competition winner, while others were left behind at the National Art Gallery to collect what's called 'colour', in newspaper parlance. No one was expecting he would have to make a phone call to far-off Europe.

One journalist talked to the judges, while the social writer worked the room making note of who was there. Ignoring the mainly male architects and politicians, she was looking out for those B-grade celebrities whose exploits provided fodder not just for the three tabloid Sydney newspapers, but also the staider broadsheet that was the *Sydney Morning Herald*.

Actress Barbara Wyndon was spotted. She'd made her name the previous year starring in the courtroom drama *Witness for the Prosecution* at Newtown's Elizabethan Theatre. The Elizabethan Trust had only been created a few years earlier, in homage to Elizabeth II's first visit to Australian shores in 1954 and in the belief that a new Elizabethan age was about to dawn in Australia. Such optimism had added to the momentum for those advocating an opera house.

The social reporter noted Miss Wyndon was the 'most excited woman in the room' when the National Opera House competition results were announced. The *Herald* photographer snapped Miss Wyndon in an elaborate headscarf standing between two men. She gazed lovingly into the eyes of her bow-tied husband, Hungarian-born architect Peter Kollnar. Kollnar, with his fellow Hungarian friend, Peter Kovac, had entered the design competition.

'I've had butterflies all day,' Miss Wyndon confessed to the reporter. 'Not only because of the competition, but because I'm doing my first TV show on ATN [now Channel 7] tonight. You know, I've got my hair in pins under this scarf.'

The social writer collected recipes of the food that had fuelled the entrants in their quest for architectural greatness. She collected anecdotes about which wives, girlfriends and mothers made midnight meals while entrants burned the midnight oil to make the competition deadline of 3 December 1956. Some cooked curries. Others constantly topped up coffee cups.

Walter Bunning had been a local favourite, being among the sixty-one Australian entrants in the competition. His wife Audrey confessed to a reporter on the phone that she had spent that morning in the city, but the tension had proven too much for her, the climax of two weeks of nerve-racking anxiety. At lunchtime she'd decided to go home to listen to the results on the air—or by a call from her husband—instead of going to the Art Gallery.

But the couple had made a pact. Win or lose, they would celebrate that night at Prince's in Martin Place—the 'in' place to eat in Sydney—just for the relief from all the strain.

• • •

As the colour and movement at the Art Gallery is being recorded, back at the Broadway newspaper office Long is talking to the *Herald* switch operator. 'I want a number in Denmark,' he tells her.

The call is to be made by radio telephone, state-of-the-art technology of the day. Notoriously unreliable, lines dropped out regularly, there were often long delays between questions, and interviews sounded like they were taking place underwater.

The newspaper's switch operator patches the call through to a central directory assistance hub in Copenhagen. Long hears some foreign language, obviously Danish, as the telephone operators try to communicate. Then some broken English explaining they will put the call through to the local operator in Hellebæk. He can't believe his luck when he gets through to the Hellebæk operator, who puts him through to the Utzon office. Then the heart-sinking news that Utzon isn't there. No matter, the operator reassures, we'll try him at home. She knows his number, he lives near her village.

Eureka! thinks Long when the operator tells him the architect's young daughter has run to get Mr Utzon.

It's only a few minutes he has to wait for the winner to come to the phone, but it seems like an eternity. It's already early evening and his bosses are getting impatient. One shoots him a look from the other side of the newsroom that says, 'hurry up'. He wants to get the scoop. Not just Sydney, but the world wants to hear from the winner.

The line crackles as Long asks if he is speaking to Jørn Utzon. There is silence, a delay, then a 'yes'. Long asks him how he feels about the news he has won the Sydney Opera House competition.

'Overjoyed,' Utzon replies.

Then he hesitates, worrying perhaps that this call might be a hoax. 'So far, the Opera House Committee has not contacted me, but I am expecting a cable at any moment. It depends on what they can advise me how soon I migrate. But I shouldn't think I would have a great deal of trouble getting a good position in Australia now, do you? It must be a wonderful country with plenty of what we have not been getting lately—sunshine.'

His wife Lis and daughter Lin walk through the door as he is on the phone. He flashes his wife a huge smile and nods, not that she needs confirmation. The fact that he's speaking in English indicates he is speaking to somebody in Australia about the competition he had entered there. Her mouth curls in a smile back at him before she races in to check on their newborn.

'Mr Utzon,' Long asks from Sydney, 'can you tell us a little bit about yourself?'

Utzon goes on. He is thirty-eight and has been a member of the Danish Association of Architects since 1942. He has done a few housing projects and small commissions. 'We have three children—a boy aged twelve, a girl aged ten and our baby son, who was born on New Year's Day this year. This news from Australia is almost as good as the news of his arrival. My wife is just as thrilled about the win as I am. I have won twenty prizes for architectural design before, in Denmark and Sweden, including six first prizes. But this is far and away the most important.'

Long takes all this down quickly in flawless shorthand. Verbatim. 'Could you tell us, Mr Utzon, how long you spent on your design of the Opera House?' he asks.

'I spent about six months, from May to December 1956. Whenever I could get time off from my other work. I studied hundreds of pictures, photographs and maps of the site. It is a very lovely position for an opera house and most inspiring to any architect. But from this distance it naturally took a great feat of the imagination to "see" it in its setting.'

• • •

By the time Utzon put down the phone from that first interview with the *Sydney Morning Herald*, friends and colleagues had started streaming into his home. The news had spread quickly.

He telephoned Erik Andersson in Sweden, one of two
brothers he'd been working with when he entered the competition. Utzon signed the work as his, although the Anderssons later
said they had worked together with Utzon on the project. Andersson raced to the Helsingborg ferry terminal in Sweden to take the
three nautical mile ferry ride across to Helsingør in Denmark,
to celebrate with Utzon. The telegram from the Opera House
Committee, congratulating him on his win, was delivered eventually via the post office. By a telegram boy. Someone else brought
French champagne. By the afternoon a party was in progress.

As the champagne corks popped, the phone rang again.
This time it was Emery Barcs, a reporter from Sydney's *Daily
Telegraph* newspaper, on the radio telephone line. He could
hear the excited chatter of Utzon's wife, children and friends in
the background as the Dane let out a large laugh down the line.
'How do you feel about your success?' asked Barcs.

'I'm terribly happy,' Utzon replied in his heavily accented
English. 'We are celebrating. There is plenty of champagne.'

'What inspired your design?' the reporter asked.

'The beautiful pictures I have received of Sydney Harbour—
all sorts of pictures, not only of Bennelong Point, but also of the
whole harbour. It must be one of the most beautiful spots in
the world. I have dreamt of it so much. Then came the idea with
that roof. Do they like it in Sydney?'

Barcs assured Utzon they did. Then he asked what he'd built
so far and what he intended to do with the 5000 pound prize
money. Another great boom of laughter came 12,000 miles
down the phone line, Barcs reported.

'Of course, I need all the money to come to Australia and
I'll bring the whole family. It's a long way and it will cost a lot
of money. But I hope the fare won't take the lot of it. What do
you think?'

After assuring Utzon he would have some pocket money left over from the prize money, Barcs asked whether he would like to come to Sydney for good.

'Not sure, depends . . . at least I mean I want to go for a long time. I mean, it depends whether they want me permanently. An opera house is not built in a day, you know—not even in Australia.'

The revellers are getting noisy. Utzon has to shout down the line to say farewell. 'Thanks for ringing me. Was a nice thing to do. We are very, very happy . . . au revoir, in Sydney,' and he laughed again.

When he hung the telephone handpiece back on the wall in his house in Hellebæk, Utzon was euphoric. Knocks on the door followed; more people arrived, carrying bottles of champagne. They drank France's finest from flutes as they toasted the good news.

• • •

The stream of well-wishers would continue after Andersson arrived on the ferry from Sweden and well into the Tuesday night. At one point, Utzon stepped outside into the cold in order to calm his mind, which was racing as fast as a sailboat with its spinnaker unfurled. As always, it was to nature that this man returned whenever he wanted to feel at one with the world. The simplicity of the natural world soothed him.

There was a reassuring rhythm to life in this place not far from the sea that he called home. Its harsh winter climate would slowly transform into the euphoria of spring and then into beautiful long summer days, when soft sunlight would stretch well into the night. He thought back over what had led him to this moment, undoubtedly one of the high points of his life so far.

What the newspaper reporters hadn't unearthed in those first phone calls was that Utzon was dyslexic. 'I was the second dumbest boy in my class at school,' he would later joke. But in years to come, many would wonder whether the fact that he predominantly thought in pictures, rather than in words, was a key to his brilliance. Perhaps that helped him imagine something into existence in a city he'd never seen on the other side of the world. During long nights, he'd sketched plans, working his left drawing hand until it cramped. For hours he'd pored over the tidal charts of Sydney Harbour in the same way that he'd studied similar charts as a young Sea Scout. Yet most important was his capacity to imagine on paper the opera house he proposed to build. Although he didn't like to read, he had soaked up information about Sydney like a sponge.

But now, he was thinking about another competition in another time and place—this one, a competition he had lost. It was in his childhood home of Aalborg, where his love affair with boats and building beautiful things had begun.

● ● ●

Chapter two

Chapter two

The young Jørn

A sole seagull's forlorn cry echoes across the water of the Limfjord, as young Jørn struggles to control the mainsail of an old wooden dinghy. He is at the bow of the boat, pulling on the ropes, while his older brother Leif is back at the stern on the tiller. The wind is whipping down the waterway and they are gathering speed. They are skippering a small boat in a Sea Scout regatta in Jutland, and they are winning the race.

Both boys are impeccably dressed in their Danish Sea Scout uniform: their sailor's caps are perched perilously on their heads despite the wind, and their twirled neckerchiefs are kept neatly in place by their woggles, the loops of leather that are a requirement of Lord Baden-Powell's boys' movement. Jørn is eight and Leif is ten, but already the love of the sea and sailing boats pumps through their veins.

This is no surprise, given that their father Aage is the naval engineer at Aalborg's shipyard. Aage trained as a ship's engineer first in Denmark, and then at Armstrong College in Newcastle, England; he is a well-respected community member in this industrial city 400 kilometres north of Copenhagen. An athletic man, he's a hunter and a sailor who likes to take his boys on expeditions. His winters are spent shooting—both clay pigeons for pleasure and deer, elk and other wild animals for food. He teaches his young sons how to use shotguns in the nearby woods. From a young age Jørn has often drawn what he sees on these shooting expeditions, and his early illustrations show a prodigious talent. This has given his parents some relief, as their second son didn't really talk until he was about four.

Summers are spent sailing, no matter how cold the weather or the water. On this day the naval engineer is standing on the waterfront, watching his boys as the wind fills their dinghy's sails and carries them swiftly along the waterway.

Aage and his wife Estrid, whose family originated from Latvia when it was part of the Russian Empire, moved here when Jørn was a baby. They have a third son Erik, who is aged two and is back at their rented home with his mother. It is an overcast summer's day in 1926. The weather can be challenging in this part of Northern Europe, but Aage is the sort of father who feels this is no excuse for his sons to stay indoors. He rarely has trouble coaxing his boys out of their home and into the fresh air, as he has done on this day of the Scout regatta.

Clouds are a particularly favourite natural phenomenon for Aage, and over time he will teach all three of his sons to read them, just like tide charts. To know that cauliflower-shaped cumulonimbus clouds can produce thunderstorms and heavy rain, and to be cautious when they recognise a shelf cloud, as it is often a harbinger of strong winds. With his long naval experience, he has seen many fine sailors come undone because of their inability to act upon the signs that were written in the

clouds. He believes sailing is like building boats: one part pragmatic, the other part poetic.

Aage insists his sons respect nature, that they surrender to
its greater powers and learn to properly read the sky and the sea.

Perhaps because of northern Jutland's seafaring past,
learning to read the skies has always been a crucial skill for
anyone who wanted to sail there. It was a survival skill, part of
the Danish DNA since Viking days. Everyone wanted to avoid
having their vessel become a shipwreck like those off the coast of
Skagen, a hundred kilometres north of Aalborg and Denmark's
northernmost point, which is a graveyard of wrecks destroyed
by high seas and sailors who failed to read the signs in the skies.

'Always keep your head in the clouds—literally,' Aage
advised his sailing sons as they set out this day to attempt to win
the race. 'Read them—don't daydream when you are out at sea.'

His sons heed his advice on most things, but especially
sailing. On the day of the competition, Aage watches on as the
two skilfully steer their boat despite their youth and relative
inexperience. There's a strong offshore breeze, and the water is
teeming with jellyfish—both the *vandmænd* (blue moon jellyfish) and the *brandmand* (red firefighter jellyfish). Any Sea Scout
in Denmark knows a sting from a cold water jellyfish tentacle
can hurt so much it will ruin a summer's day. It's a strong moti-
vation not to fall in.

Aalborg (the name means 'eel castle') is a bleak industrial city in northern Jutland whose deep port is dominated
by commerce. The herring fishing industry is centred here, as
are the naval shipyard, the Dansk Sprit factory (makers of that
Scandinavian alcoholic staple aquavit) and the Obels tobacco
factory. The unmistakable aroma of tobacco hangs heavy amid
the cloud-laden skies that dominate in winter and often summer
too. The white sails of small craft are a welcome respite in an

otherwise busy working port. Each day after the school bell
rings at Klostermarksskolen, the private primary school the
Utzon boys attend, it's to the water they go for pleasure—entertaining themselves either at their father's shipyard, 5 kilometres
east of the city centre, or on the deep harboured waterfront
where they sail or float the model boats they have built with
their father. Jørn loves the freedom sailing provides: the silence,
the chance to escape the drudgery of school life. He loves the
feel of the wind tousling his hair and the way his skin tingles
and tightens from the saltwater spray. But the Sea Scout sailing
boats frustrate him and his brother. They are old, shoddily
crafted boats—a point of contention for the boys, who are both
keen competitors.

On this day, when it looks like a win is certain, they are
all smiles and confidence. They wave to their father onshore.
His mouth moves into a half grin. He's privately proud, and
waves back.

The brothers tack and jibe, harnessing the wind to manoeuvre
their boat at just the right angle, adding some excitement to this
otherwise grey day. They are now coming to the finishing line
and are well ahead of the rest of the pack.

But, just as they are picking up speed and look to be
winning the race, their boat starts taking on water as a wind
gusts down the channel. Suddenly their boat capsizes, through
no fault of their own. This has happened before time and time
again. However well they rig their craft before setting sail, nearly
all the Aalborg Sea Scouts have at some point been ousted from
their vessels due to choppy conditions combined with unsatisfactory naval engineering.

Out they go into the Limfjord. The cold water takes their
breath away. It's hard to know what hurts more: the disappointment of losing the race or the jellyfish sting.

They finally clamber back into the boat and negotiate it to shore. Their father catches up with them dolefully dragging the vessel onto dry land. 'These boats are useless, there must be a way to design something better to sail,' Jørn complains. 'Can't you build a better boat?' he asks his father.

It's not the first time the young sailors have complained about the Sea Scouts' poor-quality dinghies, but this is the first time Aage vows to do something to remedy the problem. Their father is a firm believer in the pursuit of healthy outdoor sports for young boys and he doesn't need poor equipment as an excuse for them not to participate. As an active Aalborg Yacht Club member, Aage sponsored their new clubhouse, built from a scrapped steamer's steering house in his own shipyard. Like his sons, he knows the boats are their main handicap in racing.

'All right,' he placates them. 'Let me see what I can do.'

• • •

Before Jørn's birth, Aage Utzon was already a renowned wooden boat builder. In 1915, with a friend called George Berg, he designed his first boat, a *spidsgatter*, a craft that is pointed at both ends just like the Viking vessels of long ago. It was streamlined—especially crafted so that it slipped through the water smoothly, unlike the scout dinghies his sons were forced to sail in—and was called a 'crow-dinghy' in Danish, because its bow was pointed like the beak of a bird. The two friends later fell out. They had competing claims over who had designed the boat and they also had different methods of working. Berg, an experienced sailor, tended to base his designs on his sailing experience.

Aage was more theoretical and experimental. He was never hesitant; after so many years of boat building, he always knew what he wanted to do. His mantra was: observe, experiment, improve. Observe, experiment, improve. And to bear in mind the solution was only the next experiment away, which is the curse and blessing of every perfectionist. In the year Jørn was born, he designed a boat called a Shamrock, another sharp-sterned boat. Like his son, Aage had difficulty reading and writing; instead, he spent a lot of time outdoors hunting or sailing, usually daily.

Aage was a keen observer. Perhaps it was his life as a hunter that had developed these observational skills. In the process of boat building he often lay on his stomach on the deck of one of his boats when it was out at sea, with his head over the side of the ship to observe the water's current flow along the sides of the hull. He was particularly focused on studying the sea current flow around the hull; it was crucial for speed and sailing smoothly. In his mind, the next boat could always be a little better; he was all about optimising. It was a part of Jørn's upbringing to observe, to experiment and to improve, just like his father. The perfect solution was only ever one more experiment away.

During his many years as a boat designer—professionally and for pleasure—Aage developed his own method, which was largely based on his observations of nature. He came up with the idea for his *spidsgatter*'s bow after watching ducks swimming and the way the water parted while they glided over the water.

'Always look to nature, you'll find your solution there,' were his wise words for even the most complex of design challenges. This piece of advice he would give often to his workers at the shipyard, and later to his sons. Jørn would find it inspiring on many occasions. Nature was a panacea for all problems, his father felt.

The Utzon approach to boat building was his approach to building anything. He could not get it simple enough, which explains why his boats were only ever described as elegant. Everything in them is connected with the main form. When you construct boats for competition, he'd say 'perfection is the goal'.

By day he worked in the shipyard and at night he designed sailboats at home, often lying on the floor of the family home to make full size line drawings. Not just sketching them but making wooden models. The models were the key to his success—and his boys were recruited into model making too, a skill Jørn would come to be grateful to his father for later.

Aage would toil into the wee hours—his fingers carefully manoeuvring the tiny wooden pieces into a magnificent model of the boats he dreamt of making. Like a jigsaw puzzle the pieces would all eventually come together. It was laborious work, but a lot was learnt—not just by the boat builder, but also his boys.

Jørn would watch on in awe, observing the care his father took drafting perfect curves for the hulls of his boats so that they were watertight. Like the method used to build larger ships at the shipyard, Aage would use geometric templates known as French curves to carefully create the wooden curvature of these pleasure craft. Boat building, it is said, is an act of throwing money into the water; it's one of the most expensive pastimes you can choose as a hobby. But it's an obsession that borders on compulsion for most who practise it. Aage Utzon was no exception.

Many Danes in Jutland have inherited the skill and love of working in wood, as their Viking forebears had done crafting seafaring boats. It's much the same skills another carpenter, Ole Kirk Christiansen, at the opposite end of Jutland, used to craft small toys for his children out of local wood, which led to the creation of the Danish toy empire Lego. Wood turning and modelling is a favourite hobby to while away the long winter hours in this rural part of Denmark.

While trying to find a solution for his seafaring sons, Utzon senior paid close attention to the other boats in the Limfjord area; particularly what the Danes called a *sjaegte*, a simple dinghy used for centuries for inshore fishing, transport and pilot operations. They were *spidsgatter* too—sharp-stern boats with a simple rigging and no boom on the mainsail, which made them easier to navigate, especially for Sea Scouts. All they needed was the slightest nudge of wind. Even a beginner could learn to sail them.

• • •

In 1929, when Jørn was eleven, his father designed what became known as the 'Aalborg dinghy', which was an improvement on his earlier efforts with George Berg. Utzon's design would eventually become the standard boat for Sea Scouts all over Denmark and Scandinavia. Champion sailors went on to win regatta after regatta in the boats Aage Utzon designed. On the Limfjord his boats became the envy of other sailors, not just Sea Scouts. An uncompromising perfectionist, Aage personally supervised the construction of all the boats he designed for the youth program. He wanted each boat built to his exacting standards. The boat's reputation grew, and it was soon in demand from racing sailors all over Europe as well as the United States.

Aage, a jovial and generous man, found a sponsor for his dinghy design and gave his drawings for free to anyone who wanted to build the boat. He became well known in the boat-building world beyond Aalborg. Eventually about six to seven hundred dinghies were built around the world. This was his contribution to the youth sailing program, and it earned him international respect in yachting circles. The name Utzon became synonymous with good boat design. You could say, as the five million or so Danes like to joke, 'he was world famous, in Denmark'.

On Sundays young Jørn would accompany his father to the local boat builders, who would receive very detailed instructions on how to build his boats. Jørn inhaled the smell of wood shavings, gazed at the wooden frames and watched and learnt from his father's interactions with the expert builders.

The hull of a *spidsgatter* was smooth, but its frame structure was visible on the inside and was so neat and perfect that it looked like the work of a fine tailor. The key to the boat's shape was in the precision with which its ribs were carved, like a whale bone corset. Aage always insisted on producing full-scale drawings for the ribs, to ensure their accuracy. This was the lesson Jørn took from his father: if a thing was worth doing, it was worth doing well, inside and out. To make a vessel watertight, you had to apply the same principles as you do to making a building rock solid. You get there only through fastidious logical steps.

This quest for perfection would stay with young Jørn, as did the task of making what seemed impossible real. It led to the creation of his own sort of mantra for architecture but also an approach to life which was exhilarating: to drive yourself to tasks that seemed impossible at first but with hard work turned out not to be; to be 'on the edge of the possible'. This would become how the Utzons—both senior and junior—liked to live.

When Jørn was twelve, not long after his father had enjoyed success with the Aalborg dinghy, Aage walked into their home after a hard day's work with a pamphlet in hand. It was an advertisement for the 1930 Stockholm Exhibition. Everyone at the shipyards had been talking about the event known in Swedish as the Stockholmsutställningen. By spring that year, it had started to create a buzz throughout Scandinavia.

Aage had no trouble convincing Estrid that bundling their boys into a train carriage and heading to Sweden would be a great adventure. Estrid was always described by others as a welcoming and warm woman, though deeply sensitive. She always indulged her husband's passions, but this was an idea she felt her boys

would benefit from. An exhibition celebrating Scandinavia, an
early incarnation of an IKEA showroom of ideas about ways to
live more simply and efficiently. Who could refuse?

Jørn and his older brother were by now at Katedralskole,
the private high school in Aalborg. Leif was a star student, but
Jørn struggled. They were both enrolled in the mathematics-
natural science stream, but maths was not Jørn's strong point.
This, coupled with his dyslexia, meant school was not his favourite place. He did poorly in exams and preferred to be out in the
fresh air, either sailing or hunting, rather than being at his desk
with books.

Estrid hoped a trip abroad might provide the sort of inspiration her middle son seemed to need. In the summer of 1930,
the Utzons took the train to Copenhagen, from where they
caught the ferry to Sweden and then travelled on by train to the
Swedish capital.

In much the way an Olympic Games transforms a city
and a nation, the Stockholm Exhibition reshaped Sweden. It
celebrated all things Scandinavian; specifically, it set out to celebrate the culture of industrialism. The idea was to modernise
the Swedish economy by leaving behind the traditional craft
methods of production and embracing the technology of mass
production that was beginning to appear in factories everywhere. As a showcase of the best products Sweden had to offer
and an attempt to reshape public taste, it was a resounding
success. It attracted more than four million visitors, 25,000 of
them from abroad. It played a major role in establishing functionalism—and the International Style—as the predominant
architectural style in northern Europe post-World War I. This
led to the movement called Modernism which, shunning tradition and embracing the new in art and architecture, transformed
much of the Western world. This was a breakthrough moment

for head architects Erik Gunnar Asplund and Sigurd Lewerentz, whose names became known throughout Scandinavia.

As a naval engineer Aage Utzon was enthralled from the moment he arrived, especially by the contents of the new domestic interiors, from furniture to light fittings. As an aesthete who looked to nature to help create form, he had often struggled to find a function for the beautiful things he admired. So, this was the first time he could see how form and function might merge, and he became a convert to the clean lines of functionalism. Modular shelving in cubic storage units sat beside leather chairs and sleek lamps in a number of the pavilions, all designed by Scandinavians who would go on to become household names the world over. The living spaces were uncluttered, uncomplicated and light-filled. It heralded a new way of seeing interior design for the Utzon family, both parents and children.

The exhibitors embraced nature, opting for south-facing windows to let light and nature inside in the showcase of new housing alternatives. 'It consistently propagates a healthy and unpretentious lifestyle based on economic realities,' Finnish architect Alvar Aalto explained. It's easy to see the appeal for Aage, who was such a nature lover. But Jørn too walked around the exhibition with eyes as wide as saucers, embracing everything before him with the zeal of a new-found modernist, especially the entry pavilion with its exposed steel frame and airy expanse of glass that was dramatically lit at night.

Although temporary, the exhibition had a lasting impact on many budding designers. The Paradise Restaurant, where visitors such as the Utzons would stop to rest and dine, was a favourite meeting place. As creator of the entry pavilion and the Paradise Restaurant, Erik Gunnar Asplund's name was marked indelibly on the twelve-year-old Utzon's brain. Sparseness and simplicity were the goals of the new Scandinavian style.

On their return to Denmark, the Utzons embraced these ideas. Because of his time in northern England, Aage had always had a British sensibility. The furniture in their Aalborg home was Victorian era—dark, heavy mahogany and teak. Conventional, safe, middle class. But on their return from Sweden, they changed all of that with a huge spring clean (at the end of summer!). They got rid of all that sombre and impractically heavy old furniture and replaced it with simpler, lighter and more functional pieces in the new Scandinavian style. Items that everyone in the family could pick up and move if they needed to. They started to eat more healthily, and Estrid was inspired to include more fresh food in their diet, which they grew themselves or foraged for in the forests, in a national movement that would make Danish cuisine distinctive many decades later. They bought bikes to cycle around Aalborg and relished the new Scandinavian style of living simply.

It also exposed the artistic young Jørn to architecture. Previously, when he had visited his father at the shipyards, Aage would often enlist his middle son's help in drawing plans for the ships. Aage had wanted to encourage him to enlist in the navy, but his poor school grades stood in the way of him pursuing a career as a naval architect in his father's footsteps.

Jørn began to focus on his drawing and art. One summer holiday at his grandmother's house in Ålsgårde, which overlooked the coast of northern Zealand, he met a Swedish painter, Carl Kylberg. Kylberg taught him to draw in a more free-form way—not with the precision of naval architecture as his father had taught him, but in a more expressive way, using materials like soft pencils and charcoal. It liberated his drawing style. It helped him to refine his talent in a way his school lessons had not done.

In 1936 there was a knock on the door at the family home in Aalborg. It was a telegram offering Aage Utzon a promotion.

It was a new position as manager of the Helsingør shipyard north of Copenhagen, where he would be in charge of the entire shipbuilding process, not just the engineering.

By the summer of 1937, Jørn had finished school and he moved with his family to Copenhagen, where his elder brother Leif was already studying engineering. Jørn was torn between a career in art and one in architecture. On the strength of his freehand drawing, rather than his mathematical skills, he enrolled in architecture at Copenhagen's Royal Danish Academy of Fine Arts, in September 1937 at the age of nineteen. Here, he studied with some of the best and brightest young intellects of his era until an event on his twenty-second birthday that would alter not just the course of his life, but also the lives of all Danes.

Chapter three

Scandi-style

The evening of 8 April 1940 was a critical moment for both Jørn Utzon and Denmark.

It was early spring and the days were getting longer, with the sun not going down until late. The city was awash with colour: the pink of the cherry blossoms, and the purple, white and yellow of the blooming crocuses. The normally reserved Utzon was in the mood to celebrate. The slightly socially awkward architecture student was thrilled to be invited to the twenty-first birthday of a surgeon's daughter from Jutland, the same region where Utzon was raised.

When he'd started studying architecture, he was the youngest and least mature in his class. He was initially shy, and coming from northern Jutland meant he was the butt of jokes in cosmopolitan Copenhagen.

His friend and fellow architecture student Halldor Gunnløgsson was only a month older than Jørn, but he was worlds

apart from the middle son of a naval architect from the rural
north. Gunnløgsson was the son of a flamboyant, divorced
Icelandic actress who was independently wealthy. When he
got drunk, which he did often, he went berserk, much like
the Berserkers, the Norse warriors he was descended from,
who, according to the Icelandic sagas, fought in a trance-like
fury. Gunnløgsson was always the life of the party after a few
drinks.

Utzon, on the other hand, was not a big drinker. More
sensitive and emotionally intelligent even at that age, he became
a practical joker as a way to survive in the intellectual milieu he
found himself in at university. Not overly academic, he was the
last person selected in the architectural faculty; even he knew
he was not a prodigy like his friend Gunnløgsson. But the two
had an intellectual rapport that made them engaging sparring
partners. As they argued architecture and drew together into
the night, they befriended another architecture student, Tobias
Faber, three years older than them both.

A few years into their degree course, it was Faber who
invited Utzon to the party on that April night in 1940. Gunnløgsson urged his friend to come; he thought he might like the
guest of honour. He told Utzon that she too was considered
something of a country bumpkin by her city friends.

Lis Fenger was vivacious and warm, an artist who had come
to the Danish capital to study commercial art. The second of
eight girls, she was one of eleven children who lived in Hjorring,
about an hour's train ride north of Aalborg, Utzon's home town.
The two young people had their rural heritage in common, as
well as a mutual love of art. On the night of the party there was
an instant attraction between them. Jørn, exactly a year and a
day older than Lis, marvelled at the fact that their birthdays
were so close together. As they parted that night, they vowed to

see each other again and to celebrate his twenty-second birthday the following day.

It turned out not to be much of a celebration, however. The next day, in the pre-dawn hours of 9 April 1940, German troops invaded Denmark and Norway by land, sea and air. Lasting a bare six hours, this was one of the shortest military operations of World War II, but it would have a lifelong impact on the architect-in-training Utzon. While they had been happily enjoying Lis' birthday celebrations, unbeknown to them and most Danes, the German military had been working through the night assembling all over Denmark. Operation Weserübung, as the action was code-named with the German Luftwaffe circling low over the royal Amalienborg Palace, lives forever in the collective memory of Copenhageners. Seventeen bombers roared overhead in a pre-dawn raid over the city, dropping propaganda leaflets, while the German infantry attacked from the harbour and succeeded in capturing the Danish royal family. By 6 a.m. King Christian X had surrendered to the Germans in return for their agreement that he would retain political independence in domestic matters.

While the Germans considered the Danes more Aryan than the Norwegians, whose access to the Atlantic's shipping lanes Hitler wanted for his U-boats, the occupation did not sit well with them. The country had been neutral in World War I. Feelings still run deep in Denmark over this period of history. In 1952 actor Danny Kaye played the title role of Hans Christian Andersen in the Hollywood musical based on the life of Denmark's favourite children's author. Danes still haven't forgiven him for singing *Wonderful Copenhagen*, the title song to the movie with the German-accented 'Copenhagen' (*Koh-pehn-HAH-gehn*) rather than the Danish pronunciation (*Koh-pehn-HAY-gen*).

It was during this wartime occupation that the Danish love

affair with Britain began. Many Danes, even today, speak 'beautiful BBC-worthy' English. The Germans claimed they were invading to protect Denmark from a British invasion, but the Danes loved Britain and saw Winston Churchill as a saviour. They listened to his broadcasts over the wireless and baited the Germans to show their allegiance to Britain.

This mild form of defiance against the Nazis was certainly a distraction from the wartime hardships. Utzon had a waggish nature and played practical jokes on the German soldiers. This endeared him to both his friends and Lis, who had fallen in love with his irreverent and amusing ways.

At the beginning of his architectural studies, Utzon had been living with his brother Leif. Their parents had moved forty kilometres or so north to Helsingør, where their father was in charge of the shipyard. The two boys lived in the apartment of a rich uncle in Nyhavn (New Haven), Copenhagen's commercial port. In the early days of the Nazi occupation, life continued as usual in this colourful part of town.

In 1940, Jørn Utzon completed his first building project. He built a plain pine weatherboard cottage on the seawall of his grandmother's house at Ålsgårde, a former fishing village on the north coast of Zealand, just 6 kilometres north-west of Helsingør. It looked out onto the coast known as Kattegat, towards the Swedish coast. This project was a requirement of his architectural studies. Simple yet elegant, it was a sign of what was to come.

Utzon drew freehand with his left hand. He loved the creative side of architecture, the art part, which is why his friends and family said he still yearned to be an artist. For his university assignments he continued his father's practice of building models, so he would know how his drawings on paper would look three-dimensionally.

As the war progressed, a domestic fuel shortage saw a night-time curfew imposed in Copenhagen. In the early 1940s, Utzon moved with his friend Halldor Gunnløgsson to the district around the Christiansborg Palace, nicknamed 'Borgen', which means 'the Castle'. In order to cope with the fuel shortages and the freezing cold, the two of them created reading groups, self-styled salons where participants could discuss their love of architecture. It took everyone's mind off the cold and helped them focus on their future profession.

In 1942, Utzon's architectural class was split in two, with half dispersed around the Danish capital, and the other half moving to Aarhus in Jutland, Denmark's second largest city. Utzon remained in Copenhagen and continued courting the doctor's daughter. He retained his sense of humour about the wartime occupation and kept up his pranks. It was his method of coping with the bleakness. The effervescent and warm Lis laughed at his jokes.

In mid-1943 the occupation forced the Royal Academy's architectural school to close. But by then Jørn Utzon had left for neutral Sweden, free from the yoke of Hitler's troops.

• • •

The reason Nordic architecture is so renowned today is thanks largely to what happened in Stockholm during the early 1940s. It was a real cradle for talent and attracted architects from all over Scandinavia—looking both for professional advancement and an escape from the domestic woes caused by the 1939 Soviet invasion of Finland and the German invasion of Norway and Denmark. Because the Allies controlled the seas, Sweden was Germany's main source of high-quality iron ore, which was vital for its war effort. Hitler realised that if he were to attack Sweden, it would have disrupted this supply for no real gain.

Stockholm had retained a special place in Utzon's heart thanks to the impact of his family's visit to the 1930 Stockholm-sutställningen. The city had become like a beacon of hope; its neutrality attracted young free spirits such as playwright Bertolt Brecht and some of the world's best architects.

Erik Gunnar Asplund, the chief architect of the 1930 exhibition, had introduced functionalist architecture to Sweden and had become one of Utzon's childhood heroes. He had died on 20 October 1940, aged only fifty-five, but Utzon often repeated a favourite story about Asplund's greatest work, the Woodland Crematorium, built on the outskirts of Stockholm. Progress had apparently been slow and disagreements between the client and architect were frequent. Asplund resigned. Often. But after each resignation, the client would recall him and accept his terms. It was a story Utzon saw as a sort of blueprint for operating with a difficult client—the architect should always set the terms.

Utzon got a job in the architectural practice Asplund had started. He'd left Copenhagen with his university friend, the often berserk Halldor Gunnløgsson, in July 1942 after he'd completed his architectural thesis. They convinced their friend Tobias Faber to join them. All had jobs, so they could leave Denmark legally.

By the end of 1942 Utzon convinced Lis to join him, and on Friday, 4 December 1942 they were married, a week before the Swedish traditional winter festival known as Santa Lucia. Both their parents and Danish expat friends attended the wartime wedding in Stockholm. It was a long dark cold winter's day and snow was heavily packed in the capital's streets. The guests sipped glugg, the mulled Swedish wine, in a toast to the bridal party.

The newlyweds moved to an apartment in Stockholm's medieval old town, Gamla Stan. This is storybook Sweden, with picturesque narrow cobbled streets and ancient buildings dating to the thirteenth century. It was while living here, on 27 September 1944, that their first son Jan was born.

Personally and professionally, it was a nesting time for the young couple. For three years—until the war's end—Utzon worked mainly on school projects. He also began a serious study of Chinese architecture, attracted by its use of inner courtyards and other design intricacies.

Utzon was to cement many firm friendships here with architects who would prop him up like bookends later in his life. They included Norwegians Arne Korsmo, a leading propagator of the International Style, and Sverre Fehn, who went on to win the pinnacle of architecture prizes, the Pritzker.

A lifelong friendship began here too with Christian Norberg-Schulz, a Norwegian architect, author, educator and architectural theorist. Norberg-Schulz and Utzon wrote letters to each other expounding their theories on art and architecture. Finnish architect and designer Alvar Aalto was also exiled in Stockholm and gave lectures there. Like many in this circle of friends, Aalto designed furniture, lamps, furnishings and glassware. Dane Arne Jacobsen, designer of the internationally renowned 'egg chair', also sought refuge here with his 'functionalist' cohort.

It was this circle of friends who sustained him, and they were to go on to become some of the greatest Scandinavian names in architecture and design. They shared ideas and enthusiasms free from the strains of war in their respective homelands. They became better architects because of these relationships. They were theoretically engaged and professionally generous with each other. They skied, had saunas, swam together in freezing cold lakes and climbed mountains in the bucolic Swedish countryside. They wrote poems, had picnics, and went for walks on the beach, free from wartime deprivations such as

gas shortages and curfews. It was a world away from the dark
days of occupied Denmark.

• • •

For those Danes who had stayed behind, a point of pride was
the resistance to German occupation by their king, Christian X.
During the war he cycled every day through Copenhagen's
streets unaccompanied by guards. Unlike in other occupied
countries, Danish Jews were not forced to wear the Star of
David, but the king wore one in an act of solidarity. He also
facilitated the transport of Danish Jews to neutral Sweden.
He embodied the Danish spirit of defiance.

Along with his friend Tobias Faber, Utzon joined the Danish
Brigade. Known as Danforce, it was a military unit made up of
Danish refugees, trained and supplied by Sweden. With the end
of the war looming, they began to prepare for their return to their
homeland. For two weeks in 1945, in the bitter cold of a Swedish
April, the two men slept in tents in preparation for this event.

On 4 May 1945 at 8.34 p.m., while listening to the BBC
news, Utzon heard that the German troops occupying Denmark
and Holland had unconditionally surrendered to Field Marshal
Montgomery. The next night he was one of the Danforce drivers
who ferried the first Danish troops to cross the Øresund from
Sweden to Helsingør, where his parents had remained. He told
his children many years later that he drove a truck containing
dynamite, so sat forward on the edge of his seat the entire way
terrified of an explosion.

As he drove south into the Danish capital, Copenhageners
lined the streets, waving the red and white Danish flag and
cheering their compatriots in a rousing welcome home. When he
saw the familiar corkscrew spire of the baroque Church of Our
Saviour, it hit him: the war was over. Utzon was home.

• • •

Chapter four

The mastermind

Friday, 4 May 1945: on the other side of the world a conductor walks onstage at San Francisco's Civic Auditorium. He struts proudly into the crowd of world leaders assembled to honour the delegates to the United Nations (UN) conference gathered in that city. He glides in to take the helm of the orchestra, clad in the customary maestro's uniform of tuxedo and tails, and is greeted with applause. Representatives from forty-six nations have gathered in California to discuss the charter to promote international co-operation. This evening's entertainment is to be a welcome respite from the heated political negotiations that have been taking place at the nearby War Memorial Opera House and the Herbst Theatre. The mood this Friday night is buoyant. An end to world hostilities is in sight. There is optimism and a longing for gentler times, when culture, not warfare, can take the spotlight on the world stage.

The grandeur of the interior of this Beaux Arts building is breathtaking. The stunning setting helps set the expectant mood. A frisson of excitement is palpable in the crowd, awash in a sea of pearls and furs taken out of mothballed wardrobes for the occasion. Opera glasses are at the ready and a few nervous coughs break out as the stage lights go down.

Risë Stevens, the world-renowned star of opera, screen and radio most noted for her portrayal of Georges Bizet's *Carmen*, takes to the stage. The soprano with the Metropolitan Opera has flown from New York especially to perform for the UN conference.

From the moment the maestro raises his baton the room is transfixed. The music transports the audience into a reverie; it's as if everyone has been longing for such a reprieve after the hardship of war. The Brits in the audience are moved by the guest conductor's rendition of Vaughan Williams' 'A London Symphony'. He brings the Americans to tears with Morton Gould's 'American Salute', and he stirs Russians to enthusiastic applause with Prokofiev's 'Classical Symphony'.

The conductor's name is Eugene Goossens. Having gained a reputation as one of the world's best conductors at the Cincinnati Symphony Orchestra, he has been given the special honour of conducting the San Francisco Symphony for the UN delegates. By the time he is coaxed into performing an encore after a standing ovation from the appreciative audience, almost everyone gathered there that night wants him as a guest conductor in their homeland.

• • •

The UN delegates in San Francisco weren't the only ones entranced by the talented musician. Women found Goossens irresistible in his youth. So attractive, in fact, that he had to hire a valet called Arthur Billings, whose job was to protect him from the female fans who would rush backstage post performance and push their way into his dressing room. They would try to cut pieces from his tie, as if he were a movie star.

'My heart just loosens when I'm listening to Mr Goossens,' wrote playwright Noel Coward of the Belgian-born British baton-wielding force of nature, who was at this time a self-styled celebrity of the classical music scene. Goossens counted Russian composer Igor Stravinsky, Australian singer Dame Nellie Melba and Italian conductor Arturo Toscanini as friends. He went fishing with painter Pablo Picasso.

Goossens started his musical career as a violinist, playing in restaurants and cinema orchestras, before studying at the Bruges Conservatorium and the Royal College of Music in London. A third-generation conductor—both his father and grandfather were also called Eugene—he made his Covent Garden debut in London in 1921. In 1923, he was invited by George Eastman, founder of the Eastman Kodak Company, to become conductor of the Rochester Philharmonic Orchestra, which provided background music for silent films. Goossens soon became renowned for his showmanship, conducting before huge crowds from the Hollywood Bowl to New York.

His then wife, Marjorie Foulkrod, was his third and nineteen years his junior; he had five daughters. 'I don't suppose there will be a Eugene the fourth,' he said resignedly after the birth of his fifth child. He was a skilled painter—mainly landscapes and pen and ink drawings—and a well-regarded composer. An aesthete, he was something of an amateur architect, whose hobby was to draw ocean liners. He enjoyed the company of stimulating people, especially 'the company of gifted, amusing homosexuals'. His close friends called him Gene; his contemporaries called him a genius. This was the

man whose vision would ultimately lead to the creation of the
Sydney Opera House.

• • •

A year after the San Francisco performance that had wowed
the world leaders, Eugene Goossens came to Sydney as a guest
conductor with the ABC's Symphony Orchestra. He'd been
invited by ABC Managing Director Charles Moses, a fellow Brit
who'd heard of Goossens' reputation in classical musical circles.

'Colonel Moses', as he was known at the time, was attempting to establish an ABC symphony orchestra in each of the six
Australian state capitals. He convinced the ABC commissioners
this was a worthwhile project, given that these cities' councils
would make a significant contribution to the running costs.
Sydney's symphony was the first and he wanted it to be the
showcase for the country's classical musical capabilities.

Instead of the long restful sea voyage big stars at the time
usually took when visiting Australia, Goossens arrived in
Sydney in 1946 by air; he was thoroughly exhausted after many
days of travel. By then he was already known as one of the first
'commuter conductors', travelling the world and performing
with orchestras as a guest conductor.

During that first visit the local press was thoroughly fascinated by his exploits, and soon discovered one of his secret
passions: steam trains. When he travelled in the United States,
he often asked to sit in the locomotive's cab with the driver. He
donned dungarees when he stepped aboard the Newcastle Flyer
at Sydney's Central Station, where he was photographed riding
in the engine with the driver. During his whistle-stop 1946 tour
of Australia, he courted the press outrageously and was always
happy to pose for the cameras, even with his face covered in
grime and soot as it was that day when he alighted at Newcastle.

The Sydney Symphony Orchestra (SSO) had been formed in 1908, but after the ABC was created in 1932 the broadcaster slowly took control of the various state orchestras. In 1945 Moses had reached an agreement with Sydney City Council and the NSW government for them to share the cost of the SSO while the ABC managed it. At Goossens' concerts at the Sydney Town Hall, Moses was so impressed by the flamboyant conductor that he asked him to return as the orchestra's first chief conductor.

Despite the ABC's heavy involvement in music and literature during this era, Moses wasn't himself prominent on the cultural scene. As a former Victorian amateur heavyweight boxing champion and woodchopper, he was more of a sports fan. As a British soldier, he'd enlisted and fought in World War I, migrating with his Irish wife to Australia in 1919. A failed farmer, he tried a host of careers, including selling real estate and cars, before applying for a position as a radio announcer at the ABC. His southern English accent was considered ideal for radio. He became the ABC's sporting editor in January 1933, and by November 1935 he was general manager.

The sports-mad Moses was an odd choice as cheerleader for the high-brow Goossens. However, he was keen to broadcast the orchestras' classical music to the masses because he knew there was an eager audience, and he thought recruiting a figure such as Goossens would be a coup. He just had to convince the ABC board of the idea of permanently employing the maestro. Goossens had put a number of small orchestras on the map all over the United States, wielding his baton like a magic wand. Moses hoped he could bring that same drive and professionalism to Australia and do the same for Sydney.

But when Moses sent a telegram to Goossens offering him the job, the conductor declined. Moses then picked up the phone and called him in America via the ABC switchboard, whereupon

Goossens scoffed down the line: 'You likely couldn't afford me. I doubt you can match the sort of money I am making in America.'

Moses hung up disappointedly. He wanted Goossens, but he knew he would have to finagle some more money out of the ABC Board.

So, he used his contacts in the NSW government to scout around for a token role Goossens could fill—perhaps a job that had been vacant for some time and came with an impressive salary. Moses learnt that the role of director of Sydney's New South Wales State Conservatorium of Music (now the Sydney Conservatorium of Music) was vacant. So, he was able to combine the salary from the job of SSO chief conductor with the Conservatorium salary and thus make an offer that might realistically attract Goossens.

Moses picked up the phone again. This time he could offer a package that was in excess of £5000 for the two jobs, a sum he insisted was more than what Goossens was earning in America and even more than the Australian prime minister earned.

'I'll only accept on the understanding I can spend part of the time continuing to work as a guest conductor overseas,' Goossens said.

Moses agreed. The ABC Board did too.

• • •

Goossens arrived in Sydney on a chilly midwinter July day in 1947. He was accompanied by his wife, Marjorie, plus two daughters from his second marriage, Sidonie and Renée. A crowd of reporters greeted him on the tarmac at Sydney Airport and flashbulbs popped for photos for the afternoon tabloids.

'What are your plans for Sydney, Mr Goossens?' one of the pressmen yelled at the conductor, who by now was fifty-three and portly, not quite the ladies' man he'd been reputed to be in his early days in America.

'I intend to make the fledgling Sydney Symphony Orchestra one of the six best in the world,' he proclaimed. 'I will make its members as famous as Australia's cricket stars.' Even the maestro was aware of local pride in the exploits of batsman Don Bradman. The reporters eagerly took down his words and continued to ask questions.

The photographers, however, were more interested in his much younger, thinner and more attractive wife. A wealthy divorced socialite, Marjorie Foulkrod was a talented pianist who had been studying at New York's Juilliard School when she met her next husband; they were married in May 1946. She was thirty-four when they arrived in Sydney and she soon became known about town for her elegant clothing and sassy style. The Sydney newspapers sought her views on the latest fashions and she modelled her stylish 'continental wardrobe' for a colour spread in the *Australian Women's Weekly*.

Eugene Goossens the third and Mrs Eugene Goossens the third settled in Sydney's leafy well-to-do Wahroonga, together with Sidonie and Renée. Renée detested her glamorous step-mother, especially when Marjorie sent her off to boarding school in France due to her busy social schedule and Eugene's gruelling work regime. They were soon on the invitation list at NSW Government House and in demand at north shore musicales and eastern suburbs soirees.

• • •

Classical musicians in Sydney wanted to be, as Goossens had hinted, as famous as cricket stars. Growth in subscribers to the SSO under his reign doubled. He tapped into the mood of post-war optimism and the feeling that Sydney really needed to

become a more cosmopolitan and less provincial city; his aim
was to capture not so much the suaveness of London, but more
the liveliness of America, whose ebullience he knew intimately.

'I believe that precisely what happened after the First World
War is going to happen again,' he declared to Sydney's *Daily
Telegraph*. 'Music reached a pretty high point just before 1914,
and then everything became moribund. Suddenly a year or so
after the war a tremendous activity arose among Stravinsky,
Schonberg and the rest of the so-called moderns.' He predicted:
'The same will happen now.'

The buzz created by Goossens' arrival ensured Sydney's
Gothic Town Hall was filled night after night, with the 'House
Full' sign appearing regularly on the Town Hall's sandstone
steps on George Street to turn away newcomers. The symphony
became the hottest ticket in town. Demand for seats was so
fierce, and available seats so rare, that some of the 20,000
subscribers began to bequeath their seats in their wills. The
much-acclaimed maestro didn't suffer fools gladly and had
high standards for both his orchestra and his audience. He once
publicly shamed an audience member for coughing during a
Town Hall concert.

From the beginning of his SSO stint, Goossens campaigned
tirelessly for the creation of a new musical venue for Sydney—a
place that could handle opera, symphony concerts, ballet and
drama, just like San Francisco's famous War Memorial Opera
House, which had opened in 1932, or the 8000-seat San Francisco Civic Auditorium where he had performed for the UN
delegates. Even Cincinnati, Ohio, where Goossens worked
before Sydney, had a Music Hall that could seat 2550, and an
auditorium that ranked acoustically as one of the world's finest.
Sydney's Town Hall could only seat 2300; it was draughty, and
it had no heating nor any facilities for providing refreshments.

This meant patrons had to dash to pubs and cafes during inter-mission. Worst of all was its cavernous ceiling, which killed the orchestra's sound. Goossens claimed the building was designed for town meetings rather than concert halls. His conviction was that Australian music lovers deserved better.

The SSO was now experiencing a golden age, and Goossens wanted his charges to have a venue deserving of their talents, just as the Sydney Cricket Ground was deserving of Australia's world-famous cricketers. He vowed to make achieving that goal his next magnum opus.

Chapter five

The ordinary Joe who gave Sydney its Opera House

Late in 1947, Charles Moses is summoned by his secretary from a meeting at the ABC's federal headquarters in downtown Sydney's Pitt Street. 'Mr Goossens is on the line,' she tells her boss. 'He says it's urgent.'

Moses raises his eyebrows. 'Not again,' he says under his breath as he paces down the corridor following the waft of her Chanel No. 5 back to his office. He picks up the black Bakelite phone gingerly.

'Goossens here,' the conductor says and, without pausing, bellows, 'You must do something about getting a new opera house built.'

He goes on to list all the reasons why the Sydney Town Hall is not a suitable venue for his symphony orchestra. 'Not only that,' he concludes, 'the Old Vic is touring here next year with Laurence Olivier and Vivien Leigh, and all we have to offer them is the Tivoli.'

The Tivoli Theatre had opened in 1911 as the Adelphi Theatre. In 1932 it was renamed, somewhat optimistically, the 'Grand Opera House' and then the 'New Tivoli Theatre'. The Tiv, as it was popularly known, was located down the not-so-salubrious southern end of the city near Sydney's sandstone Central Station and Chinatown on Castlereagh Street between Hay and Campbell streets, a block away from today's Capitol Theatre. As the venue for salacious vaudeville acts, such as the high stepping of the barely clad 'Tivoli Tappers' and the bawdy badinage of 'Stiffy & Mo' and Mike Connors and his wife Queenie Paul, its reputation was occasionally interrupted by the respectability of opera, ballet, musical comedy and touring theatre groups like France's Folies Bergère and Britain's Old Vic.

It was an utter embarrassment to Goossens not to have a suitable venue with which to lure his musical friends in the northern hemisphere to perform in far-off Australia. Opera buffs were frustrated, too. At this time there was no national body like Opera Australia championing their cause, only state-run ad-hoc opera companies and the occasional visits by Italian opera and Gilbert & Sullivan troupes. These were very much poor cousins to the emerging popularity of musical comedy. In 1940s Sydney the 'high arts' were a low priority.

Since 1934 the most influential adviser to the ABC on its music programming had been the Melbourne-based and Shepparton-born conductor Bernard Heinze. Gathering around the wireless was a popular pastime for Australia's post-war population of 7.5 million people, but the standard of the sound produced in live and recorded broadcasts needed improvement and Goossens believed this could only be achieved by having better performance spaces. He had a hard time convincing others of this need. It was the sound of leather on willow, the unmistakable whack of a cricket ball on a bat, that was music to most Australian ears.

At the end of 1947 cricketer Don Bradman scored his hundredth century. This sporting feat dominated the ABC news bulletins and pre-occupied Moses for most of that year. He'd also been busy at Radio 2BL, replacing BBC news broadcasts from London with the ABC's own news department, which was inaugurated in June that year.

Until this phone call from Goossens, Moses had indulged his principal conductor, who had been in Sydney for less than six months. Despite Goossens' success in drawing large audiences to his classical concerts, many considered him a prima donna. The ABC boss was starting to think they had a point after Goossens delivered his very long list of reasons why the Town Hall didn't work.

'I am in broadcasting not the building business,' Moses retorted before slamming down the handset and returning to his meeting.

Goossens was not a man who was used to being told 'no'. He was frustrated; he knew he was failing in his boast to make his musicians as famous as the nation's cricketers. He also began to realise his requests were falling on deaf ears at the ABC. So he started to complain to journalists. They were all ears.

Goossens attacked the then NSW Labor Premier James McGirr and other 'philistines', as he called them, for not treating his orchestra with the respect he felt it deserved. This was an outburst that was particularly embarrassing for both the ABC and the Conservatorium, which were reliant on government money.

Finally, Moses summoned Goossens to his office at ABC headquarters and promised to do what he could to get an opera house, but only if Goossens agreed to one condition: that he hold fire with the newspapers. Reluctantly, the conductor agreed.

• • •

Also at the end of 1947, high on a hill in Sydney's well-heeled eastern suburbs, Peter Hall, a sixteen-year-old boarding student at the prestigious Cranbrook School at Bellevue Hill, was packing his belongings to return home for the summer break. He was an only child, the son of a postal inspector who moved often from country town to country town for his work.

Hall won a scholarship to the elite school, 'a very imposing structure which overlooks Rose Bay, Sydney, and commands a marvellous view of the harbour', as he described it to his grandmother on 14 December 1942, in his first year. It has been the school of choice for generations of wealthy NSW families wanting an Anglican education for their sons.

Hall, who had been born in the port city of Newcastle, was preparing to return to Narrabri, where his parents were now living, having just sat for his Leaving Certificate, the end-of-school exam. But as he was young for his school year, his parents had agreed to headmaster Brian Hone's request that he return in 1948 and repeat the year. Hone, a first-class cricketer who had opened batting for South Australia, often made this request to repeat to parents of younger boys who were promising athletes, thus allowing them another year to shine academically while the school continued to reap the accolades of their sporting success. In Hall's case repeating would allow him to play as number five in the school's first XI, become House Prefect and Head of Boarders at Rawson House, excel again at debating and continue as a member of the school magazine committee for a third year. At the end of 1948, he was only narrowly beaten for the coveted position of dux of the school, taking out the school prizes for French and Latin and again achieving honours in the Leaving Certificate.

Discipline and persistence were the hallmarks of Peter Hall's student days. He intended to go to university to study the Classics at the University of Sydney, with fellow Cranbrookian

Tom Heath, Hall's academic rival who had topped their final year and wanted to study architecture. In terms of school accomplishments, Hall couldn't have been more different from Jørn Utzon.

• • •

On his return to Copenhagen after the war, Utzon established his own architectural practice. He visited his hero, the Finn Alvar Aalto, travelling to work in his Helsinki workshop in 1946. He continued to enter architectural competitions without success, but, in 1947, through contacts organised via his father, he took a ferry from Denmark to Casablanca to take up a commission in Morocco. He had been asked to design a factory for a family who had won the contract to make soap for the entire French army. But by the time he arrived, the French franc had devalued so drastically that the factory was going to cost ten times the original estimate and the family no longer had the money for the commission.

Instead of returning home immediately, Utzon spent five weeks walking and hitchhiking 500 kilometres in the high Atlas Mountains and along the edge of the Sahara Desert. Here he was often invited by Bedouin tribesman to be their guest in their rammed-earth homes, an experience that would stay with him for a lifetime. In the sketches he drew during these travels, it is clear he was impressed by the simple lines of the Bedouin homes. Before he left for Morocco in 1947, he'd expressed his dissatisfaction with contemporary design in an article, 'Tendencies in Contemporary Architecture', written with his friend Tobias Faber and published in Denmark's *Arkitekten* magazine.

During this period in the late 1940s, Utzon designed lamps as a way to make money. He also applied for scholarships. In 1949 he and Lis travelled to the United States on a scholarship for several months, leaving their two young children (their daughter Lin had been born in 1946) with their parents and other family members.

Utzon's father had arranged their passage to New York, and on arrival they found a Studebaker waiting for them in port. Lis' surgeon father had operated on the nose of Studebaker's CEO in Denmark, and as thanks he arranged for the young couple to have the car free of charge.

Norwegian friends, Arne and Grete Kormso, joined them and the two couples headed off on a cross-country road trip. In Chicago they called on Mies van der Rohe, a founder of the Bauhaus and the 'Less is More' school of thought in modern architecture, but they were told he was too busy to see them.

Utzon called on Eero Saarinen, a fellow Scandinavian architect making a name for himself in post-war Michigan and who had grown up north of Detroit on the campus of Cranbrook Educational Community designed by his Finnish architect father Eliel. Eero was close friends with the acclaimed furniture designers Ray and Charles Eames—they had all studied together at the Cranbrook Academy of Art, which was based on the community's campus—and he arranged for the visiting couples to stay with the Eames' in Los Angeles, en route south to Mexico.

The Utzons and Kormsos also spent a weekend with Frank Lloyd Wright at his Taliesin East home in Wisconsin, Utzon giving the great architect a lamp he'd designed, although Wright was not overly impressed by it. The Scandinavians then travelled to Scottsdale, Arizona, where Utzon studied at Taliesin West, Frank Lloyd Wright's architectural school. But the main goal of their trip was to make it to Oaxaca in southern Mexico and the Mayan ruins of Monte Albán. The ancient Zapotec capital, Monte Albán's hilltop terrace comprises a series of steps that look out at the city of Oaxaca below. From its stone platform the entire valley can be seen from on high: every cloud, every bird floating in the breeze, and every mountain.

For the two young architects and their wives it was a memorable experience to climb the steps to the top of the temple, and muse at pre-Columbian architecture's perfect symmetry. It was a marvel to them as wondrous as the pyramids of Egypt. It was a glorious way to end 1949 and close the chapter on a war-torn decade that had been a tumultuous time for all.

The Utzons returned to Denmark with over 300 photos, much 8mm film and the Studebaker. But because of Denmark's high import taxes they swapped the vehicle for a cheaper and more practical pre-war car. Their son Jan still remembers the excitement he felt as a five year old going to the harbour to meet his parents for the first time in months. He saw the ship's captain in uniform and waved at him, assuming he was his father.

• • •

Back in Sydney in 1951, Eugene Goossens waltzed into the class of his final-year diploma students at the Conservatorium of Music, the Con, with a great fur coat around his shoulders. His students were both awed by him and adored him. He was considered pompous and autocratic. A proud man, he'd been complaining for nearly five years now about the pitiful absence of an appropriate opera/cultural facility, but utterly without effect.

Goossens always entered a room with a flounce as dramatic as a scene from one of the operas he conducted. But this day he had an announcement to make to his students. They would perform his own opera, *Judith*, at the Conservatorium's Verbrugghen Hall that year. He had tried unsuccessfully in 1929 to stage *Judith* while he lived in the United States, but this time he would try again with a far more willing cast: his students.

Among that 1951 final-year class was a young man from Sydney's north-western suburb of Epping. Richard Bonynge had come to the Con from the selective Sydney Boys High School, where he had been considered a prodigy. Although frightened by him, Bonynge also looked to Goossens as a musical mentor. To sing the title role of Judith for the Sydney season, Goossens had chosen an unknown local stenographer, twenty-five-year-old Joan Sutherland, who was forever indebted to Goossens for his personal operatic coaching and for granting her this first chance. Bonynge and Sutherland were enamoured not just of Goossens, but of each other, and a relationship soon developed between them.

Verbrugghen Hall, in Goossens' eyes, was as draughty and acoustically flawed as the Town Hall, but it was the best he could do. Its early patrons remember the sub-standard sets being so flimsy that they fell not only during performances by the students but also by the NSW Opera Company.

Goossens continued to juggle his work with the SSO, the Con and as a guest conductor overseas, all the while remaining on the A-list of Sydney's party circuit with his vivacious wife. His gruelling itinerary of country-town performances, to which the steam-train enthusiast travelled usually up front with the train conductor, kept regional classical music fans appeased.

Despite falling backwards in a stairwell in Lismore in 1953 and slipping a disc, which kept him in hospital for a month, he hardly slowed down at all. He used his hospital time to compose an oratorio, *The Apocalypse*, and then, when he had recovered, he resumed conducting in Sydney and undertook a five-month tour of Europe.

Yet, an opera house for Sydney remained his passion project. Goossens wanted a new home not just for his orchestra, but also for the next generation of Australian opera stars, who were starting to shine under his tutelage.

From his office at the Con—the castellated Gothic building in Sydney's Royal Botanic Garden that had originally been built as the horse stables for nearby Government House—Goossens would often take lunch-time walks with his secretary, Phyllis Williams. On their loop they would walk either down Macquarie Street or through the Botanic Gardens to Circular Quay, Goossens always brimming with ideas, usually about his beloved opera house project. Each time they reached Bennelong Point on Sydney Harbour, he would inform Williams, 'This is where it has to be.'

But Bennelong Point was the location of the Fort Macquarie tram depot, the turnaround point for the city's trams, and it had been acquired by the Maritime Services Board to become an international shipping terminal. Plans had already been drawn up—something that outraged Goossens.

After a good, solid seven years or so of campaigning, ABC boss Moses finally capitulated to Goossens' demands to do something. In 1954, he organised a private meeting between Goossens and the relatively new state premier, Joseph Cahill, who had won the ballot for the Labor leadership to become premier in 1952, following the resignation of James McGirr, whom Goossens had earlier accused of being a philistine.

With Joe Cahill's ascension, there was a new wind blowing down Macquarie Street, the state government's traditional seat of power. Cahill was considered a 'doer'. As Secretary for Public Works and later Minister for Local Government, he had established the State Dockyards at Newcastle and the State Brickworks, and supervised the establishment of the Electricity Authority and the Cumberland County Council.

When the two men finally met, Goossens began by complaining about the Maritime Service Board's plans to build a shipping terminal at Bennelong Point. 'Put it on the other side,' Goossens declared as forcefully as he could.

In the end, the new NSW premier was swayed by Goossens' public standing and the force of his argument. Cahill asked him, along with Moses, to join a five-member government committee exploring ideas for a cultural centre. The other three members would be the Under Secretary for Local Government, Stanley Haviland; Professor of Architecture at the University of Sydney, Henry Ingham Ashworth; and the Town Clerk of Sydney, Roy Hendy. Goossens was very happy to accept this appointment because he was assured that the biggest auditorium in the new cultural centre would be used primarily for symphony concerts and opera. In other words, it would be tailor-made for him.

The flamboyant Goossens and the new Labor leader were odd bedfellows in much the way he and Moses were. They came from different worlds, but they shared the same vision: the need for a cultural institution that would put Sydney on the world stage.

• • •

Chapter six

The magnificent lonely idea

As a gifted musician and a skilled painter, Eugene Goossens befriended many artists and architects; they seemed far more receptive to his enthusiasm for an opera house than Charles Moses. His own vision for the building boasted P&O-style windows, no doubt influenced by his penchant for drawing ocean liners in his spare time. He asked theatre designer Bill Constable to sketch it. The watercolour that Constable produced included an outdoor music bowl, much like the Hollywood Bowl where Goossens had loved to perform.

Two early supporters of his idea came from the University of Sydney's architecture faculty: lecturer and *Sydney Morning Herald* cartoonist George Molnar and Henry Ingram Ashworth, the new dean of the faculty. It was likely no coincidence they were also European: Molnar from Hungary and Ashworth from Britain.

In 1951 Molnar and Ashworth had set their fifth-year architecture students the following assignment: 'The problem:

63

an Opera House for Sydney. The time to solve it: six weeks. The site to build on: the official site—the one on the corner of Liverpool and College Streets.'

The students' proposals all went on display for a week at the elegant downtown department store, David Jones. However, the newspapers were more taken by the idea put forward by one student to locate a nightclub on Shark Island than by the plans offered for a new and permanent home for high culture such as opera.

Molnar had come to Australia in 1939 to work as an architect in Canberra. In 1945 he moved to Sydney to lecture in architecture at the University of Sydney, and in 1954 he started working as a *Herald* cartoonist. His output of black-and-white cartoons, which were published three times a week until he retired three decades later in 1984, today reads like an illustrated compendium of the ups and downs of the opera house journey.

Molnar entered wholeheartedly into the city-wide debate as to the possible location of an opera house. A popular suggestion was on top of Wynyard Station because of the advantage offered by being close to public transport. In a piece he wrote for the *Herald* in October 1954, he dismissed the 'official' site on the corner of Liverpool and College streets that he'd had his students design for, suggesting this location, where five streets converged including Oxford Street, would be a nightmare because of its heavy traffic and lack of parking.

'After working on the project for a few days it became evident that the site is quite unsuitable,' he explained. 'To spend six weeks on a design that is bound to be unsatisfactory is a waste we could not afford, so the students were directed to design an opera house to be built either in the place of the Conservatorium or in the Domain. It seems the people of Sydney are going to spend about four years of toil and many hundred thousand pounds to arrive at the same conclusion. By that time it will be too late to do anything about it. The public buildings of Sydney are not very distinguished. Especially their settings are mean (this does not apply to tram sheds, overhead railways and lavatories).'

Jokes aside, Molnar, like Goossens, felt the Fort Macquarie Tram Depot, the terminus for the city's trams, was one of the most beautifully located turnaround points for public transport in the world. In its heyday the Sydney tram system was the second largest in the Commonwealth (after London) and one of the largest in the world. In 1945, patronage peaked at 405 million passenger journeys on its 181 miles (291 kilometres) of tracks.

But the days of the Sydney tram were numbered. The burghers of the city, in their infinite wisdom, were replacing the system with buses and trains. Having at Goossens' request fended off a land grab by the Maritime Services Board, Cahill was open to suggestions about the best use of the promontory.

• • •

NSW Premier Joe Cahill had never seen an opera in his life. This unashamedly working-class man played the pianola at his home in the inner-west suburb of Marrickville, but that was probably the extent of his musical knowledge. Even as the state's top politician, he lived in the same modest brick bungalow house his Irish-born railway worker father had bought when Cahill was a child. He remained there after his marriage and the birth of his five children.

But he was an ambitious man with big plans for his state, especially his beloved city of birth. He knew from the moment he met Eugene Goossens in 1954 that they shared a vision. Cahill had been infected with Goossens' enthusiasm. In political terms, 'Ordinary Joe' was the founding father of the opera house idea.

Born within the tightly knit community of railway workers that had grown up around the Eveleigh railway workshops at Redfern, Cahill was educated at a Catholic convent first and then by the Patrician Brothers. Forced to leave school for financial reasons, he started as an apprentice fitter and turner at Eveleigh aged sixteen. Although lacking in formal education, the key to Cahill was his open mind.

As a young trade unionist, he had joined the Workers' Educational Association, attending evening lectures after work in order to develop his public speaking skills, which he put to test in debating contests as well as in his role in the railway workers' union. In 1917, aged twenty-six, he was sacked from his job for taking part in a railway strike; his personnel file was marked 'agitator'.

In that year he tried unsuccessfully to enter state politics, and then suffered a long period of unemployment before the railways took him on again in 1922. Unemployment is said to have been a formative experience for him. A grass roots militant, he was committed to the cause of collective action but accustomed to walking to the beat of his own drum. No one ever questioned his work ethic; he was driven, but not always in the same direction as his fellow railway workers.

When he finally returned to the Eveleigh workshops, he was barred from holding a union office. But this did not deter him; he simply devoted his considerable energies elsewhere. He entered state politics in 1925 in the NSW Legislative Assembly as a left-wing member of the Australian Labor Party (ALP) and with the reputation of being a convincing orator.

Throughout his political career Cahill continued to live in the area where he had been raised; he claimed this kept him grounded. But his capacity to mix in all sorts of circles was legendary: from the sandstone confines of Macquarie Street's

Parliament House to the turf of the racetracks at Randwick or Rose Hill. A regular early morning swimmer, he also liked a drink and a cigar. Above all, however, Cahill was a devoted family man. On numerous occasions he publicly stated that 'family life is the cornerstone of the State'.

They Called Him Old Smoothie is, tellingly, the title of Cahill's posthumous biography. His biographer Peter Golding sang his praises: 'What made Joe Cahill remarkable in a world of political cynicism was that essentially he was an ordinary man who was driven by a sincere conviction that all people, rich or poor, had the right to share the good things of life. That really was why he risked his career to achieve what must have seemed an impossible dream—the Sydney Opera House.'

In the same month that Cahill became premier, April 1952, Goossens' protégée, Joan Sutherland, made her opera debut singing at London's Covent Garden, having been recognised as a major talent after her role in Goossens' *Judith*. Even if the Sydney soprano had wanted to stay in the country of her birth after winning the most prestigious competition for young Australian singers, the Sun Aria, in 1949, there was simply nowhere for her to perform. This lack of opportunity had propelled Helen Porter Mitchell, who took the stage name of Dame Nellie Melba after her home town of Melbourne, to leave Australia earlier in the twentieth century. Sydney, at the time Cahill was elected premier, was a city of SP (starting price) bookies, 'colourful' racing identities (code word for criminals) and corrupt cops. It was known for one of Australia's most spectacular evening entertainments: harness racing at Harold Park Paceway, where, on one Saturday evening in 1952, a record crowd of 25,000 was in attendance. Nearby was the greyhound racetrack at Wentworth Park, another popular night-time entertainment under floodlights.

Although Cahill was a man more comfortable with a night at 'the trots' or 'the dogs' than a night at the opera, he recognised his city was changing. Since the late 1940s, post-war European migrants were demanding a different kind of culture than the one that could be found in the pubs and at the racetrack. They wanted operas, symphonies and plays, along with the kinds of restaurants and bars found in their homelands.

After his meeting with Goossens in 1954, and his formation of an Opera House Committee, Joe Cahill decided to call a public meeting on the matter. The date was set for the morning of 30 November 1954. The venue: the Lecture Room of Sydney's public library on the second floor of the late nineteenth-century Queen Victoria Building.

• • •

A purple haze descends on Sydney every November when the jacaranda trees bloom. By the time 30 November 1954 arrived, the city was engulfed in a lilac tide of flowers and an enthusiasm to discuss the idea of establishing a cultural institution. Cahill had sent invitations to the public event to a wide range of Sydneysiders, not just those involved in the arts. A shrewd politician, he knew he needed to harness support from Australia's elite with more skill than a Harold Park jockey. The guest list ranged from newspaper publishers—Warwick Fairfax of the *Sydney Morning Herald* and Frank Packer of Consolidated Press—to the directors of the NSW Chamber of Manufacturers and the Royal Prince Alfred Hospital.

The Queen Victoria Building, situated at one of the city's busiest intersections, is just across the road from the Town Hall, where the previous week Goossens had premiered to a standing ovation *Apocalypse*, which he'd written in hospital.

Outside, the din of trams rattled down George Street, but

inside the library lecture room everyone fell quiet as Cahill took
to the podium as the first speaker. They were keen to hear details
of what he had in mind.

'The people who have gathered here this morning are interested in opera and other forms of art to which perhaps many
in the community might not give a second thought,' he began.
'Experience has proved that it is always the few who have to
pioneer the way, and the government has decided to go ahead
with this project . . . Some will say that the time is not oppor-
tune to build an opera house in Sydney and that we could apply
our resources to better advantage. I have been in public life for
thirty years and there was never a time when a similar criticism
would not have been offered against any great national venture
of this nature. If such a criticism were valid, one wonders how
London ever got its Covent Garden; Paris, New York and
Vienna their fine opera houses; and Milan its La Scala, which
was destroyed during the war and has since been rebuilt.

'This state cannot go on without proper facilities for the
expression of talent and the staging of the highest forms of
artistic entertainment which add grace and charm to living
and which help to develop and mould a better, more enlight-
ened community. The Opera House should not be regarded as
the special preserve of Sydney people. It should be regarded
as something which belongs to the people of New South Wales
as a whole—or, for that matter to the people of Australia.'

He proclaimed he did not want a watered-down version
of a cultural centre—a carbon copy of something from Britain
or Europe. That would only buy into the colonial inferiority
complex, the 'cultural cringe', so common in many parts of the
globe that had been colonised.

'Surely it is proper in establishing an opera house that it
should not be a "shandy gaff",' he said, using the pub parlance

of the day, 'but an edifice that will be a credit to the state, not
only today but also for hundreds of years . . . If we in our lifetime
did nothing more than express our love of the arts by providing
a building worthy of them, even when names are forgotten, the
building will always remain as a testimony to what was done in
the year 1954 by a group of citizens for the encouragement of
talent and culture.'

There was silence at first. The audience was clearly inspired
by Cahill's vision. Surprised too, perhaps, by the former rail-
wayman's passionate oratory in support of the fine arts. A few
started to clap; others joined in more enthusiastically.

Eugene Goossens spoke on behalf of the Sydney Symphony
Orchestra, followed by the governor of the Commonwealth
Bank, Dr HC Coombs, nicknamed 'Nugget' because of his short
stature (he was 5 feet 3 inches tall) and solid gait.

Coombs spoke on behalf of the Elizabethan Theatre Trust,
which he had convinced the conservative Menzies federal
government to create in the wake of Queen Elizabeth II's first
royal visit to Australia earlier that year. 'I am certain,' he assured
the premier, 'that if you succeed, your name will live for the
next 400 years as the head of the government that put the opera
house there.'

Newspaper proprietor Warwick Fairfax spoke of the
'ticklish matter of finance' and suggested it might be an uphill
battle to get the public to pay. A spokesman for the Parks
and Playground Movement, whose slogan was 'Hands off the
Parks', railed against the suggestion that a five-acre expanse of
The Domain be used as the site for the opera house.

Then Mr Gale of the Workers' Educational Association that
Cahill so loved took to the stage: 'I congratulate the premier
on this important decision. To make the venture politically
possible, one must avoid antagonising the country, and I believe

it is essential to enlist the support of the country people ...
The committee should consider how best to interest country
dwellers. It should be made clear that this will not be a place
for highbrows, but a place where people enjoy themselves. It
should certainly be licensed. Then with the introduction of
10 o'clock closing [of pubs], opera patrons would be able to
enjoy a drink at interval, in the continental manner ... At
present, one cannot attend a concert in the Sydney Town Hall
unless one is a subscriber, and one cannot become a subscriber
until a ticket holder dies. The committee might consider the
possibility of setting aside blocks of seats at the opera house for
use by casual country visitors.'

The following day's *Sydney Morning Herald* reported under
the headline 'An Opera House at Last?' that Mr Cahill showed
he was 'indeed in earnest and was confident of the support
of his government and party' for the opera house idea. 'That
Sydney requires an opera house is beyond dispute. That the state
government should take the lead in providing it and bear the
major part of the cost would also be accepted without question
in any European country. Yet the British tradition is very different and today England is still contemplating building its first
civic theatre in Coventry. For Sydney to go one better and build
a splendid opera house would indeed be a feather in her cap.'

• • •

George Molnar was considered the finest cartoonist of his
generation. His wit was as elegant as his art and he was fluent
in Hungarian, French, German and English. He could draw, he
could write, he could deliver Latin adages with aplomb. He was
just the man Cahill wanted to enlist for his pet project.

Molnar joined his Sydney University colleagues Professor of
Architecture Henry Ingham Ashworth and Professor of Town

and Country Planning Denis Winston, and fellow architect and occasional *Herald* architecture critic Walter Bunning at a special meeting of the NSW Chapter of the Royal Australian Institute of Architects (RAIA) held at the National Art Gallery of New South Wales to discuss the location of the planned opera house. The typed minutes of that meeting were covered with cursive corrections; clearly whoever had taken notes had struggled to keep pace with the conversation.

'There should be two major halls; one a large hall to seat 3000 people—mainly for opera, and a smaller hall for 1200 people for drama and music. No less than five acres would be required,' the minutes read. The building needed to be within central Sydney with access to public transport, and it should 'provide a worthy setting of a kind likely to enhance the architectural effect of a fine building'. 'Because of the special character and importance of this building and because another project of equal importance is unlikely to occur again for a very long time, it may be that the site should be on existing parklands.'

Many sites were considered—among them at College Street, The Domain, the Conservatorium and Wynyard Square—but, in the end, the group agreed with Goossens: it had to be Bennelong Point. 'We believe this to be an outstandingly suitable site, which, if properly developed, would provide a setting for the Opera House which would be unrivalled throughout the world,' the minutes read. 'Such a harbour setting would, at the same time, be characteristic of Sydney and provide a landmark for travellers as memorable as the Stockholm Town Hall or Doge's Palace in Venice, and as striking, in a different way, as the Sydney Harbour Bridge.'

The meeting also decided that the architect should be selected through an 'open competition (national or international) and that the chairman of assessors should be an architect of international repute, not resident in Australia and having special knowledge of similar projects'.

Bennelong Point was announced as the site for the opera house on 17 May 1955. The old Fort Macquarie tram shed would be detonated and demolished, the government said, and a competition would be launched in 1956 to find an architect.

But the issue of whether an international search should be undertaken had not been resolved and the pages of the *Herald* erupted. *Herald* critic Walter Bunning favoured keeping it local. Molnar argued for an international competition: 'We want for Sydney the best Opera House that can be built. This must mean an international competition. Apart from getting the best brains to ponder our problems, the worldwide interest centred on the Opera House of Sydney will be a good advertisement for Australia . . . A competition by invitation . . . invites only those architects whom you expect to have the best answer to your problem . . . Yet the magnificent lonely idea may still escape.'

Ultimately Molnar's argument prevailed; international it was to be. The premier established a committee chaired by Henry Ingham Ashworth to act as the client. By all accounts Ashworth, a self-important Englishman, was a bad choice as chair. Had Cahill chosen differently, the building of the Sydney Opera House might have been freed of at least some of the drama that later plagued it.

But it was another self-important Englishman, Eugene Goossens, who suddenly presented Cahill with a huge and unexpected scandal.

Chapter seven

'Sex, magic' and the maestro

Eugene Goossens was bored. The flamboyant conductor had grown tired of the battle for his public passion project and his wife Marjorie was abroad, yet again, on one of her regular extended visits. So, he began to focus on his private passion: black magic . . . and sex.

Browsing in a Sydney bookshop, he'd picked up a copy of a book by Rosaleen Norton, known as the 'Witch of Kings Cross'. The artist, a notorious Pan worshipper, had created her own coven of witches and was 'known to the police' because of two previous prosecutions for obscenity. With its references to paganism and ritual, *The Art of Rosaleen Norton* appealed to Goossens' long-standing interest in the occult, as did her drawings of devils and demons with their sexual undertones.

Goossens slipped the slim volume under his newspaper and discreetly paid for it. He later wrote her a letter and visited her at home for a 'cup of tea'.

Goossens must have been astounded at what he saw when he walked into Norton's Brougham Street den.[1] The walls were decorated with occult symbols and there was a makeshift altar she used for her coven's rituals. The flat was less than five minutes' walk from the rehearsal rooms where the conductor worked almost daily with the Sydney Symphony Orchestra. He soon developed a sexual relationship with both Norton and her lover Gavin Greenlees. In staid Sydney this was risky behaviour.

Goossens became obsessed by 'Roie', or 'Roiewitch' as he called his Bohemian, bisexual lover. When he was away on tour, he would pen her infatuated letters in which he referred to 'S.M.' ('sex magic'), frequently outlining the vivid details of his sexual fantasies with her. He would also draw provocative pictures.

'Anonymity is still best,' Goossens wrote in one note to Norton; 'without mentioning my name (which you will never do, in any connection)', said another. And then the hasty instruction scribbled beneath one of his characteristically lewd sketches in the corner of an aerogram: 'DESTROY ALL THIS'. But Norton kept the lurid letters in a bundle hidden in the back of a sofa at Brougham Street. Whatever her reasons, it was a decision that would eventually cost the conductor his career.

• • •

On 9 June 1955 Goossens was awarded a knighthood for his services to music. This brought great kudos to the ABC, Charles

---

1　In what follows—the calamitous fall from grace of Sir Eugene Goossens—I am indebted to the research of David Salter and, in particular, his article, 'The Conservatorium Director and the Witch', first published in the *Good Weekend* of 3 July 1999. Readers interested in the definitive account of this misadventure are urged to visit http://www.smh.com.au/good-weekend/gw-classics/the-conservatorium-director-and-the-witch-20150702-gi3h8y.html.

Moses, the SSO, the Conservatorium and the NSW government. Yet while he was being celebrated publicly, privately Goossens was becoming increasingly remote. There were questions, always, around his marriage. He felt trapped within a small circle of social elites in a city that was prudish and puritanical. He very much looked forward to going to London to meet the Queen for his investiture—as well as to frequent some of his favourite adult book stores.

In September 1955 two Sydney petty thieves, Frank Honer and Ray Ager, were shopping around a roll of undeveloped film stolen from the coven at Rosaleen Norton's flat. The price they set was £200. The editor of *The Sun*, the afternoon tabloid owned by the Fairfax family, had the film processed, but he decided the photos were 'too hot' for publication.

No doubt sensing a journalistic opportunity, however, *The Sun* arranged for the photos to find their way to the NSW Police. Vice Squad detectives quickly recognised Norton and Greenlees in the staged, but undeniably obscene, sado-sexual poses.

Honer and Ager were arrested, and police obtained admissions from the two would-be porn merchants that the material had been stolen from Norton's Brougham Street flat. Two days later, the Vice Squad swooped and arrested Norton and Greenlees at their home, charging the artist and her poet with 'making an obscene publication' and 'the abominable crime of buggery'.

During her arrest, Norton dived down the back of her lounge, no doubt to search for the letters.

'They're not there,' she said.

'No. I've got them,' Detective Bert Trevenar replied. He claimed he'd already been given the bundle of Goossens' letters by an anonymous 'informant' who'd infiltrated the coven.

The afternoon newspapers splashed coverage of the Brougham Street arrests—'Artist is questioned' and 'Artist faces charge over obscene film'—complete with pictures of Norton being dragged off to police headquarters. Not surprisingly, Goossens feared implication and hurriedly destroyed his private collection of pornography and black magic paraphernalia, probably by burning it in the backyard incinerator of his Wahroonga home.

'During the investigation I obtained information involving Sir Eugene Goossens, the then conductor of the Sydney Symphony Orchestra, with Norton together with photographs and letters,' Detective Trevenar said in his report of the raid. 'These letters clearly indicated that Goossens was involved in the practice of Pantheism [sic] and the resultant sex perversion with Norton and Greenlees. Detective Inspector Walden directed me to take the necessary steps to complete the investigation into Goossens' connection in these matters.'

Goossens had already left Sydney to collect his knighthood at Buckingham Palace. In the 1950s, the resources of the NSW Police did not extend to tailing globetrotting musicians, so the Sydney detectives called on their connections at *The Sun* to use their Fleet Street connections to tail the conductor. An exclusive for *The Sun* was guaranteed on his return. The newspaper had Goossens followed in London, where he was seen making unorthodox purchases in grubby newsagencies and bookshops in Soho and around Leicester Square.

On 7 March 1956, as Goossens began his journey home, the Vice Squad received thirty-six hours' notice from *The Sun* that he was on his way. Detective Trevenar was told his flight number, arrival time and, as a bonus, was told the conductor would be carrying a briefcase that 'probably had indecent photographs'.

On 8 March the Vice Squad briefed colleagues in Customs and suggested senior officers be at Sydney's Mascot airport the following morning to meet Goossens' Qantas flight and that they search his bags and 'even his person if required'. Only then, once the conductor was legally back in Australia, would the NSW Police be able to question him about the letters and photographs found in Norton's flat.

• • •

It was a rainy Friday morning when customs inspectors confronted Goossens on his arrival from London at Mascot airport.

'Do you have anything to declare?' asked Inspector Nathaniel Craig.

'No,' replied Goossens.

'What is in your briefcase?' one of the officers asked.

'Oh, that's only my musical scores,' he told them.

The officers asked to open the briefcase. They found seven brown paper parcels, including envelopes marked 'Beethoven' and 'Brahms'. The star of the SSO began to sweat profusely.

Six hours of questioning later, the material in the briefcase was revealed to be not musical scores, but pornography, masks, a film viewer and some incense sticks. They were concealed in heavy paper sealed with adhesive tape. Goossens had clearly gone to great effort.

Of this collection, 837 photographs, a set of prints, eight books (including *Sharing Their Pleasures*, *Continental Flossie* and *Nancy's Love Life*) and one spool of film were, in the opinion of senior customs officers, 'likely to constitute a breach of Section 233 of the Customs Act' (prohibiting 'the possession or importation of blasphemous, indecent or obscene works or articles').

'I welcome the seizing of them,' Goossens told the officers that day.

From his coat pocket, he handed over a document titled *Sex Magic*, which he confirmed he had copied out in his own hand. At first, he blamed his London valet, Arthur Billings, but the sheer volume of evidence soon reduced the great conductor to silence. By the end of the ordeal, he appealed to the customs officers for mercy.

'Gentlemen, I beg of you not to let this be known; if I could make amends some other way.'

The city's major newspapers were waiting to ambush the conductor as he was whisked away from the airport by the police.

At police headquarters, in the first-floor offices of the Vice Squad, Goossens faced his second harrowing interrogation of the day. Detective Trevenar showed him the letters found at Brougham Street. Goossens confirmed he had written them.

'There is repeated mention of "S.M. Rites" between you and Norton and Greenlees, made in the letters. What is that?' the detective asked.

'Our mutual interest in magic led to the occasional practise of a certain magic ceremonial. I was distinctly influenced by it and was induced to take part in certain manifestations which might come under the heading of "Sex Magic" . . . which is a ceremony involving sexual stimulation in a minor manner as I have more fully described to Detective Trevenar,' his statement read.

Trevenar's separate record of interview, written up on the same day, records the earlier interrogation relating to 'Sex Magic'.

'I said: "How is that rite conducted?" He said: "We undressed and sat on the floor in a circle. Miss Norton conducted the verbal part of the Rite. I then performed the sex stimulation on her." I said: "How did you do that?" He said: "I placed my tongue in her sexual organ and kept moving it until I stimulated her."'

The mysterious ritual 'Sex Magic' was nothing more than Goossens' euphemism for oral sex.

• • •

'It is difficult to imagine a worse case,' Mr JD Holmes QC said, as he outlined the Crown's case against Sir Eugene Goossens in the Court of Petty Sessions in Martin Place on 22 March 1956.

The conductor's counsel was the colourful criminal barrister Jack Shand, considered the best of his era and likely paid by the taxpayers via the ABC coffers. Shand pleaded guilty on his client's behalf to having imported prohibited goods, and read a statement from Dr George Blaxland, who said Goossens was in a state of physical and mental collapse at his Wahroonga home and would not be fit to attend court.

Shand then called the ABC's Charles Moses to the stand as a character witness. The two may have been foes on opera house matters, but Moses had enormous respect for Goossens, as he told the court.

Shand: 'Would you say the defendant has done very much for Australian music?'

Moses: 'Undoubtedly. I would say the engagement of Sir Eugene Goossens from a musical point of view was one of the most fortunate things that could have happened for this country.'

It wasn't a trial in the proper sense. Shand's job was to keep Goossens out of jail and confine any punishment to the maximum fine (£100). He was successful in both these goals. Goossens was forced to resign as conductor of the SSO and director of the Conservatorium.

The scandal spread quickly through Sydney, and was soon gossip fodder for newspapers across the nation. There was talk his marriage had been troubled for some time, a truth perhaps confirmed by the fact Mrs Goossens—now Lady Marjorie—was holidaying solo in Europe when news broke of her husband's arrest. While 'resting in a convent near Paris', Lady Goossens denied rumours of a separation and vowed to stand by her husband no matter what happened. 'I have offered to come back if necessary to give evidence on his behalf,' she said.

Despite Lady Goossens' promises, she didn't come back to Sydney. Instead, her husband boarded a KLM flight for Rome under a false name—on his sixty-third birthday, a fact an accompanying journalist, who was paid by his paper to follow the conductor to Italy, drew to his attention en route.

Goossens' solicitor, Mervyn Finlay, relayed the following final message to Australia: 'It is my misfortune that I allowed myself to be used to bring prohibited matter into this country as a result of persistent menaces I could not ignore, involving others.'

The *Daily Mirror* reported that Sir Eugene and Lady Goossens were reunited in a dramatic scene at Rome airport. 'When the couple reached Nice they booked a double room at the Hotel Massena, and Sir Eugene ordered the hotel staff not to let anyone see him, or to accept phone calls.'

But the harmonious reunion was short-lived. The marriage broke down almost immediately. Lady Goossens had enrolled her stepdaughters in educational institutions in France, but this was an alibi to cover her own liaison there with a Polish count. She left Goossens, who returned to the United Kingdom alone and in disgrace. Despite calls in Australia to have him stripped of his knighthood, this did not happen.

While Goossens and his supporters in Australia claimed he was set up, blackmailed perhaps by Norton and Greenlees, the scandal followed him for the rest of his life. He never returned to Australia. 'The great services rendered by Sir Eugene Goossens to Australia, and Sydney in particular, have apparently been forgotten overnight,' letter-writer W Wager observed in the *Sydney Morning Herald* on 15 March 1956.

Sir Eugene Goossens was not the only person involved with the creation of the Sydney Opera House who would never see it

built. Nor was he the last to have his reputation destroyed in a
flurry of controversy. He was simply the first.

• • •

With Goossens gone, the competition to find an architect for
an opera house continued. Perhaps because of its stunning
location at Bennelong Point, 881 entries were registered. Of
these, deposits were received and competition books sent to
722 possible entrants from forty-five different countries. By the
cut-off date of 3 December 1956, 233 entries had been received.
A reporter in the *Daily Telegraph* quipped that 'entries for the
State Opera House design make an interesting design display in
themselves . . . if the worst happens they could just about build
the Opera House out of the packing cases'. This was a stagger-
ing result for a competition at the far end of the world.

Entries were received from Germany, Morocco, England,
Iran and Kenya, as well as one from Yugoslavia, still in the
communist bloc. Sixty-one entries came from Australia, including one from *Herald* architecture critic Walter Bunning and
another from a post-war émigré called Harry Seidler. George
Molnar also entered through the firm Stephenson and Turner.
His vision was in the shape of a Manly ferry, in keeping with the
location's nautical theme.

• • •

'The promoters invite all architects, who are members of their
respective Architectural Institutes in any country in the world to
submit designs in competition for—a proposed National Opera
House, to be erected on Bennelong Point, Sydney, Australia,
in accordance with these conditions and the annexed appen-
dices', the competition's guidelines—as the twenty-five-page
booklet known as the 'brown book'—announced. Entrants who

submitted a deposit of £10 would be sent the conditions, which would be refunded to those architects who submitted a bona fide design. The 'winner would need to become registered in NSW as an architect under the Architects Act (1921–46) before he can be appointed'.

Three of the four assessors—Henry Ingham Ashworth, who had originally been involved in selecting the panel, Leslie Martin and Cobden Parkes—came together for the first time on 7 January 1957. Sporting the artistic accoutrements of the era and looking like a 1950s barbershop quartet (braces and all), they smoked pipes or cigars and wore bow ties and kerchiefs. Affectation was writ large. Tobacco smoke as well as pomposity hung heavily within the room in the Art Gallery where the trio gathered that first day.

Manchester-born Ingham Ashworth had been in Sydney for only five years when Premier Cahill asked him to become chairman of the judging panel in 1954. He'd attended Manchester Grammar and Manchester University before serving as a soldier in India and Burma in World War II. At the University of Sydney, he was not popular with students. He was perceived as too British and conservative, and held traditional views about the role of women that discouraged female students. He has been described variously as 'a second-rate, self-important Englishman' (Sydney architect Don Gazzard) and 'a complete blunderer who thought he was Churchill' (Sydney architect Philip Drew).

Fellow Mancurnian Leslie Martin, the first chair of architecture at Cambridge University, had been born a year before Ingham Ashworth; he also had attended Manchester Grammar and Manchester University and the two men were acquainted. During World War II, Martin supervised the rebuilding of damaged British railway stations. But he is best known for his work as architect of London's Royal Festival Hall, and his experience with this project is the likely reason he was asked to be on the judging panel in Sydney. A form-over-function kind of architect, he looked to the angular clean lines of Scandinavian architecture for inspiration; Finnish architect Alvar Aalto was said to be an early influence on him.

Cobden Parkes, son of the five-time NSW premier and 'Father of Federation' Henry Parkes, was the only Australian judge. The Balmain-born Government Architect worked as a draughtsman before serving both at Gallipoli and on the Western Front. Having lost three fingers after being wounded at Gallipoli, he rejoined the Department of Public Works on his return to Australia and studied architecture at Sydney Tech at night. A man of conservative tastes, he had worked on the portico and great reading room of the State Library of New South Wales (fine examples of classicism) and had absolutely no notion of modernism.

The fourth member of the judging panel arrived late, but it was he who was to provide the most decisive voice. With Scandinavian sensibilities, Eero Saarinen was the wonder boy of American architecture. Everybody wanted his advice and big American corporations such as John Deere and IBM paid him handsomely for it. It was considered quite a coup to have even persuaded him to join the panel.

When he swanned in four days late to the judging room, his task was to convince his fellow judges that they should all sing from the same song sheet.

Chapter eight

Gentlemen, here is your opera house

Aline Louchheim, the associate art editor and critic for the *New York Times*, fastened her seatbelt as her plane started its descent into Detroit Metro Airport. It was a wintry day in January 1953. She'd come from New York to write a profile on the Finnish-born Eero Saarinen, who was emerging as one of America's most promising architects.

Aged thirty-eight, Louchheim had cultivated a quality in herself that her newspaper colleagues described as 'intelluptuous'—possessing a combination of intelligence and voluptuousness that many found irresistible. This made her a great reporter—people usually told her too much.

Saarinen was forty-three and the quintessence of 1950s architectural panache, a man's man of modernism who wore suits and bow ties and smoked a pipe. He'd shot to prominence with his General Motors Technical Centre in Michigan and Missouri Gateway Arch, the world's tallest arch at

180 metres. He possessed what his fellow Finns call *sisu*, an ability to pull something out of yourself you didn't think possible. In his adopted home, America, they called this 'guts' and determination.

A workaholic, he averaged a steady twelve-hour day. Working on the Floating Staircase, the centrepiece of the General Motors (GM) building, Saarinen walked into his office at 8 a.m. on Christmas morning to ask: 'Where is everyone?'

'It's Christmas Day,' one of the few colleagues at work explained.

'Blah . . . so what,' the driven designer replied.

Despite his snappy appearance, the celebrity architect was something of a mystery. He was not communicative, except— according to Balthazar Korab, one of his employees—at 'martini parties', where he was known to sketch some of his best ideas on napkins. (Korab went on to be an entrant in the Sydney Opera House design competition.)

So, it was with some trepidation that Louchheim donned her fur coat and gingerly descended the stairs onto the icy tarmac. Saarinen met her inside the airport terminal and drove her in his company car to the GM building in the suburb of Warren.

A second-generation architect, Saarinen had been born in Helsinki in 1910 on his father, Eliel's, thirty-seventh birthday. Saarinen senior was Finland's foremost architect and had designed his country's pavilion at the Paris World Fair of 1900. He brought art nouveau to the masses, his early work culminating in his design for the Helsinki Central Railway Station in the style of Scandinavian National Romanticism. He later designed a set of postage stamps and Finland's bank notes. Saarinen's lakeside home and design studio, Hvitträsk (White Lake) in the woods west of Helsinki, was like a fairy-tale castle inspired by the epic Finnish poem *Kalevala*.

As in Sweden, the Finnish art and architectural world was tightly knit. In time Hvitträsk became an artistic hub, its visitors including the Finnish composer Jean Sibelius, Austrian composer Gustav Mahler and author Maxim Gorky fleeing Russian police. 'Sounds of piano playing and high-pitched gaiety were heard in the big living room late into the night,' wrote Aline Louchheim of the house in a 1948 profile of Saarinen senior for the *New York Times Magazine*.

Eero Saarinen had been raised beneath the vaulted ceilings of this extraordinary family home. Falling asleep each night under those curves and cupolas gave him a deep understanding of the strength of the vault, an architectural form that found its way into all his major architectural works and furniture design. He also admired other architects who embraced the curve.

In the early 1920s, Eero's father entered a competition to design the headquarters for the *Chicago Tribune*. He didn't win, but with the US$20,000 prize money for being runner-up, he boarded a boat with his family bound for Ellis Island, New York.

Eero was thirteen when the family arrived in the United States in 1923. Settling in Chicago, the Saarinens were part of the Scandinavian influx that shaped the look and feel of America's Midwest, which over the years became a magnet for the masters of modernism, in both architecture and design. From the Prairie School (whose most famous proponent was Frank Lloyd Wright) to the skyscraper, the Midwest ultimately influenced the shape of modern cities throughout the world. Its auto companies, too, became design academies with tremendous impact on tastes worldwide.

Saarinen senior took a job teaching architecture at the University of Michigan in Ann Arbor, and was then invited to design Detroit's prestigious Cranbrook Educational Community. Eero, an architectural prodigy, became an understudy to his father, a master's apprentice. At seventeen, he designed a line of pink chairs for the Cranbrook campus. Thus began the creation of some of the most iconic pieces of modern design, classics such as the Swivel Tulip Chair and the Reclining Womb Chair. After graduating from Cranbrook, Eero studied sculpture in France, and then architecture at Yale, before returning to work in his father's office.

In 1947 the Jefferson National Expansion Memorial Association launched a national design competition for a monument at St Louis, Missouri, to honour Thomas Jefferson. Both Saarinens entered. When the telegrams announcing that Saarinen & Associates had won the $40,000 competition arrived at their Detroit office, champagne was ordered to celebrate what was assumed to be Eliel's victory. It wasn't until the following day that they learnt the winner was in fact Eero's Gateway Arch, a stainless-steel structure envisaged as a monument to the westward expansion of the United States. It subsequently became the internationally recognised symbol of St Louis and cemented Eero Saarinen's star status. The GM project at Warren only confirmed his genius.

General Motors had initially approached Saarinen senior in 1944 to design its Technical Center. Postponed until after the end of World War II, in 1949 Eero set to work on the project in collaboration with his father, who died shortly afterwards in 1950.

Completed in 1956, the 710-acre campus comprised thirty-eight buildings, none of them more than three storeys high, set among a landscape of 13,000 trees. It was a modernist's dream. Among its innovations were Eero's masterpiece the Floating Stairs, located in the GM Research Labs and Design Studio, and its windows based on the mechanical sealing gasket used on car windshields, a technique now used the world over in office construction. The American Institute of Architects ultimately hailed the GM Technical Center as the most outstanding architectural project of its era and described it as the 'Versailles of Industry'.

With work proceeding on both the St Louis and General Motors projects, their visionary creator was rapidly developing a reputation that would place him in the pantheon of modernist architecture, joining Le Corbusier, Walter Gropius and Frank Lloyd Wright. Which is why the *New York Times* was sending one of its best reporters to learn more about this rising talent.

• • •

When they met in 1953, Aline Louchheim and Eero Saarinen were both married. Aline's husband was back in New York with their two children and nanny; Saarinen's wife Lily was at home with their two children in Michigan. But both were instantly swept off their feet, Aline first by the brilliant designs for the GM buildings and then by the man who had created them. They made love the same night.

By the time Aline's profile, 'Now Saarinen the Son', appeared in the *New York Times Magazine* on 23 April, they were having an affair. Nearly a year later they would marry, and she would become Mrs Aline B Saarinen, moving into Eero's remodelled Victorian farmhouse in Bloomfield Hills. They had a son, Eames, named in honour of Eero's best friend, designer Charles Eames.

Saarinen's second marriage was said to be a meeting of minds. Aline gave up her journalism career to became 'Head of Information Service' at Eero Saarinen & Associates, and her husband's loudest cheerleader. With her beguiling manner, she helped captivate the corporate chiefs, ambassadors and university presidents who became her husband's clients. She pitched his projects to the magazine editors for whom she had previously worked.

On 2 July 1956 Saarinen appeared on the cover of *TIME* magazine. He was then working on the wing-shaped thin shell roof of the TWA Flight Center at New York's Idlewild Airport (renamed John F Kennedy Airport in 1963). His two ultra-modern designs at Boston's Massachusetts Institute of Technology (MIT)—the Kresge auditorium, especially its glass curtain wall, and the MIT chapel—were garnering praise. 'Saarinen sleeps, eats and dreams architecture, and reduces just about every experience in life to architectural terms', *TIME* reported under the headline 'The Maturing of Modern'. 'Last week, as his wife watched with fascination, he casually turned over his breakfast grapefruit, began carving out elliptical parabolic arches which he then carried off to the office to see if they might do as an idea for the office model of T.W.A.'s new terminal at Idlewild.'

The story was read by architects the world over, perhaps even by Jørn Utzon in Denmark, and most likely Henry Ingham Ashworth in Sydney. Which is how this man of the moment in the design world came to be invited to join the panel to help decide the winning entry in the international competition to design the Sydney Opera House.

• • •

It's easy to see why Australia awaited Eero Saarinen with breathless anticipation. In the week leading up to his January 1957 arrival, Walter Bunning wrote a gushing profile of him for the *Sydney Morning Herald*:

> Eero Saarinen, at the age of 46, is an architect of world stature whose works include public buildings, churches and concert halls ranging from the vast research laboratories of the General Motors Company at Detroit to the new cave

where a pool enters its mouth. This adds a sense of mystery
in keeping with the spiritual nature of the building.

In design everyone senses Saarinen's concern with the
environment of his buildings. For example, in the design
for the United States Embassy in London, he has captured
the classical dignity of the Georgian town houses lining the
Bloomsbury Squares but this building uses contemporary
materials in an original way. It is the sensitivity to environment in addition to his concern with pure form and
simplicity which places Saarinen high in world esteem.
The key to Saarinen's flow of ideas is to be found partly
in his father. Eliel was a famous Finnish architect who had
carried out notable buildings in his native Helsinki and had
won the second prize in the Canberra planning competition
before going to America in 1921.

[Eero Saarinen's] designs are marked by a very individual approach to each problem, for he is not a follower of
any of the recognised contemporary schools of thought. In
a country where Walter Gropius, Frank Lloyd Wright and
Mies van der Rohe are regarded as leaders of architectural
thought and have established a wide following, Saarinen
stands apart and unique. He likes to suit each building to
its setting and surroundings in a way which denies any
dogmatic rules of design, and because of this overriding aim
it is difficult to discern the general principle upon which
his buildings are developed. He is the one leading architect
who is always likely to surprise with his unique solution to
a problem.

On Friday, 11 January 1957, Eero Saarinen arrived with
Aline at Sydney's Mascot airport. The pair had travelled via
Indonesia, taking several days to make the journey from the

United States. It was a humid day and they went straight to the Australia Hotel, regarded as 'Sydney's premier hotel', *the* place to stay and the place to be seen.

Aline rested after the long journey, but a freshened Saarinen shot down the grey and white marble stairs of the hotel's Castlereagh Street entrance and walked briskly up Martin Place and across The Domain to the Art Gallery of New South Wales to join the judging panel.

The three other judges were by then well advanced in the business of culling entries, a process that had begun the previous Monday, 7 January. It was exhausting and exacting work.

Professor Ingham Ashworth had met Sir Leslie Martin at the airport when he arrived the previous Monday from San Francisco and they had started judging immediately. A room at the art gallery had been especially cleared of paintings so plans could be displayed on the walls. According to the *Daily Telegraph*, they discarded a hundred designs in one day. By the time Saarinen arrived, they had selected ten 'possibles'. They were met with silence from Saarinen as he spent the morning poring over the short list.

Cobden Parkes could see Saarinen was unimpressed. 'Lunch, perhaps?' he suggested.

Parkes shepherded him to a little kiosk across the road from the gallery. Despite being tired from his long trip, Saarinen asked Parkes to take him on a short tour of the city.

They walked down to Mrs Macquarie's Chair in the Royal Botanic Garden on the edge of Sydney Harbour, to see Sydney at its sparkling best. Parkes pointed out the sandstone glory of NSW Government House and a few other landmarks. But Saarinen was uninterested; his focus seemed to be elsewhere. 'No, never mind that! Let's not think about anything other than the opera house site. Where is it?' he asked.

Parkes pointed out the site—on the other side of Farm Cove, where the First Fleet convicts had landed, with its backdrop of the Sydney Harbour Bridge.

Saarinen set to work. He pulled an old envelope and a 4B pencil out of his pocket and made a pencil sketch of Bennelong Point with a vague outline of a building standing on it. What he saw before him, he later confessed to Parkes, was what he considered one of the best sites in the world for an opera house.

'One of its great merits is the absence of surrounding buildings, leaving the architect free to break all the traditions of previous buildings in Sydney if he wished to,' he told the *Herald* in an interview published on 12 January. 'Sydney will undoubtedly have an Opera House which will be known throughout the world,' he proclaimed.

Back in the judging room, Saarinen skimmed through the entries rejected before his arrival. He retrieved one and was immediately struck by its originality. He stood back to take in what he saw. Then he looked at it up close to view it in detail. With a flourish he declared in his heavy Finnish accent: 'Gentlemen, here is your opera house.'

• • •

It took ten days—from 7 to 17 January—for the panel to make its final decision. 'Short in days perhaps, but we made up for it in hours,' Cobden Parkes later told the *Herald*.

'We had an extremely difficult job choosing the design,' Ingham Ashworth confessed many years later. 'After all, we weren't choosing Miss Australia or something equally boring.'

Eero Saarinen was a veteran entrant in international design competitions and was well used to the rigours of the judging process. He was also a master of the late arrival—letting others do the difficult work of culling while he took all the glory in the decision.

'It was almost a night and day job except a Sunday morning we took off to go to Palm Beach,' Saarinen told the press conference before the winner was announced. 'Usually an international contest of this kind can be judged in three to four days. The requirements of your Opera House competition called for such detail that it has taken a lot longer to judge. But a most pleasant job to work on. The judging has been most cordial. And you can say that our choices were unanimous. Absolutely unanimous.'

But the truth of the matter was that had Saarinen not retrieved entry number 218 from the pile of rejected designs, the shape of modern Sydney would be different today. He pressed with all his energy for this entry to receive the first prize against every argument raised by his fellow judges. In the end their conservative tastes yielded to Saarinen's modernist sensibilities.

Whatever prompted him to champion this entry as forcefully as he did remains uncertain. What is certain, however, is this: in one decisive move, he transferred entry number 218 from oblivion to the edge of the possible.

* * *

• • •

Chapter nine

Chapter nine

And the winner is . . .

The exterior walls of the classically elegant Art Gallery of New South Wales pay homage to great European masters such as Donatello, Rembrandt, Raphael and Giotto. Were it not for the white cockatoos screeching raucously overhead, from the outside this could be any art gallery in any city in the Western world.

On 10 December 1956, it was closed to the public—except for the court housing its Australian Collection, including paintings by Arthur Streeton and Tom Roberts. The world's eyes were still on Melbourne, where two days before the city had hosted the closing ceremony of its successful Olympic Games. In Sydney, gallery employees were busy stripping artworks from the walls to make way for the hundreds of opera house competition entries that were to remain on those walls, shielded from the general view by standing screens erected by Department of Public Works employees, until the announcement. Much work had gone into these preparations. Since the previous year, the

competition chair Henry Ingham Ashworth had been corre-
sponding with the Art Gallery trustees about the judging.

The public exhibition of the opera house competition entries
would be on display from 29 January until 15 February 1957,
running concurrently with the gallery's major drawcard—the
Archibald Prize, from 19 January until 17 February.

On Friday, 18 January, the four judges handed the sealed
envelope containing their selection report to the Opera House
Committee chairman, 'Silent Stan' Haviland, in an informal
ceremony at the ornate Victorian Renaissance Revival–style Lands
Department building on Bridge Street. Often lovingly referred to
by Sydneysiders as one of the 'sandstones', this old government
building had been the beating heart of public life since the late
eighteenth century. Its Doric, Ionic and Corinthian pilasters, with
its 'onion' copper-domed clock tower and its entranceway for
horse-drawn carriages, could not be stylistically more different
from the modernist sleek lines of the winning entry, whose scheme
number Haviland now clutched in the yellow manila envelope.

'The architect has made good use of quite new materials,
I think we can say,' Professor Martin said in the press conference before the announcement. 'It is a building which will have
to stand for a number of years. And it is the sort of design which
will be appreciated in the future.'

'Is there anything . . . a little appetiser you can offer?' one
of the journalists begged.

'I'm afraid that's all I can say,' Martin replied apologetically.

The four judges were the picture of 1950s fashionable
elegance that day, just as they had been most days during the
judging. They wore silver sleeve garters to keep their shirt cuffs
from soiling, and Brylcreemed their hair slickly into place. They
wiped their brows with crisp white linen handkerchiefs to stop
the sweat pouring down their faces this sticky summer's day.

Saarinen, a stocky, intense and bespectacled man, had a stutter that became more noticeable the more nervous he became. And that day he was nervous. Not only had he put his professional reputation on the line by so forcefully arguing the merits of the winning entry, but there was a lot at stake—not just for him, but for Sydney as a whole and the nation as well. While Aline was swimming at Bondi and exploring the city, her husband was playing through the possible reactions to the choice he had championed.

'There'll be criticism, of course, but you can't do a good piece of work without criticism,' Saarinen hinted.

Up until this point, the judges only knew the winner and runners up by their entry numbers. It was only after the handover at the Lands Department that prize winners' names were revealed in the strictest of confidence. First prize was £5000, second £2000 and third £1000.

The next day, a Saturday, with squally north-east winds heralding bush fire danger, the international judges, Sir Leslie Martin and Eero Saarinen, flew to London. Martin was going home, and Saarinen and his wife were taking the long way to the United States via Europe.

• • •

The winning drawings submitted as scheme number 218 were simple and light on detail to the point of being only diagrammatic. In order to convey the genius of this design to his fellow judges, Saarinen had sketched two more detailed drawings in crayon to convince them. They were subsequently signed by Saarinen and inscribed 'to J. J. Cahill, Premier NSW'.

Henry Ingham Ashworth commissioned his architectural colleague Arthur Baldwinson at the University of Sydney to create a watercolour of the winning scheme for the public announcement.

Saarinen may have been able to convince the judges of the winner, but Ingham Ashworth was not so sure he'd be able to convince the public and politicians on such sketchy drawings. Baldwinson placed the building in situ on Bennelong Point.

Sydneysiders sweltered in the week following the handover of the winners' envelope. They longed for the cool change of a southerly buster, and the familiar sound of wind rattling Venetian blinds in homes across the city.

The tension created by the unrelenting heat was matched by the expectation of the announcement of the winner of the opera house design competition. Other than the first concert by the American rock 'n' rollers Bill Haley and his Comets the previous week, the city was preoccupied by little else. The announcement was to be broadcast live on ABC Radio and on TV, which had been introduced in Australia just the year before, in 1956.

Architect Bertrand James 'BJ' Waterhouse, president of the Art Gallery, opened the ceremony to announce the competition winner at 3 p.m. on Tuesday 29 January 1957. He'd come from his home at Neutral Bay on the north side of the harbour, where he ran a private architectural practice.

'One of the greatest charms of an architectural competition is that one never knows at all what the results will be. I remember another architectural competition, many years ago, when all the Gothicist dons of England competed for the Liverpool Cathedral,' he began. 'All and sundry were sure that a certain prominent don who had done a great deal of important work would win. But it proved to be Sir Giles Gilbert Scott, then aged twenty-one. So, we never know. We might find some young man here who has produced something of real architectural value. Hence the excitement.'

There was certainly excitement in the room that day on Art Gallery Road. The audience wondered if the Yorkshireman was hinting that a local architect had won? Walter Bunning's chest was already bursting with pride; any more and the buttons on his cotton shirt would have popped off. As the *Herald*'s architectural critic, he thought he was the favourite and no doubt hoped that his glowing praise of the visiting judges might have helped him to gain their favour. But their decision had already been made by the time he interviewed them.

It seems unlikely that BJ Waterhouse knew the identity of the winner any more than the audience. A trained architect, his specialty was residential design. He'd made a name for himself in 1925 for the textured stucco walls and shuttered windows of a yellow house called Nutcote in Neutral Bay that had been commissioned by May Gibbs, Australia's favourite children's author famous for her classic book about two gumnut babies called Snugglepot and Cuddlepie. If Waterhouse did have any inside information, he wasn't letting on.

Reporters were seated at a table below a florid Italian painting by Carlo Cignani called *The Five Senses*. A curious George Molnar was in the crowd too; like the reporters, he had been given the assessors' report and was quickly scanning it for clues. It described the winning design ('The white sail-like forms of the shell vaults relate to the harbour as the sails of its yachts . . .'), but no names were mentioned.

There was a restlessness in the room as entrants, reporters, photographers and cameramen wriggled impatiently in their seats.

'There are two French words on the plan,' said a photographer who had been given behind-the-scenes access to take shots of the winning design, 'if that means anything.'

'Is the winner a Frenchman?' asked one of the press pack.

'Well, at least a Continental,' another replied.

George Molnar, having studied the assessors' report, ducked behind the dais; after a quick survey of the drawings, he matched the winner with the number on the assessors' report. He didn't have a name; he just knew it wasn't him. 'If it hasn't got wings, it hasn't won,' he blurted to the waiting pressmen.

The Opera House Committee chairman, Stan Haviland, moved onto the dais. He explained how the four judges had worked through over two thousand drawings—each entrant had submitted around eight to ten double elephant sheets. 'It is interesting to know that at all stages of the adjudication, the assessors amused themselves by trying to guess the nationality of the winner—and they were all wrong.'

At 3.15 p.m. Haviland handed over to Premier Cahill, giving him the vital envelope plus the two rough sketches drawn and signed by Saarinen. Cahill, always the master of understatement, was showing himself to be also the master of suspense. Having turned sixty-six the previous week, he was clearly excited to be taking centre stage to announce the winner. Although he was no trained thespian, his years spent honing his public speaking skills at the Workers' Educational Association and in debating societies had taught him a knack for creating dramatic tension.

A movie camera started purring behind a battery of arc lights; the ABC was filming. A press photographer hurried across the floor. The moment of enlightenment was nearing. But Cahill was in no hurry to open the envelope. He scanned the crowd; he knew when he had the audience eating out of the palm of his hand. 'I'm confident that everyone, once having seen the winning design, will think the prize money well spent,' he said.

At 3.22 p.m. Cahill paused. 'Before announcing the name of the person who submitted the winning design, I shall run the risk of trying your patience by making one or two general remarks . . .'

A whisper ran through the crowd. Toes were tapping, ties were loosened, gentlemen removed their jackets, and sweat poured down the faces of the men gathered in the non-air-conditioned gallery. Ladies removed their white gloves, mopped their brows and fanned themselves with the assessors' report. Sighs could be heard around the room. The crowd was getting impatient.

At 3.27 p.m. Cahill paused again. 'Before I announce the prize . . . if I can just for a moment take your minds back to a meeting two years ago in the library building when it was decided that this project should be put into hand . . .'

• • •

At Denmark's Kronborg Castle, on the other side of the world, it was 7.27 a.m. The fifteenth-century castle situated at Helsingør was immortalised as Elsinore in William Shakespeare's *Hamlet*. The Bard describes its winter weather this way: 'the air bites shrewdly . . . it is a nipping and eager air'. On this January day in 1957 the Dannebrog, the Danish flag, flapped in the wind as fishing boats left the Helsingør shore.

Kronborg Castle sits starkly on the edge of the Danish peninsula that juts out of the narrowest point of the Øresund, the sound between Denmark and Sweden. Helsingør is, of course, home to the shipyard where Aage Utzon worked. Built on the 'sandy tongue' at the mouth of the sound, it is surrounded by water— the inlet at its entrance serves as a moat with a drawbridge. Kronberg's elegant green copper turret reaches like a stalactite skyward from the castle's massive fortifications, built from sandstone. It had been to this promontory that Jørn Utzon went when seeking inspiration for his submission to the biggest competition of his career so far, to design the Sydney Opera House.

By 1957 Utzon had sent entries to at least twenty competitions over the course of twelve years. These had ranged from bids to build London's Crystal Palace to the design for a Danish crematorium. He had won seven of the twenty competitions, but none had resulted in a commission. He had long ago stopped himself from investing in the idea of winning.

One competition had been particularly close to his heart: the design for a Swedish affordable housing project that used courtyards. Utzon loved Chinese courtyards—closed on the outside, but open to a central interior—and had included them in his entry. He won first prize, but the project did not go ahead. He took his prize-winning plans to the mayor of Helsingør, who commissioned the Kingo project: sixty-three affordable houses on 4 hectares of land. Kingo and his own home in Hellebæk had been his major accomplishments up until 1957. To keep his business afloat he designed lamps, notably the U336 pendant lamp, while he was working on his Sydney proposal.

For six months the Sydney competition occupied his waking thoughts and ignited his creative fire. He was curious about this city on the other side of the world that he'd never visited, and he spent weeks researching the site. He went to the Australian embassy in Copenhagen to watch an 8mm film about Sydney. He browsed the embassy's books and brochures. He wrote away for maritime charts and pored over them late into the night.

At Kronborg Castle he paced out distances, his long legs stretching to count the metres as he tried to picture Bennelong Point. While walking around the castle's ancient walls, he realised that the Sydney Opera House would be like Kronborg: viewed from all sides. He had often sailed around the Kronborg peninsula, observing the castle from all angles, so knew the Sydney Opera House could not have an ugly side. It needed to be beautiful from all angles. Around, above and below. From a ferry on the harbour or from a car on the Harbour Bridge.

Taking some inspiration from the white sail boats scurrying over the waters around the castle, he went back to his office at

Helsingør with a window looking out onto a serene pond. He
glanced at a white swan and thought how the arc of its white
wings provided a beautiful form, a small but significant symbol.
He decided shells would cover the two halls in his project that
would be placed side by side and raised on a podium like the
Zapotec city of Monte Albán in Oaxaca. It would be beautiful
from all angles.

Utzon thought about this concept for many months and
drew some sketches. His entry was one of the last to arrive—
number 218 in a field of 233. He likely gave it little more
thought until that January morning when he and his wife went
walking in the Hellebæk forest, and a call came from a newspaper reporter that would change their world.

• • •

In Sydney, the premier continued to play the crowd, but at 3.29 p.m.
he opened his envelope and announced: 'The design awarded
the first premium is scheme number 218; the design awarded the
second premium is number 28; and the design awarded third
premium is scheme number 62.'

Cahill hesitated. 'Those are the numbers,' he said, noticeably
flustered. 'I'm afraid I haven't the names. Whether somebody
will tell us . . .'

Stan Haviland quickly stepped forward and found another
document in the premier's envelope.

'Design awarded first premium,' read Cahill, 'is scheme
number 218, submitted by Jorn Utzon—the correct pronunciation is *Yawn Ootson*—of Hellebæk, Denmark, thirty-eight
years of age.'

The crowd erupted. Disappointed entrants mingled in the
room. Others made their way to take a closer look at the winning
entry displayed on the art gallery walls. At last the winner had a

name, but who was he? Did anyone know anything about him? How might they contact him? The committee members tried to find an address and phone number to give to reporters, while Stan Haviland arranged for the official cable to be sent to Utzon notifying him of his win.

At 4 p.m. an audio recording of the two absent judges in conversation with Professor Ashworth supporting their decision was played. Eero Saarinen, the stutterer, explained in his Finnish-accented American drawl why such a controversial entry had been chosen. Lesley Martin—who would later become Sir Lesley—conceded that the winning sketches were minimal, but that they had the makings of one of the world's finest buildings. 'In my opinion the winning design was a great building and one which would work. I think the shell vaults of the roof will give an impression of the sails of yachts,' Professor Martin said.

Saarinen explained the design's most appealing feature was that, as a total concept, it was an outstanding piece of art. He did concede, however, that it would not conform with what most people presently had in mind as an opera house. 'All Gothic cathedrals had used the interlocking shell vault system, but theirs had been made from stone,' he said on the crackly audio tape. 'The system of this winning design is in use in Italy, Brazil, Madrid and America.'

In concluding the ceremony, the premier explained that the assessors expected some criticism of the design they had chosen. 'It is not my intention to enter the lists on that score at any time. I shall leave controversy of that nature to those better qualified than myself,' he said.

But he did defend the decision to build an opera house and the choice of Bennelong Point. This criticism, he said, was 'something that the government and I will have to face'. Sydney, a city of nearly two million people, still had no place for the large-scale presentation of music, choral works, opera or ballet, he said. This was 'regrettable'. 'To those who say that this is not the time to commence such a project, I would say that to postpone a decision would turn an immediately desirable work into an urgent necessity in the not too distant future. In the meantime, music and theatre would be in danger of languishing through lack of official encouragement, and suitable sites would become a fast diminishing commodity. I am sure that most will agree that the government's decision was not rash or ill-considered.'

And so it was that a man whose only musical instrument in his Marrickville home was a pianola assured the future of a performance space for classical music in his hometown. If Cahill could be accused of playing it up for the crowd that day, it was only a preview of how this Sydney saga would unfold.

Chapter ten

Poetry or pastry?

Entry 220 by the Austrian-born local architect Harry Seidler was one of the last to be received, even though it probably had the shortest distances to travel: a mere 6 kilometres or so from Sydney's eastern suburbs to the Lands Department in the CBD.

Seidler, a thirty-three-year-old Harvard graduate, committed modernist and 1951 winner of the Sulman Prize for architecture, had made a name for himself in Sydney for his residential buildings. He was also known for his dapper grey suits—more Brooks Brothers than Savile Row—and snappy style. Coming to the attention of the *Sun-Herald*'s women's pages, he was nominated as one of Sydney's ten best-dressed bachelors and was noted for his love of 'gay bow ties, soft shirts' and the fact he paid a 'lot of attention to his shoes'.

He and his five-man team worked on paid residential projects during the day. Then from dusk till dawn over many nights they finessed their entry in the small design studio

under his Point Piper house in order to meet the competition's
3 December deadline. Conceived according to Seidler's taste
in the Bauhaus style, his team's submission was a functional
building and far from flamboyant—very correct, with excellent
sight lines and acoustics (advice was received from a famous
acoustic engineer). It was commended by the judges, but it
wasn't among the top three.

On the day of the announcement Seidler raced to the Art
Gallery from his Point Piper studio, arriving just before 3 p.m.
He could see his arch rival, the *Herald*'s architecture correspondent Walter Bunning, already seated and sidled his way through
the crowd to take a place at the back of the room.

When he finally managed to take his first look at the winning
design, he stepped back to view the entry from a distance.
The sketch by Baldwinson had captured the sweeping vista of
Utzon's white sails reflected on Sydney Harbour, but Utzon's
plans were sketchy. The assessors were correct: 'Simple to the
point of being diagrammatic'. 'Nothing more than a magnificent doodle,' *TIME* magazine's US-based Australian art critic
Robert Hughes would later say.

But Seidler didn't dismiss the design immediately as so many
would do. He told a reporter: 'The winning design is poetic. It
is a piece of poetry. It is magnificent. I am quite staggered by
it. The jury should be commended for having the courage to
award the prize to it.' While disappointed his entry had not
won, he could appreciate the scope of Utzon's design. And he
thought the name of the Dane was familiar.

Back at his studio he pulled down a book from his book-
shelf. *Building and Home* had been published not long before in
Switzerland, Seidler himself featuring for the modernist houses
he'd designed in Sydney, including the Sulman prize-winning
house he'd built for his parents.

As he flicked through its pages, he found photos of a house Utzon had designed in Middelboe, Denmark. In a beautiful low-lying setting close to water, the house had attracted wide interest because of the novel technique Utzon had employed in its construction. Its skeleton consisted of an ingenious system of prefabrication with regularly spaced posts and beams made of pre-cast concrete sections, and walls of glass and prefabricated timber panels.

Journalist after journalist called Seidler wanting to know what he could tell them about the mysterious Dane. 'Have you ever heard of this man?' they asked.

'Certainly. He's a Danish architect. I've seen his house. His house is in a book that also has some houses I built in it, and I think it [Utzon's design] looks terrific,' Seidler said.

It was hard for local architects to accept the idea that this stranger was coming to Sydney to build such an important local building. Many noses were out of joint.

Walter Bunning found Utzon's win hard to stomach. In 1945 his book *Homes in the Sun* had advocated better designed homes, communities, towns and regions to suit the Australian environment. The great Australian architectural critic Robin Boyd called him 'the best known architectural publicist in the country'.

In 1946 Bunning joined Charles Madden to form Bunning and Madden. The firm would design many public and private buildings in Sydney and Canberra, most notably the National Library of Australia in Canberra. But in 1957 Bunning was best known for having won the 1949 competition to design Sydney's Anzac House. One of Australia's first curtain-wall buildings, it subsequently won the Royal Institute of British Architects' bronze medal.

Like Seidler, Bunning had inspected the winning design closely. 'It looks like an insect with a shell on its back which has crawled out from under a log,' he declared to reporters looking for his thoughts. Perhaps he was a sore loser?

A rumour had circulated that the wife of one local contestant was so confident of victory that she had organised a cocktail party that evening for 125 guests somewhere in Sydney. But the only celebrations in the hours after the announcement took place in Denmark.

• • •

The party in Denmark at the Utzon house had indeed been a big one, although not large in the number of attendees.

Erik Andersson, who with his brother Henry ran the Swedish architectural practice where Utzon worked as a freelance conceptual designer, jumped straight on a ferry to Helsingør to join the celebrations, bringing with him more French champagne to add what had already been consumed.

They partied into the night, but Andersson had to get back to Sweden before daylight. All the ferries had stopped so Utzon, emboldened by the champagne, found an old pilot he knew from his father's days at the shipyards. They begged him to make a special trip back to Sweden to deliver Andersson home.

'I told him your brother was a very important industrialist in Copenhagen,' Andersson joked later as he recounted the tale of the evening of the Opera House win.

'And I said you were the Lord Mayor of Helsingborg,' Utzon would add, as to why he needed to get home urgently. In reality the win, as much as the champagne, had both probably gone to their heads.

• • •

In Sydney on the trams and trains that early evening, commuters discussed the shock announcement. The editors of the afternoon tabloids had kept their presses open for the news. *The Sun* splashed its front page with a headline that declared 'the most beautiful theatre in the world' had won the Opera House competition. 'Because of its very originality it is clearly a controversial design,' the assessors were quoted as saying. 'We are however convinced of its merits.'

The following day, 30 January, the two major Sydney morning newspapers reported that Utzon had studied hundreds of photographs and maps of the site for six months. Their front pages carried Baldwinson's sketch of Utzon's design.

'Cheapest to build', the *Herald* boasted on its front page. Quantity surveyors had examined the ten leading entries and declared Utzon's design by far the cheapest to build, estimating it would cost £3.5 million. It was later revealed they'd never seen a building of such scale before and had spent only twenty minutes examining the drawings.

The day after Utzon was declared the winner, the Opera House Committee announced that an appeal to fund the '£3,500,000 National Opera House' would be launched within two months. It was assumed this would be enough time for Cahill to get the approval from his caucus to publicly fund the project; it turned out he would need nearly five months.

'The Utzon opera house should put Sydney in the forefront of world architectural discussion,' the *Daily Telegraph* editorialised. The head of the ABC, Charles Moses, was quoted as saying: 'Wherever artists and architects meet, they'll discuss this wonderful structure.' Privately, he had been shocked when the bold proposition won, and he doubted the NSW government would ever give the green light for the building.

Moses, like Premier Joe Cahill, had been infected with Eugene Goossens' enthusiasm for the project, but he knew Cahill would face enormous opposition particularly within the Labor Party, a party for the workers rather than the high arts. He knew the matter would be a lively topic of debate at the party's State

Conference due in May, and he doubted Cahill would be able to convince its delegates. Not to mention his caucus.

'The government will never accept this—it is so unorthodox . . . I would have expected the Premier to be more excited about a more orthodox design,' Moses later said. But on that summer day he held his tongue. He didn't need to add to the already loud and long list of public critics in the days following the announcement.

In the *Herald* one woman described the design as looking like 'a piece of Danish pastry'. An architect said: 'It doesn't thrill me at all. I think it is messy.'

Mr WL Hume, secretary of the Parks and Playgrounds Movement, who had been so vocal at the library meeting Cahill had chaired back in 1954, was disgruntled that the city had lost yet more parkland. 'The design would occupy the whole of the site at Bennelong Point. We were given to understand that the small reserve at present existing would be preserved. We are very disappointed.'

The *Sydney Morning Herald* was flooded with 'an unending stream of letters' by people who 'have been stirred into applause or scornful laughter'. Every letter published on 1 February concerned the Opera House. It was described variously as: 'a wonderful piece of sculpture'; a 'haystack covered by several tarpaulins which are being lifted by a strong wind'; 'a ray of hope'; 'the New South Whale or Moby Joe'; 'the Loch Ness Monster'; 'a sink with plates stacked in readiness for washing'; 'some large lovely ship of the imagination'; 'a flock of white seagulls alighting on the harbour'; 'a hideous parachute which we cannot fold up and put away'; 'Goossens' folly'; and 'a 25th century Bluebeard's lair, its ominous vanes pointed skywards apparently only for the purpose of discharging guided missiles or some latter-day nuclear evil eye. Words fail.'

Words may have failed that letter writer, but the critics kept finding them. On 12 February, barely a fortnight after the announcement, *Herald* columnist Eric Baume hinted at early ennui: 'I suppose you have opera house indigestion. So have I. Never have so many words been produced in the correspondence columns about so little.'

The design was the most polarising building project ever undertaken in Australia. In Sydney, arch rivals Seidler (in favour of Utzon) and Bunning (against) were invited to debate the design at a gathering of architects on 22 February. Frank Lloyd Wright, probably the best known American architect of that era, dismissed the design as reckless. 'This circus tent is not architecture,' he claimed in a comment piece penned exclusively for *The Sun* newspaper. 'God help us all,' he exclaimed in the telegram heralding the arrival of his opinion piece. The king of international architecture wanted the final word, but ultimately that would lie with Premier Cahill, and his ability to convince his caucus.

• • •

The Opera House Committee met on 12 February to discuss many things, but most importantly item number six, the merits of the building's proposed name—'the Opera House'. There was a feeling the word 'opera' might prejudice the appeal for funds, given that the building would only be used for opera for two months of the year.

On 13 February the *Sydney Morning Herald* reported that 'The National Opera House is intended to be renamed prior to a public appeal for funds', and made its own suggestions including National Festival House and Sydney Musical Arts House. It then ran a naming competition, as did the *Australian Women's Weekly*. Submissions to the *Weekly* included:

Melody Mansion, Sirius Gleam, The Harbourage Auditorium, The Corroboree, Harmony Hall and White Sails Opera
House. Aurora Musicalis, Macquarie, Cahill, Bennelong Hall
(and its inevitable abbreviation to Ben Hall, after the famous
bushranger) were all canvassed by *Herald* readers. The most
popular suggestions were 'the Sydney Opera House' or 'if the
Queen would permit it, the Royal Sydney Opera House'. By
early March, the *Herald* declared its support for Queen's Hall
or Prince's Theatre.

In the end, the committee decided the name Sydney Opera
House would remain.

• • •

The display entries at the Art Gallery continued until mid-
February. Visitors crowded twelve-deep around Jørn Utzon's
prize-winning design. So popular was this display that scores of
people had to leave without clapping eyes on it. The Archibald
exhibition was a welcome recipient of the overflow.

Former Cranbrook student Peter Hall was among those who
caught the tram to St Mary's Cathedral and trod the shady path
under the canopy of Art Gallery Road's Moreton Bay figs to
the exhibition. The twenty-five-year-old university student was
living as a boarder at Sydney University's Wesley College, now
studying a combined architecture and arts degree. A scholarship
with the NSW Department of Public Works paid for his architecture studies, but it required him to work in the Government
Architect's Office during university holidays.

Hall took photos of the plans and the Baldwinson render-
ing and noted the name and address of the Danish architect. He
was impressed by what he saw of the winning entry, an impression that would last a long time.

• • •

News of Utzon's winning design was published around the world in the weeks and months following his win. In London, an accomplished engineer called Ove Arup saw the story about his fellow Dane in *The Times* the day after the announcement. He wrote to Utzon to congratulate him and to offer the services of his firm. 'If you don't know who the hell I am you may think it very odd that I write to you. You may be right,' wrote Arup, founder of Ove Arup and Partners, then emerging as one of the world's leading engineering firms.

Two days after Arup penned his letter, Jørn Utzon flew to London and met with competition judges Leslie Martin and Eero Saarinen to discuss the next steps. Martin suggested engaging an engineer and introduced Utzon to Arup.

By the time Utzon got to London, journalists from around the world had started to arrive at his family home in the forest seeking an interview. One of them was Australian George Richards. Then a cadet on the Sydney *Telegraph*, Richards had won a trip to Europe and £100 spending money on a Jack Davey radio quiz show. He had left Sydney at the end of 1956 and was in Copenhagen in 1957 when the announcement was made in his home town. With two friends, also journalists, he rented a car and drove to Utzon's home in hope of an exclusive interview.

The architect was in London with the judges, but Lis was there with a house full of wet kids. She was kind enough to give the three young men a cup of coffee, but she was not keen about the invasion of her privacy. This would be the first of a lifetime of such intrusions for the Utzons.

• • •

On 16 June 1957, a Saturday night, Joe Cahill stood on the stage of the Sydney Town Hall. He knew that the course of the evening would determine whether or not the Sydney Opera House would be built.

For months, there had been political wrangling over formally approving the building of the Opera House. To deflect possible criticism, in heated and passionate debate during a special Labor caucus meeting on 1 May, Cahill stressed that the project would be financed by the running of special lotteries. This would mean that there would be no impact on public works or revenue commitments. More than fifteen caucus members spoke—many against the proposal. A motion supporting the early construction of the project and the launching of a public appeal for funds was passed by just 24 votes to 17. But Cahill knew his plan could still be scuttled, as another motion opposing construction was scheduled for June. In a stroke of strategic genius, he declared he would refer the decision on the Opera House to the ALP State Conference in June.

Since the announcement of his win, Utzon had been working on a scale model of the building he had conceived; he had vowed not to come to Australia until he knew the project would be funded. Leading up to the crucial June conference, he sent photos of his scale model to Cahill. 'With all my best compliments on your fine fight for the new Opera House and for a richer life for your people, and with kindest regards,' he wrote.

From the outset, opposition to the idea of an opera house had been vocal and strong. In the blokey backrooms of the conference, some delegates were spoiling for a fight. They argued that homes for the poor were more important than a home for the arts. Cahill told the *Daily Telegraph*: 'If we are not prepared to take a bit of a risk, we are not worth our salt.' It was a wish more than a threat.

In a heartfelt plea from the stage of the Town Hall, the premier told the assembled delegates that Labor 'can decide to ignore the arts and sciences', but 'that is not the Labor way of doing things'. The project 'would make not even a perceptible ripple on our financial ocean', he promised. Labor would deliver 'a great cultural centre' and still fund homes for those who needed it.

But it was Labor women—the Women's Organising Committee and one female immigrant in particular—who convinced the mainly male conference delegates of the merits of an opera house for Sydney. In April, the Labor Women's Organising Committee conference had recommended: 'Homes as well as an Opera House—we appeal to the NSW government to immediately launch an appeal for funds to commence the building of an Opera House.'

In opposing this position on the floor of the state conference, JW Thompson, the member for Leichhardt, argued that opera houses were only for 'hoity-toity people' and would be 'only something for the people with minks and diamonds, and not what ordinary people want'.

Miss N Napper of the Clothing Trades Union shot back at the member for Leichhardt: 'Many working women these days have furs, although they may not have diamonds. Are we going to bring up our children in an atmosphere of rock and roll, or of better things?' There was applause. 'We may not be able to pay for the stalls or the boxes, but we can certainly afford the circle,' she continued in an impassioned speech, and explained how the small island of Malta, where her parents lived, was home to the world's third biggest opera house.

The legendary Kath Anderson, the secretary of the Women's Organising Committee and wife of the Waverley mayor, supported Miss Napper. The intention was to have a public appeal for funds, she said. 'It would give those who cry out for an opera house the opportunity to subscribe.'

The motion for adoption of the women's committee's recommendation to endorse the opera house proposal was carried by a majority of voices. The Sydney Opera House would be built thanks to Labor women.

Once it became official Labor Party policy, opposition from Cahill's parliamentary colleagues now became more muted. But this did not stop the member for Monaro, JW Seiffert, from bitterly attacking the proposal to build and fund the Opera House at the caucus meeting of 3 July and claiming it gave preferential treatment to the 'super class' of people. He accused both the *Sydney Morning Herald* and the *Daily Telegraph* of only supporting the building of an opera house because it would provide a cheap source of programs for television stations ATN 7 and TCN 9, each owned by both newspaper's respective proprietor.

Cahill said he hoped the project would not need 'one penny' more of the state's consolidated revenue than the initial £100,000 the government had already pledged. In the end, caucus voted overwhelmingly in favour of building the winning design.

Stan Haviland sent Utzon a cable confirming the project had been approved. Utzon sent the scale model to Sydney and boarded a plane in Copenhagen with his Swedish partner Erik Andersson for the long flight to Australia.

It would take until 25 September for the caucus to approve the quarterly lottery that would fund the opera house. By that time much had changed—the Sydney Opera House had become the talk of world architectural circles, Peter Hall had graduated as an architect and Harry Seidler, one of Sydney's most eligible bachelors, had met Penelope Evatt, who would become his wife.

A lot had happened in the eight months since Jørn Utzon's design was declared the winner of the Sydney Opera House competition on 29 January 1957. But none of it compared to the pace of the drama that commenced on 29 July 1957, the day Jørn Utzon first set foot in Australia.

• • •

Chapter eleven

Bennelong pointers

A group of twenty-five Danes bearing red-and-white flags greeted Utzon and his Swedish business partner Erik Andersson when they arrived at Sydney's Mascot airport. The Danish Consul, Henning Hergel, was among those who waved as the pair crossed the tarmac. Utzon, who had travelled tourist class and was wearing a grey suit, grey suede shoes and a black and white tie, towered head and shoulders over the rest of the passengers on the Qantas flight. The small and jovial-looking Andersson seemed to follow him as eagerly as a fox terrier.

A sinus infection had delayed Utzon in Fiji, but now he wore a huge smile. As warm as spring sunlight, some said.

'Lanky Jorn looks like a young Gary Cooper, only better looking,' the *Australian Women's Weekly* reporter Ronald McKie wrote. 'I think he bears a striking resemblance to Sir Edmund Hillary, the conqueror of Everest,' was the verdict of the *Telegraph*'s veteran war correspondent, Ronald Monson. Utzon was tanned and tall—they agreed. But how tall exactly? Age and height were the specifics their editors always wanted to know.

Emery Barcs, in his interview published in the *Telegraph* the day after the prize win, had written: 'Utzon is evidently a great Viking of a fellow—6 foot 9 inches tall with a tremendous laugh.' The cables from Denmark reported this height, too. The press entourage decided this should be checked.

'How tall are you, Mr Utzon?' yelled Monson with the bravado of an old hack. 'Can you stand back to back with the Consul?' he asked.

Utzon's eyes flickered with amusement. He was happy to oblige.

Henning Hergel, who claimed to be 6 feet 2 inches (about 1.8 metres), stood back to back with his fellow countryman. Utzon was pronounced 6 feet 4½ inches (about 1.94 metres) by the diminutive 5-foot-3-inch (1.6 metre) Andersson, who had to stand on a chair to measure them. Photographers loved the spectacle and snapped the shot; Utzon's relationship with the local media was off to a promising start.

Speaking softly, in heavily accented but perfect English, Utzon explained how he had come to Australia to realise his greatest dream.

'Who did most of the work?' one reporter asked.

The Dane, in what was to become known as his self-effacing style, said his Swedish partner had had a big hand in the design.

'Jørn did most of the work,' Andersson countered, 'and it is our practice for the one who does most of the work to sign the plan, so he signed it.'

'How will you build your opera house scheme, Mr Utzon?' yelled another journalist.

The Opera House roof would be several inches thick and covered with almost-white ceramic tiles. 'I've been in Berlin recently and seen a congress hall with such a roof spanning 240 feet, and it was only 3 inches thick. Your opera house is the talk of Europe. After I had won the competition I travelled the continent looking at other opera houses. Everywhere I went architects and music lovers were wildly enthusiastic about the fact that Sydney was going to have an opera house of such an unusual design. Many marvelled at the fact that it would be the same size as the new Metropolitan Opera House in New York.'

'How long would it take to build?'

Final plans would be completed within eighteen months and the building could be built within two years, Utzon proclaimed.

Fighting jetlag, the two Scandinavians were whisked away in a waiting car to their city hotel.

• • •

The next morning Jørn Utzon saw Bennelong Point for the first time. 'The fronds of date palms that grew in a circle behind the Macquarie tram shed were flailing in a strong north-westerly wind. Beyond a low sandstone wall, the harbour was flecked with foam,' wrote Gavin Souter, the *Herald* feature writer who accompanied the two architects on this historic occasion.

Also there were Henry Ingham Ashworth, Charles Moses and Stan Haviland. When Moses leant forward to shake Utzon's hand for the first time, the ABC general manager remarked on his height. 'A perfect 1500-metre man if ever I've seen one,' he joked.

'I never run a yard more than I have to,' replied Utzon.

Perched high above the site on the Tarpeian Way, the path above the sheer rock face cut along the north-west side of Macquarie Street in the Botanic Garden, they took in the splendid view of both the harbour and the promontory.

Utzon was blown away by the location and almost literally by the nor'-wester coming off the harbour. 'It's right,' said the Dane as his hair and gabardine coat blew wildly in the wind. Like a good sailor he scanned the horizon, from the Sydney Heads to the Circular Quay ferry terminal. He took in the vista of the harbour, the clouds, the Harbour Bridge—everything he could from this high vantage point. 'It's okay. This is the way they placed temples in the old days. It's absolutely breathtaking. There's no opera house site in the world to compare with it . . . This site is even more beautiful than in the photographs from which I worked.'

The blustery gale made it not only hard to hear, but also hard for Souter to take notes. Utzon explained he wanted a house that seemed to grow organically out of the landscape. To find such a shape, he had looked at flowers and insects. He spoke about Mayan platforms and Kronborg Castle, which stood on a point only a few miles from his home.

'It was not really the same. At Kronborg, part of the horizon is open; here the site is more intimate because the other side of the harbour is so close. Kronborg Castle is a big heavy structure with high towers and, as the ferry runs around it, the towers seem to move,' he explained to Souter, as he watched a Manly ferry rounding the point on its way to Circular Quay. 'The House will have several shells behind each other so that when you move past, they seem to move too.'

Later that day, over sandwiches with Souter in the genteel surrounds of the Australian Club, the country's oldest gentle-men's club, Utzon and Andersson outlined their ideas for 'The House', as they called their creation. The first conception of the vaulting concrete shells had come from organic forms, Utzon said—flowers and insects.

Photographs and colour slides of the harbour and Bennelong Point had helped them visualise the location, they explained. But more helpful had been a conversation with two Australian equestrians on their way to Sweden for the 1956

Olympic competition (because of Australia's strict quarantine requirements, the equestrian events were held in Stockholm). They described the colour of the water, the way it lapped on the shore, and the general geography of the harbour. They had been even more helpful than the tide charts of Sydney Utzon obtained in Copenhagen, he said.

'What do you think of Frank Lloyd Wright's criticism?' Souter asked.

'He would not bother attacking it if he were not interested in it,' Utzon replied, noting the praise from architects such as Richard Neutra, whom he'd visited in Los Angeles on his way to Sydney.

'Don't let me be a self-praiser,' Utzon cautioned. 'Self-praise stinks in Denmark.' In Denmark, Jante's law, a concept similar to Australia's tall poppy syndrome, downplayed individual success.

To those who dismissed his design as 'modern foolishness', he said their criticism didn't interest him, echoing his own father's openness to the spirit of the new. 'We ride in automobiles and we fire rockets. Why should we build in the Victorian style today?'

He pulled a glossy black and white photograph of his opera house model out of his briefcase and tapped on it as if to emphasise his point. 'This is "our time" style. It is our own,' he told Souter. 'That is how it will be at Bennelong Point. You must belong to your surroundings. When we design for Copenhagen, we are Danes; when we made this scheme for the Opera House, we camped on Bennelong Point. We were Bennelong Pointers.'

• • •

Utzon and Andersson also met Joe Cahill that same day. In subsequent years Utzon was fond of describing his first exchange with the premier.

'Do you think you need the help of other architects?' Cahill asked.

'No,' the Scandinavians replied in tandem.

Uncomfortably seated behind a green felt-topped mahogany desk, the premier produced small drinking glasses to toast the Opera House.

'When can you start?' Cahill demanded.

The design of the shells had not yet been solved and he would prefer to find a solution before commencing, Utzon told him.

'That's not what I asked you,' Cahill retorted. 'When can you start?'

Stunned by his forthrightness, neither Utzon nor Andersson knew how to respond.

'Would it be possible to have the plans ready within eighteen months?' Cahill suggested.

'All right, we will do it,' Utzon replied, putting down his barely touched glass to shake the premier's hand. Utzon still wasn't much of a drinker.

'Mr Utzon is like a breath of fresh air,' Premier Cahill said after their meeting. 'He seems to bring a new outlook to the whole scheme. His carefree way of being able to answer "yes" and "no" straightforwardly to all questions impressed me greatly.' To intimate observers, Utzon and Cahill were simpatico.

Cahill promised to demolish the tram sheds and lay the foundation stone before the next state election, which was due after March 1959.

Appearing on Buzz Kennedy's *TV Talk Town* later that week, Utzon optimistically declared that Christmas Eve 1960 might be the opening date for the Opera House.

● ● ●

Ronald McKie, the *Australian Women's Weekly* staff reporter, also sat down that week for an interview with the 'dashing Dane and the smiling Swede'.

'Although my name is pronounced *Yawn Oot-sun*,' the Dane explained in good English, 'Erik can never say it properly, he's Swedish—that's his big trouble.'

Erik sat up primly, placed a hand over his heart, and bowed like a puppet.

'I am Swedish, but not stiff Swedish,' Andersson said.

'I am so happy his English is worse than mine,' Jørn said. 'I can now do all the talking.'

Andersson's eyebrows raised, nearly losing themselves in his hair.

'From now on it will be joost like always,' he said through laughter.

Andersson is a 'more disorderly person than I am, if that's possible,' Utzon claimed. 'He drops his clothes on the floor and he snores.'

'Jørn is the ideal type of family man who will appeal to Australians,' Andersson countered. 'He does not drop his clothes on the floor and he snores.'

Asked where the idea of the building came from, Utzon told McKie he often walked in the forest to think and relax.

'In the forest is a small hill which my children use for skiing and below the hill is a valley which forms a natural amphitheatre. The amphitheatre inspired me. I realised one day it was almost identical with the shape and size of the opera house we were trying to design.'

Andersson agreed.

'With our staff and families we put up white marker-points in the valley and up the slope of the little hill. Then we all played the part of the audience—arriving at the opera house, climbing our seats, departing. This method gave us distances, heights, the entire conception, the dream.'

Andersson nodded violently.

'That is true. It was a dream, because Jørn is an artist. He sees as others do not see. He is also a man who has found the secret of living—of combining work, play and family life.'

But it was Utzon's family life that interested many Australian women, so much so that reporters were sent to his home in Denmark. In the same month as his visit to Sydney, the *Herald*'s women's pages remarked on the 'coconut coloured rugs' covering the cement and tiled floors, and the stone fireplace that was hooded with gold leaf aluminium and often used as an indoor barbecue.

In Sydney, *Woman's Day* reporter Patricia Scholer interviewed the 'long, narrow, dark Jørn Utzon of the intense manner' and 'Toby-jug faced' Erik Andersson. Utzon told her a perfect house needed a good kitchen with easy-to-clean surfaces and easy access to other living areas, and a view if possible. Like the other journalists who had talked to them, Scholer was impressed by Utzon and Andersson. Though shy, both men had won over the suspicious Sydney press.

But they had one more thing to do during this first visit to Sydney: sit the exam to become registered as NSW architects (a competition condition). Needing some coaching from local architects, the Danish Consul Henning Hergel was forced to explain all this to a thousand music lovers who had gathered at North Sydney's Independent Theatre for an opera evening in the architect's honour. 'They are both very anxious to pass and have spent all weekend working hard,' the consul explained to the disappointed audience.

Utzon and Andersson passed the exams and were duly registered as NSW architects. The course of history might have completely changed if they had failed.

• • •

Chapter twelve

Kiss and sell

'Is this some kind of joke?' Premier Cahill deadpanned when he got a sneak peek at the meticulously created model of the Opera House during Utzon's first visit to Sydney. To be displayed in a glass case in the Town Hall, it was the centrepiece for the launch of the Sydney Opera House Appeal to raise money for the construction of the building.

Completely unsolicited, Peter TC Chow of Pymble had already made the first contribution to the Opera House Appeal (£10) in February, the month after Utzon's win. Like Mr Chow, many Sydneysiders were eager to contribute. As well as the Labor Party caucus pledging to fund the Opera House with a lottery, Sydney's Labor Lord Mayor Harry Jensen also pledged to launch a fund-raising appeal.

This is how Jørn Utzon and Erik Andersson came to be seated under the flags of Sweden, Denmark and Australia on the stage of Sydney Town Hall on the afternoon of 7 August 1957.

With them were the chairman of the Opera House Committee, Stan Haviland; the chairman of the ABC, Sir Richard Boyer; Premier Cahill; Lord Mayor Jensen; the leader of the state opposition, Pat Morton; and the vice-chancellor of Sydney University, the distinguished historian Professor Stephen Roberts.

A wildly enthusiastic crowd of 2500 people packed the Town Hall, stamping their feet, clapping and cheering as Harry Jensen read out a list of first contributions that included the Sydney City Council with £100,000 over five years.

Town Hall officials said the audience was the most emotional they had ever seen at a public meeting. Hundreds of people waving banknotes swarmed the clerks who were receiving donations. Pens were passed around to write cheques.

An emotional premier told the applauding audience: 'We are determined that this building shall be finished. We need only a continuance of this present mood to ensure that in the not too distant future a mighty Opera House will stand on Bennelong Point, to prove to the world that we Australians have pride in our culture second to none.' The building would be the most outstanding of its type in the world, he said. 'However, the name Opera House has given rise to a misconception that it will be used only for grand opera, which would interest only a fragment of the community. The facts are that the two halls which will be included in this project will be used for opera performances for a maximum of only two months a year. The use of the title Opera House has become so widespread and general in recent months that we thought it best to preserve that name. I hope that it eventually will become known as the Royal Sydney Opera House. Representations will be made to Her Majesty for permission to use the prefix Royal and it is our hope that she will approve.'

'I want to impress on everyone that this building will be available to all members of the community,' Cahill continued to the wild support of the audience. 'The ordinary working man from the day will be able to go there just as well as those in more favoured circumstances. There will be nothing savouring—even remotely—of a class-conscious barrier and this project will stand as a monument of democratic nationhood in its truest sense. I will give you my complete assurance that the money for this building can and will be found without any prejudice in any degree to education, housing and health.'

Utzon took to the stage, his speech frequently interrupted by applause. 'My partner and I have difficulty in expressing how welcome we feel here. I hope we have answered all the letters we have received from the day we got the message telling us we had won the competition; those letters showed us how much you wanted this Opera House deep in your hearts. Now it's up to you to pay for it—that's the easy part.'

Opposition leader Pat Morton chipped in with the first donation and he was followed by the premier himself, who gave a cheque of £50. Mayor Jensen—popularly known as 'Headline Harry' because of his keen eye for what we today would call a 'photo op'—announced that the Elizabethan Theatre Trust would donate the profits from the gala performance of *Tosca* on 13 September to the appeal.

Joan Hammond—the Pymble Ladies' College–educated, 1929 NSW state junior golfer turned opera singer—took to the stage to sing the aria 'One Fine Day' from the opera *Madame Butterfly* to the rapturous applause. ABC chairman Sir Richard Boyer paid tribute to the role played by Goossens in furthering the cause of the Sydney Opera House.

The appeal raised £235,500 in just over half an hour (a sum the equivalent of nearly half a million dollars).

Inspecting Utzon's model in the Town Hall foyer, actress Ursula Jeans declared to a *Herald* reporter, 'I think it's a

21st cultural birthday present to the people of Australia.' Her enthusiasm matched the warm mood of the crowd as they filed out of the Town Hall and down its sandstone stairs into the windy August evening.

• • •

Later that night, beneath the glorious crystal chandelier in the Lord Mayor's reception room, an impromptu 'kissing party' took place where kisses were traded for cash. Among those selling their smooches were soprano Joan Hammond, her manager/lover Lolita Marriott, the Sydney Symphony Orchestra's flautist Elaine Shaffer and the wife of its American violinist, Ruggiero Ricci.

Erik Andersson started off proceedings by offering £50 to kiss Miss Hammond. The two of them kissed each other delicately on the cheek before Andersson hastily wiped away the lipstick mark.

Jørn Utzon was next, topping his partner's effort by offering £100—£50 each to kiss Miss Shaffer and Mrs Ricci. As the tall Dane bent down to kiss Mrs Ricci, she quipped: 'I am reducing the fee. The normal price is £100.'

The mayor—also known as 'Handsome Harry' (when not making headlines)—announced Opposition Leader Pat Morton had given 15 guineas to kiss him. 'I'll see you later about that, Pat,' he joked.

'Very much later,' replied the opposition leader above the laughter.

This was a most flamboyant kick-off to a fund-raiser for a public building, but it raised £295 and showed the exuberance so many had for the idea of the Opera House.

And it wasn't just Sydneysiders. A Melbourne resident sent along a donation, commenting: 'Here is an opportunity for us to repay Sydney for its generous attitude to our Olympic Games effort. Let us make a gesture of goodwill to show them that our interstate jealousies don't really count in matters of this sort.'

Indeed, the opera house captured the imagination of people all over the world. A week after the fund-raising launch, film producer Mike Todd announced he would be visiting Sydney in October with his wife, actress Elizabeth Taylor, and planned to donate half the proceeds of the Australian premiere of his film, *Around the World in 80 Days*, to the Opera House Appeal. In what was dubbed the 'Party of the Year' by the *Australian Women's Weekly*, guests 'in satin and mink mingled with New Australians in brightly coloured national dress' at the Mark Foy's Empress Ballroom to celebrate the film's release—and raise £7604 for the appeal.

Utzon had received more than 800 letters since his win, mainly from Australians and mostly congratulatory. But one, a love letter of sorts, offered a warning as well. Penned by Lis Utzon, she knew her husband and how intensely he threw himself into projects. She was worried that this one would break his heart. Writing to him in Sydney from their home in Hellebæk, she warned him that building an opera house on the other side of the world would not be 'a breeze'.

That blustery nor'-wester during his first glimpse of Bennelong Point may well have been a harbinger of what was to come. But Sydney was buoyed by Utzon's first visit, so much so that it was willing to place a bet on him.

• • •

Out in the bush the bottlebrush was flowering, and farmers were preparing for a long dry summer. In Melbourne the talk of the town was Straight Draw, the horse that had won the Melbourne Cup, the race that stopped the nation. But in Sydney it was all about how to get a ticket in the upcoming Opera House lottery.

On 25 November 1957, the queue outside the Lotteries Department snaked down Barrack Street when the first tickets went on sale. More than 1250 tickets were sold on the first day alone. Lottery office workers answered over three thousand telephone and mail inquiries, and there hadn't even been any advertising. Within a month, the 100,000 £5 tickets in the first Opera House lottery had been over-subscribed.

'This indicates a special public response to the purpose for which the lottery is being conducted,' declared the director of NSW State Lotteries, Charles Theodore Tallentire, who had previously been Premier Cahill's private secretary. And in a newspaper interview just after the lottery was launched, he commented: 'For many people a lottery ticket represents a contribution to the Opera House appeal.'

What better way to fund major infrastructure, it was reasoned, than to profit from punters' penchant for playing the odds?

• • •

The first Opera House lottery draw took place on 10 January 1958. Lotteries had been conducted in NSW since the 1930s to help fund hospitals and to commemorate special events like the opening of the Sydney Harbour Bridge, but this was the richest lottery ever held in the state, with its three prizes of £100,000, £50,000 and £25,000.

A brand new wooden barrel made from Queensland maple bound in leather straps and with glowing brasswork had been donated to the Sydney Opera House by the Tatts Group especially for the occasion. It was brought into the new auditorium of the Lottery Office in Barrack Street with great fanfare for this much-anticipated event. 'Silent Stan' Haviland was chosen to draw the three main prizes. Broadcast live on radio and TV, the giant barrel, loaded with 100,000 wooden marbles numbered one to 100,000, began to spin to an enormous din. On the table in front of Haviland were a large long-handled spoon, several little trays and a long-handled set of tongs. Lottery officials were on hand to help.

Haviland was handed the tongs. The barrel ceased revolving, the straps were released, and the trap was opened. Haviland dug in the tongs and withdrew one of the wooden balls.

Before the hushed crowd, he held up the winning ball and dropped it into the spoon, which was offered to the State Lotteries Director. He picked up the ball between his thumb and forefinger, held it up and read out the number.

Reporters raced to find the winner. The chase led them to a harbourside home. Fifty-two-year-old Oswald Sellers' two-storey brick mansion was on one of the city's most desirable streets, Wolseley Road, Point Piper. One of the city's wealthiest residents, Sellers already had a housekeeper, a gardener and a chauffeur. He was a company director in a host of enterprises, most notably the Hoadley's chocolate empire, famed for giving Australia the marshmallow-filled chocolate wafer delight known as the Polly Waffle as well as the Violet Crumble. According to his ward, sixteen-year-old Caroline Edwards, 'He went white when he heard the news and raced out of the house.'

'A hundred thousand quid is a lot of money,' Sellers said at the impromptu press conference outside his house that night. He had bought several tickets and he wasn't sure which had won. The well-known businessman was deeply suspicious of journalists, so the reporters were surprised by his initial response.

'Now, boys, you have got the story. Ask me any questions,' he proclaimed. But when asked where the winning ticket was, Sellers replied, 'Who do you think you are quizzing? Go to hell!'

The minutiae and melodrama of each lottery draw became perfect fodder for the front-page splashes of the afternoon tabloids. Reporters from the *Mirror*, the *Telegraph* and *The Sun* would find themselves in hot pursuit of the winning ticket holder. Company cars would be stationed ready north, south, east and west of the city to be despatched to the winner's address for the doorknock interview.

The Barrack Street draws were broadcast live on radio station 2KY. The punters who listened to the station for the horse races loved it. Rice-paper-thin Sydney Opera House lottery tickets sealed in an envelope as a Christmas or birthday present became as ubiquitous as a lucky jade plant at the front door of many Sydney suburban homes. ('Jade by the door, poor no more,' the saying went.)

In a period that ultimately spanned almost thirty years, the Opera House lottery raised $102 million. That's 496 lotteries. And 496 winners. A lot of potential front pages.

Meanwhile, back in Denmark, Utzon was about to take a gamble himself. He sat down at his desk, took out a pen and paper, and began to write a letter asking for help from one of his heroes: 'Cher Monsieur Le Corbusier . . .'

Chapter thirteen

• • •

Chapter thirteen

With a little bit of bloomin' luck

More than a year after Utzon's win, there had been no progress towards the commencement of construction of the opera house. But 1958 was to prove pivotal on a number of planning and preparation fronts.

On 29 January, the anniversary of the announcement of Utzon's win, there was interest in Denmark in purchasing 1000 lottery tickets if the Lord Mayor of Sydney delivered them in person to Copenhagen's Lord Mayor. Jensen never made it to Copenhagen City Hall, but local Danes in Sydney supported the fund raising by donating money from recitals they held.

In March and April of 1958, Utzon returned for his second visit to Sydney. His partner Erik Andersson had dropped out of the project by then. The Swede had not enjoyed his stay in Australia, he later confessed to Utzon. In 1957, Australia seemed a very long way from Scandinavia. Instead, Utzon arrived with Ove Arup, the Danish/British engineer who had so impetuously introduced himself to Utzon the day after his win and was now a partner in this venture.

Although Arup had a strong Danish accent all his life—his father was a Danish veterinary surgeon and his mother Norwegian—he was also *terribly* British. By day he toiled at his Fitzrovia office with slide rules and log tables, in his Savile Row suits and dark-rimmed glasses. But at night, after a hard day's work, he loved nothing more than to settle down after dinner with a cigar, a good port and a game of chess.

Ever the builder, he tried his hand at designing chess sets. One of his designs was packed into an elegant chess tower; another was so exquisitely small that it could be worn as a necklace. He believed that chess sets, much like the buildings he helped to shape, should be both functional and aesthetically pleasing.

Arup's enthusiasm for design—whether of a chess set or a city building—was obvious. A poet and practical joker too, it is little wonder that he and Utzon formed an immediate bond. With a twenty-three year age difference, their relationship was more like father and son than work colleagues.

Before their trip to Sydney, Arup regularly visited Utzon both in his Helsingør office and in the home office he'd built at Hellebæk using some of his prize money. They worked through the difficulties of trying to turn a concept into a reality.

In Sydney, they chose to stay at Bondi Beach. Utzon, a keen body surfer, had been there on his first visit. He'd heard of the balsa surfboards a team of American surf lifesavers had brought to Australia for the Melbourne Olympics and was eager to give them a go.

The main purpose of this visit was for Utzon and Arup to present the 'Sydney National Opera House' report to the NSW government and the Sydney Opera House Executive Committee. Known as the 'red book', it outlined Utzon's vision in practical terms with drawings, photographs and commentary on structure, acoustics, mechanics, electrics and theatre technique. Except when he was swimming, Utzon was seldom without his personal copy of the book. Twenty-five copies had come with him from Denmark, and another hundred were sent before construction would begin.

'I have been doing nothing but eat, sleep and work on "The House" with a lot of people at the office. And now we know how it will be built,' he told reporters as he thumbed through his copy of the red book.

He had plans for a preliminary noise survey of the site so that the two main halls could be thoroughly insulated against noise from one another as well as from the harbour. A Swedish producer, Sandro Malmquist, had been brought in as a consultant in theatre technique: 'I wanted a theatre man, not a technician,' Utzon said. The red book outlined a revolutionary stage machinery system: 'Until the last few decades the stage had in principle not been subject to any change for 200 years or more—apart from the development of the technical auxiliary equipment,' Malmquist wrote. 'Now this is no longer so. We have broken out of the snail shell of the baroque-theatre and have discovered so many more ways in which to play theatre.'

While Utzon's plans were taking shape, the site at Bennelong Point remained untouched and people were growing impatient. The job of reducing the brilliant concept into 'concrete loveliness is proving very tough,' the Sun-Herald's London correspondent reported on 17 August 1958. The Sun's attention had been diverted to what it called 'a 50,000 pound soup opera'—a plan to build a restaurant in Frenchs Forest in the north of Sydney based on Utzon's uncopyrighted design that would also have a drive-in restaurant next to it on 60 acres of native bush.

That same month, the NSW Department of Public Works paid Johnman Construction £984 to demolish the Fort Macquarie

Tram Depot at Bennelong Point. Built to resemble a battlement, the depot had sat idle since 1955, when the decision had been made to use this site for a cultural centre. Demolition started on 18 August 1958 and continued until that December.

Progress was painfully slow and fell well short of expectations. A *Sydney Morning Herald* editorial on 1 September 1958 asked, why had there been so little progress since Cahill announced his plan for an opera house in 1954? 'Our cultural white hope may turn out to be only an architectural white elephant,' the newspaper lamented.

The *Mirror* in its afternoon edition later that day scoffed at the *Herald*'s editorial and turned its back on the whole project: 'Amidst a good deal of chatter, the point emerges that *The Herald* is anxious about lack of progress. This anxiety is not likely to be shared by the overwhelming majority of the public. To put it bluntly, lotteries to raise funds for the Opera House are being put to the wrong use.'

Later that month the *Telegraph* jumped on the bandwagon, claiming the Opera House Appeal was costing more money than it raised. This led to the resignation of the fund's publicity and executive officer, Mr A Palmer. Lord Mayor Harry Jensen conceded that the demand for Opera House lottery tickets had dwindled, but he predicted that all this would change when construction began.

Supporters of the project hoped that would be soon.

• • •

Jørn Utzon spent most of 1958 in Denmark trying to find ways to build the exterior of the Opera House. This was proving difficult and disheartening for both him and Arup, and their teams of architects and engineers. Although he had vowed to move to Australia as soon as he won the competition, Utzon's wife

Lis felt it unwise to move their family until all the engineering issues had been sorted. She reasoned: why disrupt the children's schooling until it was absolutely necessary?

In late October 1958, no doubt as frustrated as everyone else by the lack of progress, Utzon turned his mind to the interior. He sat down at his desk and penned a letter to one of his heroes, Charles-Édouard Jeanneret-Gris, the Swiss–French architect better known as Le Corbusier:

> Cher Monsieur Le Corbusier,
> I have long wanted to write to you to thank you for all
> that you mean, and have meant, to me and I allow myself
> to send you my project for the Opera of Sydney . . . It
> would be an immense joy if I could be assured of your
> participation in the decoration, the tapestries and the
> paintings, of this edifice and I pray to you to let me know
> if you could make something for it in one form or another.
> At the same time I ask if I could obtain permission to buy
> some of your oil paintings and tapestries . . .

He received a favourable response and subsequently he and Lis travelled to Paris to meet with 'Le Corb', as he was nicknamed, to talk tapestry. It is believed Utzon also approached the Frenchman's good friend, Pablo Picasso. Utzon commissioned from Le Corbusier a one-of-a-kind 6.5-square-metre wool tapestry titled *Les Dés Sont Jetés* (The Dice Are Cast). In the same way that Chagall had painted the ceiling of the Paris Opera, Utzon clearly wanted works by the great modernist masters to grace his interiors in Sydney. Weavers from Aubusson, the 'tapestry town' in central France, set to work on the commission in 1959.

The two architects met twice and correspondence between them (written between 17 November 1959 and 1 October 1960) traces a series of payments made by Utzon to Le Corbusier for 'sketches for the Sydney Opera House', a 'sample of tapestry by Monsieur Le Corbusier for the Sydney Opera House' and 'sketches and samples of tapestry made in connection with the Sydney Opera House'. It seems this sample was not completed specifically for the Opera House, but more as a sample for the sort of work Le Corbusier could offer. When it was completed it was sent to Utzon's Hellebæk home, where it hung on the dining room wall.

Clearly, the Utzons still showed no sign of moving to Sydney.

• • •

There was very little action at the Bennelong Point site until the beginning of 1959. In the lead-up to that year's March state election, Premier Cahill, sensing that time was of the essence, invited the television cameras into his office to film the signing of the contract for the Opera House foundation work to begin. Located on the second floor of the Treasury building, the Queen Anne–style room—inspired by late seventeenth-century English interiors, with high-panelled Australian cedar wainscot, heavily moulded plaster ceilings and a marble chimney open fireplace— had a dramatically different aesthetic from the building he was agreeing to commence work on at Bennelong Point.

Standing behind the premier was a handsome Dutchman named Dick Dusseldorp. 'This is a great day for NSW and Australia,' Cahill proclaimed as he signed the contract for the podium with Dusseldorp's construction firm, Civil and Civic.

The two men walked down the hill to inspect the site at Bennelong Point. 'I've watched brick by brick being taken from the old tram shed that was here, and I'm going to watch brick by brick of the Opera House go up,' Cahill told Dusseldorp. Although the premier had been unwell—he was a heavy smoker and had developed a heart condition—there was an extra bounce to his step as he wandered back up Macquarie Street to his office that day.

Cahill knew he was taking a gamble to start work before they actually knew how to build the Opera House, but the people of Sydney could wait no more, he told Utzon. With an election in less than a month, the premier knew people needed to see progress if he was to stand any chance of being re-elected.

On 25 February, a group of locals, mostly pensioners, delivered a petition to the NSW Attorney-General claiming the project was illegal under sections 34 and 37 of the *Public Works Act 1912*; they wanted to take out an injunction to stop it. Earlier, in January, Actors Equity (a professional performers' union) had asked the government to abandon its plans entirely, suggesting there was a better use for the money for the arts than this building.

But Cahill remained unperturbed. A cable was sent to Jørn Utzon in Denmark: 'WORK TO BEGIN NEXT MONTH STOP YOU ARE CORDIALLY INVITED ALONG WITH YOUR WIFE TO GRAND OPENING MARCH 2 STOP YOURS JOE'.

Jørn and Lis Utzon flew into Sydney in late February 1959.

• • •

The NSW Police Band struck up the *My Fair Lady* hit, 'With a Little Bit of Luck', at the sod-turning ceremony to mark the beginning of building at Bennelong Point on 2 March 1959.

'An inspired choice,' quipped Syd Deamer, the journalist responsible for 'Column 8', the whimsical but traditionally anonymous column that then graced the front page of the *Sydney Morning Herald*. 'Wasn't that just the thing?' wrote Deamer, '—with a little bit o' luck in the Opera House Lottery and a little bit o' luck all round, the multi-million job will be finished.'

Drizzle fell from a low bank of dark clouds and several times threatened to interrupt the hour-long ceremony, wrote *Herald* journalist Evan Williams, who attended as a third-year cadet. He would go on to become a junior roundsman at the NSW Parliament and, in later years, would follow the political drama of 'the House' closely.

Premier Cahill presided. Also present were Lord Mayor Harry Jensen, Deputy Leader of the Opposition Robin Askin (who, in 1971, changed his name to Robert Askin) and most members of state cabinet. Sir Bernard Heinze, who had replaced Goossens as the director of the Conservatorium, Charles Moses and Henry Ingham Ashworth were also there.

But it was Lis Utzon whom the crowd was most interested in. Dubbed 'the most comfortable woman at the ceremony' by the *Herald*'s women's pages, she was stockingless and wore rubber-soled flat-heeled yellow sandals with a cool white cotton dress and a pull-on straw hat. Other women shot her envious glances as their high-heels sank into sand, and grit worked its way into their shoes.

As cameras clicked, Mrs Utzon clutched a bouquet of white carnations and scarlet nectarine flowers—Denmark's colours—the Vice-Consul for Denmark had given her. Mrs K Henning Hergel, wife of the Danish Consul-General, had a more unusual present for the Utzons: 'an Aboriginal didgeridoo'.

The proceedings did not begin on schedule. Opera House Committee chairman Stan Haviland explained that the Deputy Opposition Leader, the most senior non-Labor politician expected to attend, had been unavoidably detained. 'Mr Askin has some important messages to give us, and we can't do without them.'

Askin was busy campaigning for the upcoming election, just weeks away on 21 March. That week there had been a scandal for the Coalition to deal with: the NSW Country Party leader, William Davis Hughes, had resigned because he had been found to have lied to parliament about having a science degree. Hughes was now hospitalised with a gastric complaint—most likely an ulcer because of overwork due to the elections, doctors said— and it was unclear how he would fare at that month's election, or if he would indeed remain a candidate for his Armidale seat.

When proceedings eventually began after Askin's late arrival, messages of goodwill and admiration from all over the world were read out. They included a note from the architects of the United Nations building in New York, namely Oscar Niemeyer, and none other than Le Corbusier himself, who wrote: 'The design is very beautiful and we hope it will be built.' Utzon was no doubt thrilled.

The premier took his place on the podium. 'Many controversial issues will be raised in the coming election, and, to some extent, no doubt, the electorate will be influenced by what is said upon these issues . . .' Cahill said with the same oratorical skills he displayed at the Labor Party state conference two years earlier. 'I am glad to say however that the Opera House is purely non-political.' He vowed it would open on Australia Day, 1963.

'The time for controversy is over,' Mr Askin proclaimed. 'It only remains for us to work together in a spirit of goodwill, and raise the necessary finance to bring this magnificent concept into being.' The message from the prime minister, Robert Menzies, was relayed through his representative, Les Bury. He hoped 'this great project—so imaginative in scope—will be carried through in good speed'.

Cahill moved from the official dais to a large sandstone tablet to lay the plaque Utzon had had made in Denmark. Then the architect and the premier screwed a large metal bolt into the centre of the plaque. It would mark the point from which all measurements for the construction would be taken. Cahill bent down to kiss the plaque.

The premier then raised his hand and a siren on a nearby police car sounded. Six workmen with pneumatic drills and a large bulldozer immediately went into action preparing the site.

In next day's 'Column 8', Syd Deamer noted: 'Mr Jørn Utzon, the architect of the whole business, was on the dais—and that's all. Nobody mentioned him and they failed to introduce him to the audience—even failed to mention the charming plaque he had designed for the occasion and brought from Denmark. But his reward was the stream of unstinted praise which dominated the messages received from the world's leading architects.'

'The Opera House is [Cahill's] baby and, in or out of office, he's not going to let it starve,' Deamer continued. The Opera House was indeed his 'baby'. And on that Monday morning in March, no one was happier than him to attend its christening.

Chapter fourteen

• • •

Chapter fourteen

A mini Greek tragedy

Robin Askin, the latecomer to the sod-turning ceremony, was a New South Welshman through and through. He grew up in inner city Glebe and loved rugby league and gambling. As a soldier in World War II he was known as 'Slippery Sam' for his poker-playing skill; as a politician he took the name 'Bob' Askin. A bank teller turned businessman, he joined the Liberal Party in 1947, and was elected to the New South Wales parliament in June 1950. He was deputy to Liberal leader Pat Morton at the 21 March 1959 state election just weeks after work commenced at the Opera House.

Despite widespread predictions that the political pendulum would swing against Labor after eighteen years in office, Cahill won a record third term as premier. His victory was largely due to his own personal efforts and his skill as a campaigner in the new medium of television.

The Cahill the public knew was a born performer, but to

his Labor colleagues he was a man of few well-chosen words. He liked a drink and a cigar—often late at night in the parliament's billiards room. He was a shrewd operator—a numbers man who ruled the NSW Labor Party with an iron fist but kept it cohesive. This was the approach he took to his pet project, the building of the Opera House.

But the Liberals sensed at the 1959 election that not everyone was happy with the Opera House project, particularly country voters. They could see that there was potential to make this an issue at the next election if progress remained slow and costs mounted.

In July 1959 Morton was deposed as party leader and Askin was elected unopposed. He sold his Manly printery and became the first Liberal Party leader devoted to the office full time. Like Cahill, Askin was shrewd and knew how to play the public. He would prove to be a formidable political opponent.

'First, last and always,' Askin declared, 'I am a politician—a professional politician.'

• • •

Peter Hall graduated from the University of Sydney in architecture in 1957 and then arts in 1958. At university, Hall was an eager student, active debater and a fine sportsman, captaining the university's first-grade cricket team. He became friends with his architecture lecturer and *Herald* cartoonist George Molnar, the two playing squash together.

In his final year of university, Hall won the Board of Architects Research Bursary and the newly established Hezlet Bequest Travelling Scholarship. This allowed him to travel overseas, and after graduating in May 1958, he left Australia for England and travel throughout Europe. In London he worked with what he called 'a fairly bad firm of architects', and there he was joined by Libby Bryant, whom he'd met while they were both studying architecture at Sydney University.

A few years younger than Peter, Libby, or Lib as she was known, was the talented oldest child of Bowen and Prudence Bryant. Born in 1935, she was descended from strong female stock. Her grandmother, Millicent Bryant, had in 1927 become the first woman to earn a private pilot's licence from the Australian Aero Club of NSW. On 2 June 1959 Libby and Peter were married in London's St Bartholomew's Church. The two young Australians were charismatic and creative. He drew brutalist buildings and she worked for fashion designer Mary Quant, who appreciated Libby's keen eye for colour, particularly in the bold prints then coming out of Scandinavia.

After their wedding, they headed off on a grand driving tour of Europe. Arriving in Denmark, they visited the office in Hellebæk of the much-talked-about Sydney Opera House design competition winner. Hall even looked into the possibility of getting work in Utzon's office but, as he told friends later, he 'could not stay long enough to make it worthwhile'. In a letter home to his good friend and mentor, the Government Architect Ted Farmer, dated October 1959 Hall wrote: 'Jørn Utzon, whom I visited, though a very good architect, is not outstanding in Denmark, so high is the general standard. Only Arne Jacobsen [designer of the Egg Chair] is nationally known, and his work is most impressive.' He declared Denmark to be the home of the best contemporary architecture.

In a long, previously unpublished letter home to her parents, Libby wrote fondly of the Utzons.

Jørn Utzon has been really wonderful to us, greeting us as great friends, giving us meals and so much of his precious time. As you can imagine he has a vast amount of work to do, and wants very competent people to assist; but the work is involved and he wants to take on people at this stage (two he thinks) to work here with his office until all the Opera House drawings and details are finished, and then to return to Australia to supervise actual work there.

So that was our predicament: the offer of quite a wonderful job (pay is low in Denmark) here for about 20 months and then a very responsible position in Australia. But Peter is quite sure he must be back next year, being keen to do his own designing and for other things too. Utzon is rather anxious now to have Peter, and is contemplating the idea of 6 months only, but we feel too it isn't worth beginning with him if only to withdraw just as he became well associated with the vast thing. As yet only the structural ideas are solved, Arups, the Engineers in England are completing their drawings now (Arup is also a Dane, but as his business in London, is perhaps the greatest structural engineer living). All the details are yet to be solved!

We are both terribly impressed with Utzon; he is now about 39 or so, and just starting really on a remarkable career. He's built very little in Denmark, we think must have been working in a large firm all this time, collecting his thoughts, and travelling between times to all parts of the world: now he has suddenly burst out with superb designs, wins huge competitions whenever he likes, and has a large very competent group of architects working under him in his beautiful office at Hellebæk. He is building 137 banks in Persia! All in some way repeating the original idea—an inspired one—and the Sydney Opera House, some large massed housing schemes in Sweden (a competition he won), another housing scheme of over 100 'atrium' houses in Denmark; he's just won a new competition also in Denmark for a University for Adult Workers. And so it goes on—with all this he is the most likeable, amusing and talented man with a beautiful house that he had just extended enormously to fit his wife and 3 children. There is not a vast amount of building required in Denmark, and he has cleverly got his feelers out to other parts of the world . . .

Peter thinks perhaps he might continue working with his Dept. of Works for many years. There he gets a very big wage of £30 now, with quite rapid rises, and extremely good big work to do, with little problem of fussy little clients and builders. Then later in Utzon fashion, to step out having had greater experience than he would have had struggling as a young experimenting architect on his own. They are anxious to hang on to him, and pay him half his salary all the time he is away . . .

After their time in Denmark, the couple headed south: to France, Switzerland, Italy, Yugoslavia and finally to Greece, where Libby fell sick with a nervous condition. The specialist she saw in Athens ordered her to rest and offered his home on the Greek island of Mykonos. Instead of the sea voyage home that they had originally planned, they were forced to return in an air ambulance because of Libby's health—a long and costly exercise involving multiple stops. But Hall seems to have been happy to come home and resume his job at the Government Architect's Office.

• • •

Around the same time the Halls were on Mykonos, Joe Cahill was expecting to meet a delegation of Greeks from his home suburb of Marrickville, but while attending a caucus meeting he suddenly felt unwell and started vomiting. He insisted on no fuss but allowed his son Tom to drive him to the nearby Sydney Hospital. As he stepped into his car, he said: 'I think my stomach has caught up with me.'

The premier had been 'off colour' for a few days, probably because of overwork, his colleagues thought, but in hospital he was told he'd suffered two minor heart attacks during the previous week and that he now needed a blood transfusion. It was thought he had a gastric ulcer, too. Before the transfusion, Cahill called his Minister for Public Works, Norman Ryan, to his bedside, and made him promise not to let the Opera House fail. 'Take care of my baby,' he joked.

Cahill died unexpectedly in hospital from a third heart attack the next day, 22 October 1959. He was sixty-eight. Labor, Liberal and Country Party members of parliament—all fierce foes in the bearpit of state politics—wept openly when the news of Cahill's death was announced in the chamber. His friend Cardinal Norman Gilroy led the requiem mass at the state funeral at St Mary's Cathedral, which was attended by more than three thousand people. As Cahill's funeral cortege travelled the 17 kilometres to Rookwood Cemetery, city streets, including the entire path of Parramatta Road, were packed with more than 200,000 people, their heads bared and bowed in respect.

• • •

Ove Arup had been born in Britain in 1895, but he was educated in Denmark and went to Copenhagen University in 1913 to study philosophy and mathematics. He switched to engineering in 1916—something of a middle ground between the arts and science—and upon graduation went to Hamburg, Germany to work for the Danish structural engineers Christiani and Nielsen, specialists in reinforced concrete. From there he was transferred to the firm's London office in 1923.

Concrete claimed Arup as its champion more by accident than design. In the early 1930s he met Russian modernist architect Berthold Lubetkin, who was looking for a way to build a cylindrical concrete drum for the Gorilla House at London Zoo. Ove assisted Lubetkin and then designed the concrete ramps for the zoo's penguin pool. In the late thirties he set up a construction company with his cousin, Arne Arup, and during World War II they built concrete air raid shelters and the temporary portable landing piers, known as Mulberry Harbours, used by the Allied troops for the 1944 D-Day landings.

Like Utzon, Arup was a perfectionist who would go to great lengths to find the right solution. But, unlike Utzon, he was a strategist—as are many chess champions. He bridged the two very different worlds of architecture and structural engineering.

From the outset, Arup did his utmost to build the Sydney Opera House according to the architect's original plans. He dedicated a team of fifty-five engineers in his London office in Fitzroy Street to solve its mathematical and engineering problems and regularly travelled from London to Hellebæk, where Utzon maintained an office in an old row house and a staff of nine. With pressure building from the NSW government, their major pre-occupation was how to construct the roof. This extraordinary idea of Utzon's became their shared vision.

With the death of the premier who had championed the Opera House and a new and more aggressive opposition leader itching to break the previous bipartisanship, the Opera House site was still just an enormous hole in the ground. The 1960s would bring very different pressures. The time was ripe for political play.

Chapter fifteen

Rising up to the Aztec gods

Bazil Thorne's picture was plastered all over page one of the newspapers on 1 June 1960, the day he won the tenth draw of the Opera House lottery. He wore a broad smile as he triumphantly waved his hat in one hand and the winning Opera House lottery ticket in the other. Bob Heffron, who had replaced Joe Cahill as NSW's Labor premier, was thrilled to see that people had resumed buying Opera House lottery tickets to 'swell funds' now that building had begun at Bennelong Point, just as had been predicted. The £100,000 windfall for Thorne, a travelling salesman, and his family was welcome news—both for them and for the government.

Over at Clontarf, on Sydney's north side, Stephen Bradley stared enviously at Thorne's photograph. Here he was, a Hungarian immigrant who, with the burden of a thick foreign accent, was struggling to find a permanent job so he could pay his bills and support his family. And there was Thorne, on easy street, smiling gleefully at the cameras. It didn't seem fair. Bradley soon hatched a plan and headed to Bondi: 79 Bradley Street to be precise. Here, he began closely observing the Thorne family's daily routine. On 7 July he kidnapped the Thornes' eight-year-old son, Graeme, on his way to school at Scots College, and demanded a ransom for his return. 'If I don't get the money, I'll feed him to the sharks,' Bradley threatened in a call made to the Thorne residence from a public phone box at the Spit Bridge. Graeme Thorne's kidnapping shocked the country. It was the first abduction/ransom case in Australia. The agonising wait for the Thornes was played out dramatically across newspapers, television and radio as the nation followed their painstaking ordeal.

When the young boy's body was finally discovered just over a month after he went missing, he was still in his school uniform but wrapped in a picnic rug. Forensic tests on a dog's hair found on that Onkaparinga blanket proved to be from Bradley's Pekingese dog. Police, following a tip-off from the Clontarf postman, found Bradley's house but he'd already left Sydney with his family on the P&O liner *Himalaya*. He was arrested when he went ashore in Colombo and flown back to Sydney, where he was charged with the murder of Graeme Thorne and sentenced to life in Goulburn Prison.

After Graeme Thorne's death, 'Not for Publication' became a box that could be ticked on every Opera House lottery ticket entry form.

• • •

Early in 1960, Sydney Mayor Harry Jensen had suggested an Opera House Arts Festival to mark the building's opening, which he hoped would be in 1963. But from Denmark Utzon sent word that he doubted the project would be finished by then. It was so beautiful that time shouldn't matter, the architect stressed.

While Sydney-based Danes continued to back their countryman and the Opera House with a further £700 donation (they hoped that other Sydneysiders would follow their show of support and make further donations), Askin started to see a political opportunity emerging and accused the government of bungling the project. He pursued this line in parliament, saying: 'The prime reason why now, despite our misgivings, we are continuing our support of the project is that if we don't lend our support we will make our state a laughing stock in the eyes of the civilised world.'

The construction firm Civil and Civic was now running into problems with stage one: the building of the podium that was rising like an ancient Mayan pyramid in the middle of modern Sydney. The underground work for this was the chanciest part of the whole Opera House project. Because the stage machinery was to be built into the bowels of the building, owing to its heavy weight, it had to be incorporated into the design. There were other logistical issues also causing hold-ups.

Since the day when journalist Martin Long had phoned Utzon for the *Herald* to relay to him the news of his win, the Opera House had become his specialist subject. A musicologist with an interest in Elizabethan music, he followed the construction of the building and wrote expert commentary for his new newspaper, the *Telegraph*, as the building progressed.

In an article published on 12 April 1960, Long reminded his readers that the construction site was nearly 6 acres, the area of twenty average city buildings, or three rugby fields laid side by side: 'The site itself was described as probably the worst in Sydney. Bennelong Point was mainly man-made—the part that stretched to the rocky islet separated from the shore in the days of the First Fleet. Normal drills would not work in the erratic rubble and so special percussion drills had to be used.' He reported that harbour seepage had been a constant problem and that divers had to be sent down into the tube-like steel piers to perform a pump-out before concrete could be poured. A century-old stormwater channel had had to be relocated, as did some power lines without interrupting supply. The foundations of the old car ferry wharf, from before the Harbour Bridge opened, was uncovered and, because it was extremely solid, it had to be blasted out.

Stage one was also dogged by a shortage of structural steel, because there was so much building going on in Sydney. Although the AWA Tower was still the city's tallest structure in 1960, the skyline was changing as skyscrapers were emerging. It was a race to find supplies.

But if anyone could deal with these challenges it was Civil and Civic's Dick Dusseldorp. A Dutch Jew, he had been deported from Holland in 1943 to Krakow as forced labour for the Siemens organisation. He escaped in 1944, and after the war got a job with a Dutch home construction company, which sent him to Australia in 1951 to seek out business opportunities.

On arrival, he was appalled at the plight of Sydney's building workers. He vowed to help unions ensure his building sites were places of dignity and respect. He became known as a capitalist with a socialist heart. Under his leadership, the company built two hundred prefabricated homes for Snowy Mountains Hydro Scheme workers, Australia's first high-rise building (Caltex House) and its first high-rise strata title apartments (Blues Point Tower), and would construct Australia Square, then the world's tallest building outside the United States. Not only did he win the respect of those who worked for him, he was also a regular in Sydney's small-pond social scene.

Civil and Civic's later success was based on the principle that the architect should be employed by the contractor, rather than the other way around. Dusseldorp went on to establish a financing arm for Civil and Civic and this became the Lend Lease Corporation, which changed the business model of building in Australia. He was an admirer of Utzon and architecture in general: his architect-designed home in Sydney's Middle Cove was based on Frank Lloyd Wright's organic honeycomb house.

Dusseldorp would give Australia not just everything under the sails at the Opera House but, also, at the instigation of the Building Workers Industrial Union (BWIU), he provided the stage scaffolding for the Opera House's very first live performance.

• • •

Paul Robeson was the most acclaimed African American singer in the world. He was a civil rights campaigner and a strong unionist; his father had been a slave. Because of his vocal support for Soviet communism and his comments about race relations in the USA during the McCarthy era, the US State Department refused to issue him a passport. This decision was overturned by the US Supreme Court in 1958, and he travelled the world singing about union men and the struggles of black people in his deeply resonant bass baritone voice. Whenever he could and wherever he was, he made a point of performing free for working folk.

On 9 November 1960, Robeson arrived at the Opera House construction site to perform for the Civil and Civic workers in a concert organised by the assistant national secretary of the BWIU, Ernie Boatswain. It was an unusually cold spring day and Robeson wore a black beret and a herringbone jacket with a carnation in his lapel. He was surrounded by scaffolding and workmen in shorts, rolled-up sleeves and hard hats.

It was said that Robeson had a voice of 'deep bells ringing'. His 'cosmic belch' rang out over the cavernous construction site by the harbour as the Manly ferry and a container ship cruised past. The forest red gums in the nearby Botanic Garden swayed in the breeze. There was no accompaniment; he just cupped one hand over his ear and sang two of his signature songs: 'Ol' Man River' and 'Joe Hill', the anthem about a famous American labour leader who was executed by firing squad. The workers were transfixed.

Sitting in the audience was a sixteen year old who had come down from his job at the Sydney County Council specially to see Robeson sing. With a friend, he found a way through the netted-off site and mingled with the workmen. The young unionist was profoundly moved by the working man's anthems Robeson sang that day, and this scene would stay with him for the rest of his life and in many ways inform his later public and private passions: politics and music. He would ultimately have an impact on the Sydney Symphony Orchestra in ways that nobody at that first live performance at the Opera House could have possibly imagined. But that would be more than three decades later when the young man, Paul Keating, became prime minister.

Utzon's abiding idea for the podium had always been for it to raise theatre—and opera-goers—to a different plane, to lift them spiritually above the level of their everyday lives, just as the Mesoamerican pyramids had raised the Aztecs closer to their gods. As he said in his competition entry: 'The audience is assembled from cars, trains and ferries and led like a festive procession into respective halls.' From the very beginning there had been a feeling at Bennelong Point that this was more than just a construction site, and many sensed that as Robeson sang. The podium became an appropriate metaphor for librettist Dennis

Watkins when he wrote *The Eighth Wonder*, the opera commissioned by Australian Opera that tells the story of Utzon and his creation. It also laid the groundwork for Utzon's later dealings with the NSW government, when he would be discarded like an Aztec human sacrifice.

Chapter sixteen

The spherical solution

NSW Public Works Minister Norm Ryan had taken the deathbed promise he'd made to Joe Cahill to take care of his 'baby' seriously. A former tradesman like Cahill, Ryan had worked as an electrical inspector for the NSW Public Works Department before entering parliament and being appointed the department's minister by Cahill in 1959. The two had adjoining electorates in Sydney's inner west and knew each other from Ryan's days as an alderman on Marrickville Council.

In 1960 the Sydney Opera House Act was passed and the minister for public works became its consenting authority from 1961. This put Ryan in the driving seat as the client on the project, rather than the fifteen-member Executive Committee, which had until then effectively allowed Utzon to write his own brief. In the same year, competition judge Henry Ingham Ashworth visited Hellebæk to see how work on the soon-to-start stage two was progressing and to finalise the requirements for the stage machinery. Jørn Utzon had attracted many admirers, many of them young architects who worked with him in his Hellebæk office. One, Yuzo Mikami, came from Japan; another, Jon Lundberg from Norway, oversaw the stage machinery work, which they called 'stage technique'. Yet another, Oktay Nayman from Turkey, arrived in May 1962 not long after he'd graduated as an architect in Istanbul. He was shocked to find that the office would be closed the following month, and everyone sent off on holidays for four weeks.

During an early working session, Utzon had taken a plastic foot-long ruler and bent it to show to Ove Arup the form he wanted to build the shells. They had been trying to create that concept in concrete ever since. They simply didn't know whether it was possible to build such a huge structure as the Opera House using pre-stressed concrete in the shape Utzon had drawn.

Pre-stressed concrete was the magical ingredient that was supposed to give Utzon complete sculptural freedom, but in fact it is one of the most mathematically based forms of construction and it demands great discipline. And Utzon was not strong at mathematics, which was why he hadn't ended up as a naval engineer like his father.

Ove Arup, of course, had studied maths and he understood its importance in the engineering process. He suggested to Utzon a new shape based on parabolas rather than his sleeker, freehand drawing of 1957. By 1960 and 1961 the two men were experimenting with a more ellipsoid shape—like the shape of an egg.

Arup kept pushing the need for a geometry that would allow for prefabrication. The same shape repeated over and over again would mean fewer concrete moulds would be needed to make the prefabricated parts and cheaper production costs. This had worked for him in building the Mulberry Harbours for the D-Day landings. Considered one of the greatest engineering feats of World War II, they were constructed in England and assembled like a vast jigsaw puzzle off the coast of Normandy.

Build a mould, fill it with concrete and repeat the process many times over: that was engineering according to Arup. But Utzon's shell shapes weren't geometrical; they couldn't be built in this way. It was that simple.

• • •

The scene: a summer's day in North Zealand, Denmark, 1961.

> Utzon went to the model shop alone with a heavy heart and began dismantling the perspex model, sadly thinking that it would have no use if he could not find a solution for it to be constructed in a rational way. The whole job would be cancelled after all these years of hard work. In order to save space to store the models of the shells, he stacked them together one by one, a smaller shell inside a larger one. When he finished the stacking, something struck his eyes. The curvatures of the shells, which he thought to be quite different from one shell to the other, were more similar to each other than he had thought all these years.
>
> An idea flashed in his head like a lightning in a dark sky. If they were so similar, why couldn't they be cut out from a common surface? In order to do that the curvature must be the same in all directions. What is a geometrical body with a constant curvature in all directions? A sphere!

So wrote Yuzo Mikami in his book *Utzon's Sphere*, one of the few first-hand accounts of how Utzon arrived at the spherical solution. Mikami worked with Utzon in Denmark from 1958 to 1961 before joining Ove Arup in London, where he became one of the core members of the design team for the spherical solution and tile cladding until 1967. His knowledge of the story is unclouded by any allegiance to the Utzon and Arup camps—who were said to have a differing version of events.

According to Mikami, Utzon rushed home and filled up a bathtub full of water and put his son Kim's rubber beach ball into it. He noticed the surface of the rubber ball changed colour when it was wet, allowing him to see the shapes of the spherical triangles he could cut out from the ball on the parts that were left dry. After many trials he realised that the variety of shapes and sizes available were almost limitless. Big and small, flat and upright. He could now compose the whole shell with pieces of spherical triangles cut out from just one single sphere.

The most enduring myth relating to the final shape of the Opera House's famous shells is that one day Utzon reached into the fruit bowl on his kitchen bench, picked up an orange and started peeling it. After cutting it into segments, he realised that from one sphere he could create all the segments he needed, just as Eero Saarinen had done with his breakfast grapefruit for the TWA building in 1956. Every time he cut it, the shape could be repeated. This was what Arup had been urging: repeated geometry.

However, all three Utzon offspring—Jan, Lin and Kim—dismiss the 'orange moment' as an apocryphal story that subsequently caught the public imagination. As his eldest son, architect Jan Utzon, explained: 'The persistent "orange" tale originated when my father adjusted the structural concept for the sails/roofs, from a non-geometric shape to a form inscribed within a sphere. He used the "orange image" to explain how the surface/peel of a sphere can be divided into smaller and manageable pieces that can be pre-produced and later assembled to a larger part of the surface of a sphere. Apparently his explanation, through the use of an imaginary orange, was spot on, as this story seems to have gained a life of its own.'

His youngest son, Kim, also dismisses the 'orange moment' and another 'Utzon myth'—that as a four year old, he was the one who handed his father the orange that led to the epiphany. Kim, also an architect, is well acquainted with his father's approach, having worked with him on numerous projects throughout the 1980s and 1990s. All his father did was keep on developing an idea. Kim believes he 'worked very hard for several years, together with his closest employees and engineers', to come to a solution that meant the ultimate version of the shells complied with all requirements, both practical and philosophical, in the best way possible.

However he arrived at the spherical solution to the Opera House sails, it seems clear that it was not a Eureka moment. What is certainly known is that Utzon did go to the Helsingør shipyard, where his father still worked, and asked for a sphere to be built in wood in such a way that he could piece it together like rounded wooden building blocks. He knew it would be easier to explain what he had in mind with a three-dimensional aid.

He sent his wooden sphere to Sigfried Giedion, the venerable Swiss architectural theorist and historian, who later wrote of it in the influential monthly, *Architectural Digest*: 'One day Utzon sent me . . . three hollow wooden globes from which he had sliced different segments of his vaults. This shows that the curves of his vaults are far from arbitrary. Thanks to the wooden globes, whose surface lies always at the same distance from their centre, Utzon could renounce complicated scaffolding and substitute a single movable framework. As a result, it was possible to construct the high shells from prefab parts made on the building site and put together into ribs which were then tied together in steel shoes.'

• • •

Making miniatures and mock-ups lay at the core of Utzon's architectural creativity, just as it had for fellow Dane, the carpenter Ole Kirk Christiansen, who founded the toy construction company Lego. It was a skill Utzon developed watching his father through those long winter nights in Aalborg where his office was filled with models. There were so many that before he left for Australia some of them were burnt in a bonfire.

Utzon's preferred problem-solving method was to return to nature. From his earliest days as a schoolboy, he would walk along the water's edge at the Limfjord, often clutching a little model boat designed by his father. As an adult he sought inspiration from his natural surroundings, the trickling streams and pebbly beaches near his Hellebæk home. Anyone who visited him in Denmark came to know this.

Recognising a kindred spirit and a business opportunity, Australian plywood manufacturer Ralph Symonds had visited Utzon in Denmark in 1957 not long after the announcement of his competition win. Utzon returned the visit on his first trip to Sydney later that year.

A renowned master of plywood, Symonds specialised in doing things that most people said could not be done. In 1929 he had built a plywood speedboat, the first use of plywood for marine purposes. In World War II his company had produced collapsible folding boats and pontoons for the army. He had also created the one-off giant plywood ceremonial arches that had adorned Sydney's major intersections for the Queen's first visit to Australia—giant boomerangs, topped with the royal insignia. When he visited Hellebæk, he had just formed a new company in Scotland and was looking to arrange distribution of plywood products in England and Scandinavia.

Bankrupted more than once, Symonds became rich as Sydney's boundaries expanded and new suburbs with master-built houses made predominantly out of plywood veneers and Pebblecrete were developed. Much of that plywood came from his factories in St Peters and then in Homebush. At one point in the 1950s, Symonds' Sydney factory was manufacturing the largest sheets of plywood in the world—in excess of 15 metres. He would whiz about his huge factory in a type of dodgem car driven at excessive speed.

Although considered a larrikin, in his long socks and shorts, he managed to attract the leaders of both NSW's major political parties and the Queen's cousin, the Earl of Dalkeith, along with all their wives to the 1959 grand opening of his Homebush plywood factory on the banks of Parramatta River. While he was well connected politically, he clashed with Australia's engineering establishment. He and Utzon got on like the proverbial house on fire.

Utzon was a sympathetic listener as Symonds developed his ideas for the greater use of plywood in building construction, which was being used in a host of diverse structures, from prefabricated schools for the NSW Department of Education to roofing for Melbourne's outdoor performance venue, the Sidney Myer Music Bowl. It was also used in building the stage-one podium, and Utzon was collaborating with Symonds in developing ideas for the creative use of plywood in adapting to the irregular internal shape of the Opera House.

Utzon envisaged a long and successful relationship with the maverick Symonds. He intended to use plywood in the mullions—the vertical bars between the giant panes of glass in the Opera House windows—as well as plywood for the interiors. It was something he was comfortable with because of his past experience in boat building.

The Australian architect Richard Leplastrier, who worked with Utzon as a young man, built a boat with Symonds' plywood.

'It came in a big roll and he'd banded it up with fine metal bands. I cut the bands and it sprang right out into a 50-foot-long sheet. It was amazing . . . Symonds was a brilliant guy and Utzon saw that. He knew there was no factory in the world that could make plywood in this way, other than Symonds.'

But Ralph Symonds died on a fishing expedition in December 1961 at Palm Beach; his body was found floating in Pittwater. It was front-page news. This was not just a heartbreaking tragedy for Symonds' family and all those associated with the factory; Utzon also lost a major supporter. Even beyond the grave, Symonds' friendship would haunt Utzon in ways he could never have foreseen. Utzon's loyalty to Symonds' company and his products would contribute to the Dane's undoing.

• • •

As 1961 came to an end, discussion turned to whether the organ in the Concert Hall should be pipe or electric. In the end the secretary of the Opera House Executive Committee, Ron Thomson, declared that it would be a pipe organ—but no one at the time knew the headaches this decision would entail.

Also at the end of 1961, Ove Arup, aged sixty-six, became very ill. He suffered fainting attacks brought on by low blood pressure and compounded by stress and exhaustion. It was estimated that the work undertaken by Ove Arup and Partners prior to 1962, even before construction of the roof began, totalled more than 150,000 hours. Undertaken by almost fifty engineers from fifteen countries, this was the equivalent of more than a hundred years of full-time work for a single person. His company almost went bankrupt in the three and a half years it took to find a way to build the Sydney Opera House.

Another tragedy was narrowly averted in March 1962. Excited at having solved the building's major design problems,

Utzon and Arup were eager to show the new NSW Public Works Minister Norm Ryan their plans. Utzon and Jack Zunz, one of Arup's senior London men, were booked to fly to Sydney to present to the minister and the Sydney Opera House Trust, which had now replaced the Opera House Executive Committee, the 'yellow book' detailing stage two and how the roof was going to be built.

But when Arup's technical drawings ran a week late, Utzon and Zunz had to delay their departure for two weeks. That delay saved both men's lives. The American Airlines flight they had originally been booked on to fly between New York and Los Angeles plunged into the water minutes after take-off. All ninety-five passengers and crew died instantly.

By June that year the newspapers were splashing 'shock changes' to the design of the roof on their front pages. 'Its sleek lines will be made plump, and would be covered with black stripes,' one newspaper reported. The black-tiled stripes were an idea to cover the joints of the prefabricated spherical sections. 'It will make the Opera House more spectacular,' said Executive Committee chairman Stan Haviland. 'It will accentuate the billowing sail effect,' artist/architecture lecturer George Molnar added. There was faux outrage at the shape change, but real outrage at the idea of black tiles, which Utzon later dropped.

Up until this point, Ryan had continued Cahill's good relationship with Utzon, but working from afar was starting to strain it. All communication between the Dane and his client, the minister, was via telegram, telex or letters that would take weeks to arrive. Ryan began to fear that costs were spiralling out of control.

By 1962, the Liberal opposition was claiming the government was trying to make a scapegoat out of Utzon. He was summoned to Sydney in August 1962 to explain to the cabinet the Opera House expenditures. After five hours of 'crisis' talks with the Opera House Executive Committee, Utzon said he was unable to estimate the total cost. He could only say that Sydney would be given the best opera house in the world; costs should be a secondary consideration.

Clearly managing the project from afar was not working. So, in December 1962, Jørn Utzon at last packed up his Danish home and office. *Woman's Day* journalist Anthea Goddard was despatched to Denmark to report from his 'modern as a space capsule' home. Five members of his staff—two Danes, a Norwegian, a Turk and an Australian—would come too (along with a white Jaguar Mark X the family would import from the United States). Their pet peacock, Pop, and the silver fuselage of an old aeroplane in their Hellebæk garden would stay.

Utzon headed off with his family on a three-month holiday to the United States and the Pacific on their way to Sydney, where he intended to build their dream home on a block of bushland he'd bought for £5000 on a previous visit. He also intended to realise another dream: the completion of that building on Bennelong Point.

• • •

Chapter seventeen

The end of a romance

Ove Arup stood up from his teak and leather Danish executive chair as his Australian guest was ushered into his London office. His red tie stood out against his white hair and the white rugs in the room, which was styled in dark contemporary woods and packed with primitive sculptures and larger than life Chinese wooden busts, one of which sported a panama hat. Arup sat down and sipped coffee from a mug that had the irregular design of Picasso pottery. His secretary brought in a coffee for Graham Gambie, *The Sun*'s correspondent in London, in a stylish white Danish-designed cup. Gambie had come to talk to Arup about the criticism of the mounting costs of the Opera House project.

'This petty criticism, just what sort of mentality does it take?' he asked the reporter. 'You know personally I feel very virtuous and very good about this job,' he said. 'I don't give a damn [about the criticism] ... it's so ludicrous.' Perhaps they were both crazy to take on the Sydney Opera House project, he told

Gambie. 'This is a kind of temple for Sydney. It is a monument that will provide uplift and a sense of the spiritual . . . It's quite amazing that such a young architect has been able to master such a thing. I've worked with hundreds of architects but not one of them would compare to Utzon.'

• • •

The Utzon family weren't the only VIPs expected to arrive in Sydney in March 1963. Queen Elizabeth II and the Duke of Edinburgh were also due. In 1954, when the royal yacht *Gothic* had steamed into Sydney Harbour on her first visit to Australia, more than a million spectators had lined the harbour in what was the biggest event Australia had *ever* hosted. By the time of Elizabeth's second visit, the welcome was not quite as enthusiastic. Nonetheless, more than 100,000 people packed Circular Quay to see her. A day later seventy-nine onlookers collapsed in the heat as they waited for a glimpse of the royal couple boarding the royal yacht *Britannia*. During those nine years the city had changed both in complexion, thanks to post-war migration, and composition, thanks to its growing skyline. Most notably, the Opera House was now under construction.

As Queen Elizabeth toured Bennelong Point on the first Sunday in March, she asked about the Danish architect. Olaf (Skipper) Nielsen, a fellow Dane who was Utzon's site representative, told her Utzon and his family were arriving the next day. Expressing a wish to meet him, the Queen invited Utzon to lunch with her aboard the royal yacht *Britannia*.

Jørn and Lis had just boarded a DC-7 in Tahiti with their three children. Jan, then eighteen, recalls his father being told by the air hostess that the blankets she was handing out were for first-class passengers only. They were travelling economy—a single ticket to Australia would have cost almost all of Utzon's annual salary.

The same hostess later returned with the blankets some
time later looking rather sheepish. The pilot had received a radio
message from the Queen's representative inviting Mr Utzon to
lunch. The family was requested to go straight to the royal yacht
once their plane touched down.

They landed in sweltering Sydney at 11 a.m. and the usually
cool Dane was in a lather, but not of the kind he desired. He
wanted to shave, but he had no razor with him. Lis had no
stockings with her, and neither of them had slept for thirty-
four hours. Waiting for them at Kingsford Smith Airport were
Ron Thomson, secretary of the Opera House Committee, and
Mr MS Nicklin of MacDonald Wagner and Priddle, consulting engineers at the site. After a quick freshen up and change
of clothes, the Utzons were taken straight to Circular Quay.
The children weren't invited. As the Utzons were led up the
red-carpeted canopied gangway, they were introduced to author
Patrick White, who confessed to them that he was nervous at
the prospect of meeting the royal couple. White wore his only
presentable suit—a new black one intended for attending the
theatre and concerts. 'I looked like a waiter going on duty,'
he later confided in a letter to his friend, the stage designer
Desmond Digby, about his train ride to Circular Quay. He
wasn't in the best of moods and so he was relieved to meet
Utzon. 'As handsome as they come,' he later described him.

Onboard were what could only be described as an eclectic
bunch of Sydney's prominent citizenry: the swimming star
Murray Rose; Doris Fitton, who ran the Independent Theatre
in North Sydney; machinery manufacturer James Kirby; the
headmistress of Cheltenham Girls High, Bessie Mitchell; and
newspaper proprietor Warwick Fairfax, who owned the *Sydney
Morning Herald*, and his wife Mary.

'In our nervous condition we ganged up quite a lot, and he
[Utzon] promised to show me over the Opera House,' White

told Digby. 'His wife is of that plain, dank-haired mermaid kind one sees from Denmark, very pleasant. As her English is a bit vague, she smiles.'

A few days later White and his partner Manoly Lascaris were clambering over the great tiers of concrete rising on Bennelong Point. White was exhilarated: 'It made me feel glad I am alive in Australia today. At last we are going to have something worth having . . . If only they had got on with the thing a few years earlier, so that we could be certain of having a part in it. I was particularly glad to have been shown over by Utzon, a kind of Danish Gary Cooper, although his English is a bit woolly at times, and difficult to follow. How shocking to think of those miserable little aldermanish devils attacking such a magnificent conception from their suburban underworld.'

• • •

While Jørn and Lis Utzon were struggling to make themselves understood aboard *Britannia*, their children had been taken directly from the airport to Sydney's northern beaches and the Newport Arms Hotel for the afternoon. Sixteen-year-old Lin was already tall like her father and very blonde like her mother. She was uninspired by the city she saw that Monday morning. There were few trees and not much grass. In the suburbs she saw red-brick bungalows and gardens with rose bushes, which seemed to her oddly out of place. After their long trip around the world, she was expecting something more exotic. Instead, she felt she'd arrived in a bit of England.

There was much speculation about where the family would live until they built their house. But Utzon had left instructions that nobody in the media should be told of his whereabouts. Peter Bowers, an exceptionally keen and sharp-witted young reporter with the *Herald*, contacted every source he had connected with the Opera House and visited the site. Two days after the Utzons arrived, he learnt there was a possibility they had booked into a motel on the beaches north of Sydney. He started ringing every motel listed from Palm Beach to Newport, asking: 'May I speak to Mr Utzon?'

When a motel receptionist confirmed that Utzon was indeed staying there, Bowers took an office car for the hour's drive to Newport. He knocked on the door of Utzon's darkened unit. The jet-lagged Dane had been in bed asleep but, overcoming the architect's initial annoyance, Bowers finished up with an exclusive interview. Described as 'first-rate' by his bosses, it was enough to get Bowers an 'upgrading' and a pay rise.

The subject of the interview? The gloss- and matt-finished white tiles that were to grace the Opera House sails.

Utzon claimed that all the roof's technical problems had been solved and building it would start within three months. He arched his fingers to form the shape of a shell and explained that the ribs of each shell would spread out from the base like a Spanish fan. Each rib would take only ten days to erect and, depending on its length, would be made up of nine to thirteen elements. The biggest shell would be held up by seventeen ribs, the biggest being 150 feet long. The ribs would be covered by the tiles. The ridges would feature the glossy white tiles to reflect the surrounding colours of nature—the blue of the harbour and the sky, the green of the trees. The matt tiles would be in the folds between the ridges, so would not throw a shadow over the reflective tiles. This was much better than a plain white roof, which would have no texture or expression.

'From a distance you will get a pattern of glossy tiles shining like fingernails against the flesh-like texture of matt tiles,' Utzon said. 'No matter from what angle you look [at] the Opera House roof, it will stand out very clearly—as clear as the Snowy

Mountains. As the building progresses we will go out in a boat to make sure this colour scheme will be right.'

The exterior walls and floor of the Opera House would be two-tone granite gravel, he told Bowers, probably pink and grey set in cement, rather than the sandstone as had been his original concept. He estimated the project would be completed by the end of 1965 and that it would cost £12.5 million. 'It is a very big amount of money based on a realistic study of the entire scheme. The cost compares favourably with big commercial projects in Sydney. The Opera House will be twice the size of the AMP building, which cost more than £6 million.'

The 12-centimetre by 12-centimetre ceramic square tiles were the result of three years' work by Swedish company Höganäs. Utzon had overseen the work in Sweden to produce the shiny 'ice' tiles and matt 'snow' tiles and the effect he wanted. Ultimately, 1,056,006 tiles made from clay with a small percentage of crushed stone were shipped to Sydney. They became known as the Sydney Tile.

Always the perfectionist, for Utzon the quality of these tiles was paramount. While the NSW government insisted he put the job out to tender, he'd wanted to use these tiles because they were the best he had found. Fortunately, the Höganäs tiles were also the cheapest of the quotes received.

It was his firm belief that a small detail could make a huge impact. He felt it was important that such a 'large, white sculpture in this magnificent harbour setting should catch and mirror the sky in all its varied lights—from dawn to dusk, from day to day, throughout the year.' The white exterior would be the jewel in his harbourside crown. (He'd initially intended the underside of the sails to be completed in gold leaf but gave this idea away early in the design process.)

The external appearance of the shells was to be created

by covering the concrete ribs with 4228 chevron-shaped 'tile lids'—essentially, these were giant interlocking arrow shapes, each containing dozens of Sydney Tiles. The lids, produced in a factory set up onsite, were created by placing the individual tiles into a mould that was called the 'tile bed'. The tiles would lie face down in these beds in the designated pattern of cream and white/matt and smooth. Grooves would be provided for drainage and the joints partially filled with heated animal glue to prevent grout getting onto the surface of the tiles. This was a first for Australia, and most likely an Arup solution. The backs of the tile lids were then covered with galvanised steel mesh and mortar. After a steam curing over several hours, they were ready to be installed over the ribs.

The ground-breaking use of pre-cast concrete, structural glue and early computer analysis in London for building the shells were the holy trinity that would greatly enhance Arup's world-wide reputation and that of his engineering firm.

• • •

The Utzons rented a house in Bayview, near the bush block where they had intended to build the family home. 'Opera architect starts a "boom in Bayview Heights"', the *Sydney Morning Herald* predicted somewhat dramatically in a headline. A local real estate agent was quoted saying 'land values would double overnight' when the Utzons moved into Bayview Heights, which he said at the time had 'no immediate hope of a water supply' and 'no sewerage'. Lin was enrolled at Narrabeen Girls High and started school immediately, as did her older brother Jan, who began studying for his leaving certificate at Narrabeen Boys High. Their younger brother Kim, aged six, was in primary school.

The family settled swiftly into the area, thanks partly to its sailing community. Utzon was particularly interested in the boats at the Bayview Yacht Racing Association, where he admired a beautiful boat built by a young local architect, Richard Leplastrier, then working on a house in Bayview. Utzon was taken by its fine craftsmanship; it resembled his father's work. So, when Leplastrier wrote him a scratchy letter on the butter paper used by architects for sketching, Utzon was impressed. Smudging the writing, he checked that Leplastrier had used a soft lead pencil. (According to Yuzo Mikami, Utzon cared about tools as much as he cared about his trade. His tool of choice was a green Faber-Castell lead holder.) Leplastrier was employed to help Utzon on his dream home among the 'sea of trees'.

In an interview with Margaret Jones that appeared in the *Sun-Herald* in March 1963, Utzon explained: 'At home we live in a forest, 30 miles outside Copenhagen . . . I want to keep all the trees on the Bayview site to preserve the same feeling. The house will ride among them.'

Later that month he told Barbara Richards in *Woman's Day*: 'The way I see it, the trees—and the shrubs, even—should flow in and around the house. That means building a courtyard, or a big terrace at least. Perhaps living units around a natural area. We aren't going to rush into building this house. I want to spend some months studying the climate and the living conditions and the way everybody around us does things. I did this for the Opera House, so why not for my own home?' Utzon planned to design the furniture himself. He'd also been working on designs for furniture for the Opera House interiors too.

Lin, left-handed and dyslexic like her father, didn't have the best time at school in Australia. The first essay she was asked to write was a response to the question: 'Is the Opera House a massive waste of money?' In an interview with Peter Grose for the *Daily Mirror* in May 1963, she explained that she'd argued 'many people called the Opera House a white elephant. Then

I said that I didn't think the money was badly spent, because ballet, opera and drama mean a lot to the culture of the country.'

Jan struggled with his English and had to repeat his final exams the following year, but he soon learnt to surf and both he and Lin sailed, just as they had done from a young age in Denmark. Young Kim couldn't speak English at all when they arrived. 'He's learned to say, "chewing gum" and "Coca-Cola" but not much else,' Lin told Peter Grose. Kim, dubbed the 'menace' of the family, managed to tie the reporter to the chair.

The two older children soon started to fit in socially, especially after Lin met a teenager her own age. Matt Carroll took her to his parents' Palm Beach home and invited her to join them for a Greek lunch overlooking Pittwater. They talked about literature and art, and she felt she had found her 'tribe'. (Matt Carroll was to start out studying architecture, but soon became a leading film and TV producer.)

Jan remembers building a small boat—just as his father and grandfather had done before him—on the billiard table at Bayview. Lis Utzon told the *Sunday Telegraph*'s Jan Smith in July 1963 that life was too short to spend in the kitchen, so they had a 'daily woman—very reliable' and she was thrilled to find the rented home had 'all the mod-cons like a dishwasher'. The family settled in easily. They felt particularly at home in Pittwater, probably because living so close to water reminded them of Denmark and the beaches of the Øresund. Eighteen months later, they moved to another rented house in Palm Beach.

• • •

By late May 1963, a growing tension between Utzon and Arup began to become apparent. Utzon was clashing not just with his mentor but also with the men Arup employed. Not long after his move to Australia, Utzon attempted to draw a clear demarcation, setting down unequivocally who was in charge of what at Bennelong Point. His frosty letter addressed to Arup and his two trusted confidantes began: 'Dear Sirs'. It was the beginning of the end of the romance between the two Danish men.

Jack Zunz, still in Arup's London office, naturally sided with his boss and the Arup man on the site, Michael Lewis, was in no doubt that a lot of people had been seduced by Utzon and his 'head in the clouds' approach.

As construction continued at a snail's pace after Utzon's move to Sydney, he became a convenient whipping boy for the city's press and politicians. The delays and the cost were the talk of the town—from its top end to its taxi drivers.

In the early days after his arrival, Utzon would drive from the northern beaches to the city and work at the onsite office after dropping his daughter Lin at piano lessons at the Conservatorium of Music. But, over time, this pattern changed and the time he spent at the onsite office became less frequent. While he may have appeared to the public as a dashing unflappable Dane, privately Utzon was dealing with deep personal tragedy.

• • •

One Friday afternoon in April 1964, Barry Brennan, a reporter from *The Sun*, came to the Bennelong Point office to find Utzon there. He was wearing a sports shirt of sombre grey and spotless baggy cavalry twill slacks. On the wall was a poster of the hundreds of components inside a Bell telephone, the brainchild of industrial designer Henry Dreyfuss, whom Utzon admired. It read: 'Put them together and dial anywhere'. It was pinned up as inspiration, a reminder of the complexity of the building he was trying to construct.

Caught off guard by Brennan's intrusion, Utzon quickly rolled up some blueprints he'd been looking at. The reporter asked him why the building was costing so much more to build than had been originally anticipated.

'I am the victim of politicians,' Utzon replied. 'All I have ever wanted was to create something wonderful, something magnificent in your city, which the world would admire. But I have been trapped by politicians. The trouble began right at the start, when ridiculously low estimates were issued by the government of the time. Fancy a figure of £4 million [$8 million]. How absolutely incredible. This figure never came from me. I simply submitted an idea, it was chosen, and I was asked to supervise construction. The government announced the low estimate to get initial approval.' It was the quantity surveyors, Rider Hunt and Partners, who had provided the initial estimate.

Not long after this April exchange, Utzon's older brother, Leif, died in Paris suddenly, aged forty-eight. The Dane left Australia without his family shortly after and didn't return until early June. He was gone for around eight weeks helping arrange his brother's affairs. Jørn was now the only remaining son in the family; his younger brother had died tragically in a surfing accident in 1955 in Morocco aged thirty-two. His mother had also died.

For Utzon, Leif had always been a steady rock—an anchor in stormy seas ever since their days as Sea Scouts together on the Limfjord. He was devastated by his brother's early death. It shaped how he now saw life and managed stress. In September 1964, he moved the design section of his office into Goddard's boatshed at 118 Iluka Road, Palm Beach. He put in a full clear glass window, so he could see the view out to Pittwater where the Hawkesbury River joined Lion Island. It reminded him of the view at his grandmother's house out on the Øresund.

He had time here to cogitate, to think through problems rather than rush at them like a bull at a gate. Significantly, he did not install a telephone, and this became a huge issue for his Arup colleagues, who toiled away at Bennelong Point without him. His visits to the site became even less frequent.

To take his mind off his feud with Arup, Utzon worked with Leplastrier on the plans for his house at Bayview, which was to be built as three separate dwellings.

Some time in 1964 the open doorway between the Opera House offices used by the architects and engineers was bricked up. The teams would have to make appointments to see each other. The relationship between Arup and Utzon had reached a stalemate, and it would only get worse with the election in 1965 of the Liberal Askin government. But it was someone else entirely who would force Utzon into an unwinnable checkmate.

Chapter eighteen

• • •

Chapter eighteen

The arch that changed the world

Utzon's spherical solution was all very well. The boffins in Arup's London office may have planned the Opera House roof construction on paper, and with a state-of-the-art computer that took up an entire room, but there remained the more pressing problem in Sydney: how to actually build it. The answer was Australian engineering ingenuity.

The building of the Sydney Opera House is one of Australia's, and the world's, great untold feats of engineering. It was said that, by comparison, it made the Empire State Building seem as simple to build as a garage. 'Tricky' was an understatement.

The Queensland construction company Hornibrook, which had built its reputation on bridge construction, won the contract to build the roof, and stage two of the Opera House project began on 25 March 1963—around the same time tile production began at the Höganäs plant in Sweden. Dress rehearsals for the sail erection took place in a paddock in suburban Enfield, with busy forklifts scuttling in like mud crabs to practise moving the pre-cast concrete segments.

Dundas Corbett Gore, the project manager chosen to oversee the Opera House shells, was a giant of a man—6 feet 3 inches tall (about 1.9 metres) and as burly as a front-row forward. The bald and blue-eyed civil engineering graduate from Sydney University was as big in stature as he was in personality. He employed some exceptional engineers, who really should receive more credit for making the Opera House shells a possibility.

But even before stage two began, work had to be held up for four months while the underground concrete piers were reinforced. Arup's Jack Zunz confessed that this was his fault; he'd designed them when the roof load had been expected to be much lighter. The only solution was to strengthen the concrete piers that had been sunk down through the base to support the roof. And the only way to do this was to use gelignite to blast out sixteen of the twenty piers that Civil and Civic had so carefully constructed under the podium only a few years before. A series of evening explosions rang out across the harbour for days on end. One newspaper claimed this error cost around £40,000, which in today's terms would be the equivalent of $648,000. There was a lot of rain too, which slowed the process.

The blasts were scheduled for 5 p.m. to least disturb the city. Manly ferry commuters were disrupted once, when some debris from an explosion landed on their vessel, but luckily no one was injured.

Corbett Gore went on a worldwide fact-finding mission to gather information on roof assembly and to acquire the know-how and materials needed. From the United States he picked up 'the epoxy resin idea'—using a form of super glue that would set in a few hours. Up until this time, no structure of any size anywhere in the world had been glued together. When he saw experiments by Adhesives Engineering Inc in San Francisco, he suggested the idea to Arup's London office.

He then went to France, on Arup's advice, where he ordered three tower cranes that at the time were the largest in the world. He had them shipped to Sydney in thirty parts. They were designed to carry 10 tonnes up to 100 feet in the air. From France, he then went to London to familiarise himself with Arup's plans. Returning to Sydney, he set to work.

The ribs of the roof, which splayed out like the fronds of a palm leaf, came together like a giant Lego set of 2194 pre-cast segments all glued together. Each rib segment was made by pouring concrete into thick plywood moulds made by Ralph Symonds' factory.

The first of the pre-cast roof segments was lowered into position on 22 November 1963. The Hornibrook workers and engineers began hoisting it at 6 a.m.—two hours later it was lowered into the base of the first shell. 'There was hardly any wind, which was important,' Corbett Gore told a *Sun* reporter there that day. A worker in Utzon's office recalled seeing tears in the Dane's eyes when the mouldings of the first perfect concrete segments were removed blemish-free. Some of the workers teared up, too.

The construction crew ultimately became so efficient that they made segments faster than the erection crews could assemble them. The surplus was trucked to Long Bay Gaol and stored away from the threat of vandalism. When they were needed onsite, they were trucked back.

The pre-cast segments were assembled one by one and stressed together in the same way a bridge is built. When a new segment was poised just above the last one that had been put in its place, the crew would use a stick or household paint roller to spread the epoxy resin the consistency of condensed milk over its ends. This specially formulated white resin glued the rib segments together and they were then threaded together with 350 kilometres of steel stressing cables. The tops of all the rib segments formed the ridge beam and were cable stressed together.

The ridge beam was the backbone of the building. Many years later engineers joked it was the 'secret weapon', like the winged keel on *Australia II*, the Ben Lexcen–designed yacht that won the 1983 America's Cup.

Many in Arup's team migrated to Sydney to work on the Opera House. Civil engineer Wilf Deck, who was originally from New Zealand and had worked on the ridge beam in London before coming to Sydney, was typical. Irishman Peter Rice also migrated to Sydney and, at the age of twenty-eight, found himself resident engineer in charge of one of the most complex parts of the roof construction. Rice was admired for his ability to work both as an engineer and architect and was known as the 'James Joyce' of engineering. Many decades later, the Irish Prime Minister Michael D Higgins would pay tribute to his efforts at the Sydney Opera House.

Wilf Deck recalls: 'We got the sense we were working on something special that was built to last. I feel I have contributed to the construction of a work of art, like the early art work on the cave wall in France or the Sphinx in the desert in Egypt that's been there for thousands of years. We knew this was a work of art.'

The Arup and Hornibrook engineers had to be sure that the ridge beam was strong enough so that the building wouldn't move. 'Prestressing wires' stretched from the top to the bottom of the ribs and also crossways, joining them together and eliminating movement. The cross wires were like an embroidery thread holding everything together. All of this required laborious mathematical calculation with slide rules; no computers were used onsite to build the shells.

After all the ribs had been erected, the lateral joints between them were dry-packed and the cross wires stressed. The joints were caulked with lead and everything, including the grouting of the ducts, was checked. The roof was now ready for the chevron-shaped tile lids—all 4228 of them, as Utzon had insisted. They were lifted by crane and bolted onto the roof.

The three tower cranes Gore had imported travelled on a rail bridge that progressed along the axis of the shell as each arch was being completed. Each rib segment was lowered into place using a Hornibrook-devised cradle positioned with the aid of an 'erection arch'. This engineering truss was conceived by Gore but designed by a man considered the real genius of the Hornibrook team, Joe Bertony.

• • •

Joe Bertony had been a French spy during World War II and he was twice sent to concentration camps to die. Awarded the Croix de Guerre by the French government for valour for his wartime activities, General Charles de Gaulle described his heroism to France as 'courageous discipline'. Much like the 'courageous discipline' he showed at Bennelong Point, according to his former Hornibrook colleagues.

Bertony was a painter, a scientist and an engineer as well. He probably could have earned his living as a professional photographer too; he took some of the most arresting black and white images of the construction site through his Leica camera lens. Professional photographers, such as Max Dupain and David Moore, documented the structure as it was being built and their shots have immortalised the evolving geometry of steel and concrete. But Bertony's intimate portraits of the hard-hatted construction workers reveal the joy so many people took from being part of this project.

As an engineer, Bertony used his Leonardo da Vinci-like brilliance to make initial back-of-the-envelope calculations. He would then visualise objects, construct possible solutions in his mind and draw them on paper before analysing them more thoroughly.

To a significant extent, it was Bertony's complex handwritten mathematical equations that made the roof construction possible; it took 30,000 separate equations just to work out how much stress should be applied. Everything is curved and there is not one flat plane in the entire roof, so the geometry involved was highly complex. The margin of error could be no more than half an inch (1.25 centimetres) in putting the segments together.

Most notable of all Bertony's designs was the movable steel erection arch, which was so crucial in the construction of the concrete ribs that without it building the Opera House would have been impossible. Because it was telescopic, inclinable and traversable, it enabled each roof segment to be lowered into place. Bertony wrote all his equations very quickly over six months and in beautifully rendered long-hand. Bertony was always relieved when Hornibrook double-checked his calculations. It was frightening for him to think that if he had made a mistake it might not be found in that mass of numbers. So, he welcomed the work of his younger colleague David Evans, who taught himself computer programming in order to test the calculations.

In Australia there was just one computer large enough to cope with such a complex job: the IBM 7090 located at the Long Range Weapons Research Establishment at Woomera in South Australia. This was where missiles were tested for Australia's armed forces. So, Evans would travel one week a month to South Australia and work the night shift, the only time the computer was free. At no point were Bertony's calculations incorrect.

Evans later said of his colleague: 'It could be argued that Hornibrook chief Corbett Gore could have found another person, or a team of people, to do what Joe did, but I doubt if there was anyone with Joe's genius to see how to develop the telescopic truss and to build the ribs with it, or to do a dozen other things of importance on that site. It would have taken many minds and many rounds of trial and error, and a much longer time and a much bigger budget, to get those ribs in the air if Joe hadn't been there. Other solutions would have lacked his elegance and genius. Very little of this world is totally original, but Joe's ability to find solutions and to implement them with originality, where others would not dare to go, is legendary.'

Like Utzon and Arup, Bertony and the Hornibrook team would build models to test how his ideas would work. For the erection arch, he put a little motor on the model and a push button to show how it would start and how it would get bigger as the roof progressed. While the mathematics of this was all very laborious, the actual construction, Bertony says, was simple engineering—logical and methodical.

When Bertony saw Utzon's very first designs for the Opera House, they took his breath away. In early meetings with Utzon and Arup, he told the architect he could have designed a system of constructing those original designs—it was all a question of maths. Bertony recognised in Utzon a kindred spirit: a fellow European committed to craft. Their approach—of European perfectionism—was in stark contrast to the more Anglo-Saxon approach to construction that prevailed in Australia at the time.

• • •

Just as the Civil and Civic workers had been entertained by Paul Robeson, the stage-two workers were treated to a spontaneous performance by the world-renowned Trinidad-born pianist Winifred Atwell, who'd become internationally renowned in the 1950s for her boogie-woogie and ragtime hits. She'd sold over twenty million records and was the first black performer to have a number-one hit in the UK singles chart.

Atwell arrived in a fur coat at the Opera House site one winter's day while the workers were having a 'smoko'. Her trademark old upright piano, which she took everywhere, was hoisted onto a makeshift stage where she played *Waltzing Matilda*. At first, she silently mouthed the words, but by the end of the song she was singing out loud, joined by some of the men in hard hats. She later signed autographs on their work helmets.

The Hornibrook/stage two worksite was harmonious on the whole. Indeed, one weekend Michael Elphick, a surveyor who was used to scaling extraordinary heights, taught some of the Arup engineers how to abseil on the arches. Remarkably, given that safety harnesses weren't used, no one was killed or severely injured on site during construction. Wilf Deck recalls how windy it was atop the sails, and still marvels that no one fell off.

• • •

It was during this highly productive time of building when the vaults were taking flight skyward that the relationship between Arup and Utzon reached its nadir. It was a clash over mullions, the vertical bars between the panes of glass in the windows, that caused the final collapse. Utzon wanted large plywood mullions, provided by his old mate Symonds' firm, to be hung from the roof to hold the massive window walls. Plywood had never been used in this way before, and these would be the biggest windows in the world, requiring over an acre and a half (6225 square metres) of glass.

But Arup's people told him the roof was not designed to carry that weight; they wanted the mullions to be made of steel and to sit on the ground as support for the huge plates of glass. It wasn't just the engineers who were nervous. So too were the glass-plate manufacturers—glass had never been used in this way either.

So Utzon simply hired another firm of engineers, Miller, Milston & Ferris, for a second opinion. Peter Miller, a senior partner, had worked on the lightweight de Havilland Mosquito aircraft, which were made of laminated plywood. They were probably the most brilliant planes in World War II, according to Richard Leplastrier. After the war Miller had become a consulting engineer of distinction. He was the president of the world body of consulting engineers and was awarded honours by the Australian Institution of Engineers. He was respected, and he respected Utzon's ideas. His firm saw no reason why the mullions and auditorium ceilings that Utzon had envisaged could not be prefabricated in Symonds' Homebush factory and bear the weight of the shells.

Utzon's idea was that the finished mullions and plywood interiors would be transported down the Parramatta River to the Opera House site, just as ancient Egyptians had done on the Nile when they were building the pyramids of stone. The plywood procession, from Homebush (near where Sydney's 2000 Olympics stadiums were built), was to be Utzon's way of involving the people of Sydney in his project.

Giuseppe Verdi's grand opera *Aida*, which is set on the banks of the Nile, was premiered at Cairo's Khedivial Opera House in 1871. In 1717 London, Handel's *Water Music* was first performed on the banks of the River Thames before the

king on the royal barge. Perhaps a conflation of these two historical events was what Utzon had in mind when he conceived the
idea of a flotilla of barges floating down the Parramatta River.
Utzon's imagination knew no bounds.

Mogens Prip-Buus, the only Dane still alive of those who
migrated to Sydney to work on the Opera House, explained that
the idea was for the interiors to be assembled in Homebush, then
taken by barges right to Bennelong Point, where they would be
installed by the three giant Hornibrook cranes. Arup's team,
however, fought against this: 'They were not able to work with
plywood; they only knew concrete and steel—they were only
a small firm then, not the big company they became—so their
business then was concrete and steel, steel, steel,' he said.

Utzon was by now increasingly at loggerheads with Arup's
local staff, notably Michael (Mick) Lewis, so he wrote to Arup
himself in London. Arup wrote back a conciliatory letter dated
27 February 1966, pleading for a united front in dealing with
the NSW government. 'I won't go into your accusations about
incorrectness—let's forget it. But I repeat what I said before:
it is absolutely essential that we stick together. If we don't, we
could end up with a very nasty situation . . . But let's scrap this
nonsense about "Dear Sirs" and "Yours faithfully" and secrecy
and suspicion. We are too old for that. Let's think about the
job and pull it through.'

Arup, always eager to do what he could to build Utzon's
Opera House, said he would give the concept a second chance.
But he insisted he would need to test the plywood's durability
and submit a report once his team had tested it. Utzon agreed.

• • •

Mogens Prip-Buus had started working in Jørn Utzon's Danish
office in 1958. He lived in one of the Kingo Houses, the housing

development Utzon had created at Helsingør, which even today is often described as one of Scandinavia's best examples of 'humanist homes' (communal with private inner courtyards).

Relocating to Sydney in 1963, Prip-Buus remembers going out at least twice a week to the Symonds plywood palace at Homebush Bay. He had an office there, but, because of the heat (it would often reach 40 degrees in summer) and the dust and noise, he often found it hard to draw there. But he worked closely with Ralph Symonds' technical director, Ezra Ellis. They developed what they called the *sisu* roof for the rehearsal rooms. Referencing Eero Saarinen's use of the Finnish word to describe the ideas of 'guts', they hoped performers would be inspired to pull from themselves something they did not think possible. *Sisu* was also the name Utzon's father gave to one of his boats and the business name he and Lis had used to purchase their land in Bayview. The curved plywood elements of the roof of the rehearsal room, which could be adapted for the vibrations of different instruments, had been acoustically tested as they would be for the main halls. They were working with two acoustics consultants on this: the firms Lothar Cremer and Croner Gabler, both from Berlin. The curved interior was intended to create a cosy feeling, like Utzon had experienced in Morocco sleeping under Bedouin tents.

Prip-Buus recalls Utzon working at the Bennelong Point office one day when he suddenly jumped up and wrote the words 'additive architecture' on the wall. He had coined a word for his own style of architecture, which was based on the growth patterns in nature—the things he saw in the clouds, the sky, the trees in Mexico, the tents in Morocco and in the Chinese temples and courtyards he loved. These were the repeated patterns his father had said to look for—a type of transition from the symmetry of nature into the built form.

'What he repeated often in our office was "Don't forget the principle; don't forget the idea",' Prip-Buus explained.

But Utzon was now finding it increasingly difficult to keep his own advice in mind as the situation became more fraught.

• • •

After their trip to Europe, Peter and Libby Hall settled in Sydney and Peter started full-time work at the Government Architect's Office. They moved to North Sydney and had two children, Rebecca and Marcus (known as Willy). Hall's reputation was quickly established, winning the Sir John Sulman Medal for architecture for Goldstein Hall at the University of NSW. He also completed the Macquarie University Library and the Philip Baxter College at the University of NSW.

Libby Hall became a clothes designer. Having gone to London to study theatre design, she returned to Sydney and took a job with interior designer Marion Hall Best. The two had attended the same private girls school, Frensham. Best had started to import Printex fabric in the early 1960s and Marimekko clothing when the Finnish fabric company began to develop its fashion line. Peter redesigned the interiors of Best's shops in Rowe Street in the city and on Queen Street, Woollahra.

Best had wanted Libby to take over the business, but she turned down the opportunity. Libby did, however, ask two young students, Lin Utzon and her friend Joanna Collard, to model the clothes. At nineteen, Lin was studying art at East Sydney Tech, and she embodied everything appealing about Scandinavian style. She was blonde, tall and slender—a great advertisement for the new brand of bold prints.

Jan was now studying architecture at the University of NSW, while younger brother Kim was still in primary school on the northern beaches. The younger Utzons had settled into Australia well, but things were very unsettled for their father.

When Premier Heffron retired in April 1964, Jack Renshaw became Labor premier. Norm Ryan was still Minister for Public Works, and he began to demand more accountability from Utzon. NSW voters—especially those in the country—were becoming impatient.

The stage-one base podium had cost twice as much as Civil and Civic had anticipated. Newspapers, eager for headlines to create some daily drama, ran hard with this story. Labor now gave estimates of around £17 million for completion, as did the opposition Liberal-Country Party.

An election was due on 1 May 1965. Exploiting the budget blowout, the opposition promised to rein in costs, no matter that Opera House expenditure was not coming out of the state's consolidated revenue—it was being paid for by lottery tickets. The electorate responded. The Labor Party was swept out of office after twenty-four years in power. Bob Askin's Liberal-Country Party claimed to have a clear mandate: to bring the Bennelong Point project under control.

Jørn Utzon's fate was sealed on that morning in May 1965 when Davis Hughes, the Country Party member for Armidale, woke to find himself quite unexpectedly the minister for public works.

Chapter nineteen

Plain sailing

Pittwater, with its ancient ochre-coloured cliffs and secluded bushy bays, was where the nature-loving Utzons felt most 'at home'. Like their Hellebæk house, which was in a forest 54 kilometres north of Copenhagen, Palm Beach was 43 kilometres north of Sydney's centre. Matt Carroll's parents, who had made young Lin feel so comfortable during that first Greek lunch at Pittwater, owned a terrace house in Jersey Road, Paddington. In 1965, to avoid the long commute, the Utzons arranged for Jan and Lin to live there closer to their places of study. The Utzons, senior and junior, loved the terraces of Paddington with the iron lace ornamentation on their verandahs. Jørn had bought a property in nearby Windsor Street and was restoring it with the intention that his children live there.

The Jersey Road share house occupants were friends with a host of local culturati—artists such as Martin Sharp and Peter Kingston, and writers Richard Neville and Richard Walsh.

This was the crowd who had created *OZ* magazine in 1963 and the Utzon children were embraced by them. In much the way it had excited author Patrick White, there was a sense of anticipation among this group of young Australians that the Opera House would be an inspiration for them.

Among the residents in this house was a young Australian film-maker, John Weiley, who had left his hometown of Grafton bearing the baggage of a radical raised in a strait-laced country town. He was accompanied by a mate, Bob Ellis, who fancied himself as a writer. They were both fleeing the conservative climes of the Clarence River to come to university in Sydney. They both ultimately got traineeships at the ABC. Weiley also started to make underground films with friend Bruce Beresford.

The ABC—notably through its former principal conductor Eugene Goossens and its still current General Manager Charles Moses—had been instrumental in creating the momentum for the Opera House, and the organisation stood to gain greatly when the new permanent home for its orchestra was finished. The broadcaster established a dedicated team to record its construction. One of Weiley's tasks as a trainee was to film its progress. Every weekend he would go to the old shed at the ABC's Gore Hill studios where the cameramen hung out. One of them would accompany him to Bennelong Point to film what had been accomplished during the previous seven days.

Weiley started documenting the Opera House when it was nothing more than a hole in the ground. He waded through puddles in the stage machinery pit. He got to know the building inside out—the tunnels you could crawl into and pop out on top and sail down as it took shape. He knew every crevice and curve of its creation. He even made a short feature film in the bowels of the building. By the time the podium was completed, he had recorded the buzz in the city about it. By the time the big tower cranes started to cast shadows and the shells started to take form—fold by fold, splayed like a Spanish fan—he had become obsessed by the building.

• • •

It was also in 1965 that the great pile of concrete at Bennelong Point at long last began to start looking like an opera house. The completion date was being touted as December 1969.

A night shift was introduced to complete the roof sails to hurry construction along, lit by the biggest lamp in Australia, a 6-foot (1.83 metre) long tube filled with xenon gas that blasted 20,000 watts down onto the site. The lamp gave the equivalent light of forty houses with every light turned on, the *Sydney Morning Herald* claimed. The lamp had been supplied by Germany's Siemens, the very company Civil and Civic founder, Dick Dusseldorp, had been forced to work for in a World War II labour camp.

Test after test was carried out onsite. Radioactive sodium carbonate was being pumped into the sails like a barium meal to test the concrete for possible flaws. Radiographer Noel Ross used an X-ray machine to measure the radioactive count from the shells.

Excavation of a huge basin for the carpark began that year as well. Utzon had designed the building without including a carpark. The government had not thought to ask for one. This afterthought would later cause great controversy and would prompt industrial action.

Because of the notorious winds on the harbour, and at Bennelong Point, an expert was called in to see how this might impact on acoustics at the site. Mr VJ Smith, who had worked at the Aeronautical Research Laboratory at Sydney University for twenty years, predicted winds of 20 knots would create eddies over the Opera House sails and injure people. 'Women climbing the Opera House steps could have their mink stoles blown from their shoulders into the harbour,' he predicted. Opera capes would vanish into the blue. Elderly people might be knocked down and injured by the blasts of strong winds. Windy weather could turn the opening night into something resembling a 'casualty station'. 'I advise people to ring the Weather Bureau before going to the Opera,' the expert told the *Herald*.

Herald music critic, Roger Covell, had news that was somewhat more comforting. He reported that the large-scale modelling confirmed that the acoustics would be good—and acoustic quality was what concert goers were expecting from this new building, he reminded readers. Utzon said the findings from the acoustic test by two visiting German professors were 'the most promising results I think we have had in the whole Opera House story'.

Labor's Norm Ryan was still the minister for public works. He said the most complex part of the next stage—stage three, the interiors—was the state-of-the-art backstage machinery coming from Austria. There had been previous unrest about the use of imported materials, such as the Höganäs tiles from Sweden. Utzon always followed the traditional European method of identifying the finest workmanship for each job and then developing a close relationship with the supplier, as he did with the Höganäs tiles. However, when the Coalition came to power in May 1965, supply decisions were firmly based on the tender process: three bids were requested and the cheapest usually got the work.

A model of the building that had taken seven men fourteen months to build and cost £5000 went on display in December 1964. Six feet long by 2½ feet wide (1.82 × 0.61 metres), and constructed of plywood, fibreglass and Perspex, it showed the interior of the main hall to have a colour scheme of red, white and gold. 'We want to see faces and only faces from the stage. The plan is also intended to increase the feeling of proximity between performers and audience by having no proscenium arch as a dividing line,' Utzon explained.

Conducted tours lasting one and a half hours had begun at the Bennelong Point site. Most Sundays in the 1960s, locals would teeter their way over puddles, building materials, torn cement bags and old pie crusts. Sandra Hall, writing in the *Bulletin*, reported an air of cynicism on the part of some Sydney-siders taking the Sunday tour. 'Why didn't they build a second town hall for the ABC instead of spoiling this?' said one; 'The whole thing would probably turn into a floating restaurant,' said another. Another man was impressed though, saying he could now see 'why it's taken so bloody long to finish'.

In mid-June 1965, a viewing pavilion overlooking the construction was built at the top of the Tarpeian Way—the same spot where Utzon had seen Bennelong Point for the first time. Just ten days after it opened, it was already pulling crowds of up to 2000 on weekends. A recorded message by competition judge Henry Ingham Ashworth described the concept and purpose of the building. The crush was so great one weekend in June that the 'Out' door had to be opened to allow the crowd to get inside.

That same month, the state government advertised for someone to run the Opera House. There was chatter that the job's salary, originally advertised in 1961 as £1000 per year, had risen to £4500. It would be a job for a man, the newspapers said; there was no question at the time that it could go to a woman.

● ● ●

But it was women who were increasingly on-site documenting the project, as they started to enter journalism in larger numbers in 1960s Australia. A new national daily newspaper, Rupert Murdoch's *The Australian*, was launched in 1964 as a rival to the established state-based broadsheets. Its correspondent, poet Elizabeth Riddell (known as Betty), reported from the Opera House construction, as did the *Sun-Herald*'s Margaret Jones, who wrote regular progress reports.

In July 1965, the tabloid *The Sun* sent reporter Lilla Kertesz to the Opera House to lay some tiles. A Hungarian who had 'escaped' from her homeland after the revolution in 1956, she wrote her story under the by-line 'Dinkum Aussie'. As a child she'd seen the opera houses in Budapest and Vienna, she wrote, so she was well qualified to comment: 'But our Opera House is different from these traditional ones—massive and beautiful as they are. It's so modern and exciting.'

Taken to an office on Bennelong Point, she changed out of her normal work clothes and into jeans, a shirt and a hard hat. She met the lovable black 'bitzer' Debussy, the site's pet dog that accompanied her to the casting yard where superintendent Wally Stinson showed her stacks of tiles. The tiles didn't go onto the roof one by one as she'd expected but were first set in the chevron-shaped concrete beds, which were so remarkably thin that she could see why the roof was called an egg-shell, she wrote.

• • •

It was another journalist, twenty-five-year-old Jillian Robertson, who hosted the first party on the Opera House construction site, on 27 October 1965. It turned out to be one of the wildest parties Sydney had ever seen.

Having just come back from three years of working abroad for the Murdoch press, she decided to celebrate her return with the Opera House workers. 'Coming back to Sydney—I've just returned from overseas—is like a bit of dry bread, and you need something a bit different like this. The party is fundamentally for the workers, but I've also invited everyone I like in Sydney,' Robertson said. Opera House Executive Committee chairman Stan Haviland dubbed it 'Pop at the Op', and gave permission for the party, he explained, to highlight one of the purposes of the Opera House: to present popular entertainment.

The party cost Robertson £200. One thousand guests— 600 socialites and 400 workers all wearing hard hats—consumed 500 bottles of champagne, a couple of hundred cans of brandy and dry, and hundreds of hot dogs and rolls from the Fiddlers Three Café in Cremorne. The Easybeats, Little Pattie and Sammy and the Soul Syndicate entertained the party guests, as did dancers from the Kings Cross strip club, The Pink Pussycat. For sixteen-year-old Little Pattie (Patricia Amphlett) her first close-up view of the Opera House was love at first sight.

The siren sounded at 4 p.m. to signal the end of work for the day and a blast of electric guitars marked the start of the party. By 4.15 p.m. some 250 Opera House workers were clustered high on the scaffolding sucking champagne from the bottle. As the *Sun-Herald* reported, the 'long-haired' group, The Easybeats, liked the hard hats so much they wore them on stage.

Among the guests were men wearing black eye-patches, women wheeling babies through the mud, strippers dressed in gold lamé and feathers, and some well-known names from Sydney's social set. Groupies leapt on stage and competed with the strippers in a frenzied hair-flying shake. A migrant construction worker made a big impression with impromptu palm readings for the crowd. At sundown a thunderstorm drenched the guests and rows of empty champagne bottles littered the ground as the women took off their high heels to save them being ruined in the mud.

The party was the talk of the town—at least among Sydney's small circle of socialites. It was later condemned as tasteless and criticised for the warm champagne, the cold hot dogs and the lack of toilets. The next morning, with many of the workers sporting hangovers, June Dally-Watkins, Sydney's queen of etiquette, was there with them at 7.30 a.m. to help clean up the mess.

Even though the party had sparked enormous interest in the Opera House as a venue, officials very quickly regretted their decision to let Robertson's celebration go ahead. From then on, the Executive Committee made the very firm decision that it couldn't be hired out. This was a shame, the *Daily Mirror*'s social correspondent wrote, as 'it was the best thing that has happened to Sydney for years'.

Robertson left Sydney, went on to marry into the British aristocracy and became the Duchess of Hamilton. But the memory of that first, and last, private party held at the Opera House construction site lives on for all who attended.

• • •

In 1965 Joan Sutherland toured Australia with the Sutherland-Williamson International Grand Opera Company in a triumphant sell-out return to her homeland. She had come directly from Jamaica, where she'd been rehearsing with Noel Coward to record a dozen of his romantic songs. Accompanying her was a young tenor named Luciano Pavarotti. The tour proved to be a major milestone in his career. It was not so for her husband Richard Bonynge, who had called the Australian press pack a 'bunch of orangutans'.

Sutherland was also criticised. During a speech at Sydney's Town Hall, she snapped at photographers and cameramen for making too much noise while she was trying to address the crowd. She 'nervously toyed with her white gloves and several times adjusted her heavy fur coat, obviously irked by the heat of the camera arc lights and the crowded room's gas heaters', the *Herald* reported. She started to be called 'Negative Nancy', particularly when it came to her views on the progress at Bennelong Point.

The *Mirror* reported that Sutherland had declared she would not come back to Sydney until the Opera House was built. 'We are grateful to Miss Joan Sutherland for bringing a touch of excitement into our drab lives. We now realise that what we have been missing all these years is authentic prima donna flounce,' the *Mirror* editorialised. 'Every day she reminds us the function of the prima donna is not only to sing but put on a jolly good show of temperament. Yesterday's temper tantrum at the Town Hall was a good one just to cheer up a damp and gloomy day. Miss Sutherland said she would never come back to Sydney—well not until 1980 when the Opera House is finished. We don't know why Miss Sutherland should expect the Opera House to be finished in 1980. Our personal crystal ball fails to reveal anything of the kind.'

Sutherland did make an appearance at the Opera House during this visit—at a function where the northern foyer of the Concert Hall is now located where she presented a prize to the young opera singer who had won a *Women's Weekly* singing competition. The building was still a shell without windows. It was windy and open; dark tarpaulins were used to provide protection from the cold. This time neither Sutherland or her conductor husband snapped at the press pack. Instead, they returned quietly to their cab waiting on the concourse. Soon afterwards they left Sydney for their European home.

● ● ●

Richard Leplastrier—or 'Ricardo', as Utzon called him—continued to work at the boatshed at Palm Beach. The Utzons liked to live 'in the jaws of nature', he said, a lesson that shaped Leplastrier as one of Australia's finest residential architects.

Utzon had bought a 30-foot plywood yacht from boat builders in Kirrawee, one of Sydney's southern suburbs. Lis Utzon had christened it *Kim*, after their youngest son, in January 1964. Utzon would occasionally sail it with Leplastrier, who would set up the spinnaker system on the boat for Utzon. 'He'd see the way a cloud formed over Lion Island [at the mouth of the Hawkesbury River],' says Leplastrier. 'I remember him pointing that out to me once and the cloud was like an aerofoil wing . . . The wet nor'-easter had gone up and over the island and somehow there was an inversion of temperature . . . and there was a beautiful cloud on that island and I hadn't seen it. That happened a lot and that was why he was such a brilliant teacher. He made you realise that you were looking at things, but not seeing. Even when the storms came, he was thrilled by it.'

But Utzon wasn't a very good sailor. He always respected Leplastrier's superior boating skills and let him take charge when they were out on the water. 'I mean, he enjoyed it and he loved it; but he wasn't a tactical competitive racing sailor and he didn't know the fine tuning of things, the fine adjustments or anything like that,' Leplastrier said.

The young architect loved the time he spent at the boathouse with Utzon and his team. But it was a disappointment to them all that the local council had knocked back plans for the Bayview house—because it consisted of three separate dwellings.

Utzon often took his staff to Barrenjoey headland at the northern end of Palm Beach and had them sit between two large dunes so that only the blue horizon of the ocean could be seen, framed by the curving sand. Utzon would ask them to 'Watch and wait'. Leplastrier recalls once: 'A seagull flew into view

Fort Macquarie Tram Depot in 1955, the site where the Opera House now stands. (COURTESY OF FAIRFAX MEDIA)

Fort Macquarie being demolished in 1958. (COURTESY OF FAIRFAX MEDIA)

Aage Utzon (right), designer of the Aalborg dinghy, and his son Jørn in Denmark.
(COURTESY OF BAUER MEDIA)

Some of the 233 entries received for the Sydney opera house design competition before
the 3 December 1956 cut-off date. Ron Thomson (left), secretary of the Opera House
Executive Committee, and judges Harry Ingham Ashworth (centre) and Cobden Parkes
(right). (COURTESY OF FAIRFAX MEDIA)

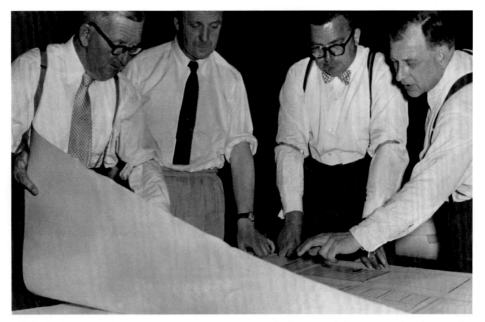

The judging panel (from left to right): Government Architect Cobden Parkes, Professor of Architecture at Cambridge University Leslie Martin, Professor Harry Ingham Ashworth, Dean of the faculty of Architecture at the University of Sydney, and Michigan architect Eero Saarinen. (COURTESY OF BAUER MEDIA)

Jørn Utzon's original entry showing the perspective from the staircase between the two halls was published in the *Daily Telegraph* on 30 January 1957, the day after Utzon was chosen as winner. (COURTESY OF BAUER MEDIA)

(From left to right) 'Silent Stan' Haviland, New South Wales Premier Joe Cahill, and Civil and Civic's Dick Dusseldorp look at the plans in Utzon's 1958 red book. (COURTESY FAIRFAX MEDIA)

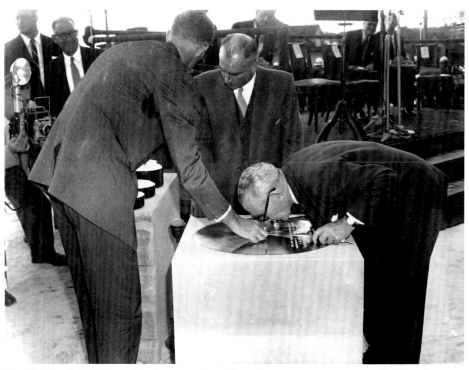

Premier Joe Cahill kisses the plaque at the sod turning ceremony on 2 March 1959 that marked the beginning of building at Bennelong Point. (COURTESY FAIRFAX MEDIA)

Mrs K Henning Hergel (left), wife of the Danish consul-general, with Jørn and Lis Utzon at the ceremony to mark the beginning of building. (COURTESY FAIRFAX MEDIA)

The Opera House fund-raising committee looking at a photograph of a building model in February 1960. (COURTESY OF BAUER MEDIA)

Jørn Utzon and Public Works Minister Norm Ryan inspect a model of the Opera House. (COURTESY OF FAIRFAX MEDIA)

Laying the Opera House floor, April 1960. (COURTESY OF FAIRFAX MEDIA)

Civil and Civic workers erect scaffolding for stage one of building in 1961.
(COURTESY OF FAIRFAX MEDIA)

Civil and civic workers living onsite in a caravan doing their washing, 20 June 1960.
(COURTESY OF FAIRFAX MEDIA)

Civil and Civic workers in 1960, not long before Paul Robeson's performance.
(COURTESY OF FAIRFAX MEDIA)

The podium rising up like a Mayan temple. (COURTESY OF FAIRFAX MEDIA)

The erection Arch at work. (COURTESY OF FAIRFAX MEDIA)

Jørn Utzon (left), NSW Premier Bob Heffron (centre) and Ove Arup (right) in Sydney, August 1962. (COURTESY OF BAUER MEDIA)

Happy days, Jørn Utzon with his co-workers Mogens Prip-Buus and Bill Wheatland. (COURTESY OF FAIRFAX MEDIA)

Joe Bertony, inventor of the Hornibrook's erection arch, with a model demonstrating how it works, 19 June 1963. (COURTESY OF BAUER MEDIA)

Utzon mobbed by the media, March 1966. (COURTESY OF BAUER MEDIA)

The Sydney Opera House on 1 March 1966, the morning after Utzon's showdown with Minister Hughes. (COURTESY OF BAUER MEDIA)

Demonstrators at the Opera House site before they marched to Parliament House on 3 March 1966. (COURTESY OF BAUER MEDIA)

Peter Hall (left) with Premier Bob Askin (centre) and Public Works Minister Davis Hughes. (COURTESY OF FAIRFAX MEDIA)

Enter architect Peter Hall, 1966. (COURTESY OF FAIRFAX MEDIA)

On the harbour enjoying the opening, 20 October 1973. (COURTESY OF FAIRFAX MEDIA)

Ben Blakeney as Bennelong atop the sail during the opening ceremony.
(COURTESY OF FAIRFAX MEDIA)

The Arthur Baldwinson watercolour of Utzon's winning entry. (COURTESY OF BAUER MEDIA)

The podium, the work of Dick Dusseldorp's employees. (COURTESY OF BAUER MEDIA)

(Above) The shell starts to take shape. (PHOTO BY KEVIN BARLOW COURTESY OF BAUER MEDIA)

(Right) Building the Bennelong restaurant, looking towards the AMP Building and city skyline. (PHOTO BY KEVIN BARLOW COURTESY OF BAUER MEDIA)

Hornibrook workers inspect plans for the erection arch ribs with the erection arch behind them. (PHOTO BY KEVIN BARLOW COURTESY OF BAUER MEDIA)

Inside the large shell. Originally designed as an opera/multi-purpose hall, it is now the
Concert Hall. (PHOTO BY KEVIN BARLOW COURTESY OF BAUER MEDIA)

The building starts to emerge, early 1966 (COURTESY OF BAUER MEDIA PTY LTD)

John Coburn and Davis Hughes with the curtain of the Moon in the Drama Theatre.
(COURTESY OF BAUER MEDIA)

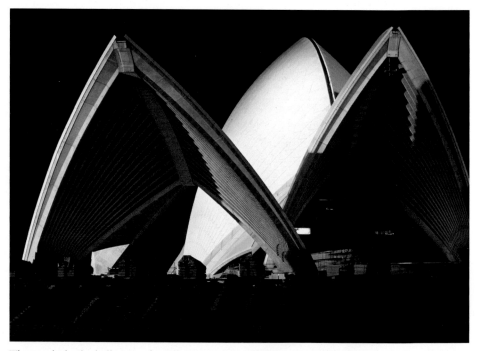

The partly-built shells were first illuminated for the 1970 Captain Cook Bicentenary
celebrations. (PHOTO BY KEVIN BARLOW COURTESY OF BAUER MEDIA)

View from western Circular Quay, 1973. (COURTESY OF BAUER MEDIA)

The Queen officially opens the Sydney Opera House, 20 October 1973.
(COURTESY OF BAUER MEDIA)

Opening night fireworks. (COURTESY OF BAUER MEDIA)

The first Indigenous lighting of the shells for Vivid in 2016. (COURTESY OF FAIRFAX MEDIA)

from behind one dune, darted across [our] field of view and disappeared behind the other. "Only show a part. Never show it all. The imagination is more powerful than reality can ever be," Utzon explained.'

Leplastrier believes Utzon was at his happiest at Pitt-water. Which was why he was spending more time there than at Bennelong Point in 1965. 'Jørn would come down to the shed and he'd be worried about something, and he'd just slowly relax and sit down and start drawing, which is what he loved doing. Whenever he'd go into town, there were problems. He'd go in his beautiful Italian-made suit. He was such a cool dresser. But he always turned up at the boatshed in a pair of shorts and Ray-Ban glasses and was very relaxed. He loved being down there [at the boatshed].'

The boathouse was a safe haven from the Hughes-induced storm that was brewing on the horizon.

Chapter twenty

Millions and mullions

'For God's sake—you're minister for public works? You can't drive a nail!' declared Davis Hughes' wife Philippa when he telephoned her in Armidale to give her news of the ministry he was about to head. As he later recalled, he was expecting his wife to say: 'Aren't you wonderful!' and 'This is great!' and 'I'm so delighted, thrilled', but instead she laughed loudly. Her husband, although respected in his electorate for his work as a teacher at The Armidale School and his tenure as mayor, was not known for his handyman skills.

Following the May 1965 election, the Liberal-Country Party formed government with the slimmest two-seat majority. The Country Party insisted that it take charge of the public works portfolio as a way of appeasing voters in the bush. 'It's such a "doing" portfolio: so important for country areas and everything from schools and hospitals and water conservation—flood mitigation, harbours and so forth,' Hughes told the new premier

Bob Askin and the leader of the Country Party, Charles Cutler, the week they were elected. Footy-loving Askin, who had no clue about opera, said the Country Party could have this portfolio, so long as Hughes took the job. Hughes claimed he had performed Chekhov at Melbourne's Comedy Theatre, produced plays, read *Ulysses* and knew classical ballet intimately.

Hughes immediately emerged as Jørn Utzon's nemesis. The personality clash between these two men is one of the most infamous in the annals of twentieth-century architecture. It pitted the old world against the new, the European way against the Australian, the broad-brush-stroke visionary against a short-term Mr Fix-It minister, a creative architect against a pragmatic politician. But to say it was just a stoush between a Danish dreamer and a tough-as-nuts Tasmanian teacher loses some of the nuance of the situation. As in all tragedies, there were good reasons for bad decisions.

• • •

William Davis Hughes was born in northern Tasmania in 1910, the eldest of seven children of churchgoing Baptists. His family lived at Sheffield, a small town south of Devonport, but his mother wanted her children to have a good education, so Hughes moved in with his grandmother to attend the selective Launceston High School. He then went to Philip Smith Training College in Hobart, and was appointed principal, aged seventeen, at a one-teacher school before completing his teacher training. He moved to Melbourne in 1936, where he became a resident master at Caulfield Grammar School and performed in amateur drama.

In 1940 he enlisted in the Royal Australian Air Force (RAAF) and rose rapidly through the ranks, ultimately being discharged as a squadron leader. In 1947 he returned to teaching in NSW and rose to deputy headmaster at The Armidale School. While his family continued to call him Bill or Billy, he dropped his Christian name when he ran for the state seat of Armidale in 1950 to avoid confusion with former Prime Minister Billy Hughes. *Hansard* recorded him as holding a Bachelor of Science degree upon entering parliament. The *Herald* reported this too. Neither were correct.

Controversy erupted in March 1959, the same month that Premier Cahill turned the first sod at Bennelong Point, when it was discovered that Hughes had never held a degree. Not only had he been promoted in the RAAF on the basis of claiming a degree, but he became a teacher in NSW on that basis as well.

As leader of the NSW Country Party at the time, Hughes had sent an official message commemorating the start of building. It would mark the beginning of a new phase in Australian history, he said: 'This imaginative structure in a beautiful setting will attract and inspire the great artists of the world and stimulate the rapid growth of our native culture . . . Country as well as city people will enjoy its benefits and people of other states will watch its progress with interest and pride.'

But soon after, as a result of the controversy, he was forced to resign as Country Party leader and remained in hospital with a gastric ulcer and a nervous condition. Without campaigning, or even leaving his hospital bed, he was returned as the member for Armidale with an increased majority in the election of 21 March 1959.

A month later he outlined the 'true position' of his degreeless status to his parliamentary colleagues, claiming only to have 'read for' a Bachelor of Science degree. 'Apparently from that more was taken than was actually intended,' he explained. Hughes had committed a fraud, yet there was a soft murmur of 'hear hears' when he gave his justification. It had been a 'brave weakness' on his part not to correct the record, he said.

• • •

On the harbour, the first hydrofoil named the *Manly III* entered service on 7 January 1965. Conventional ferries covered the 6-mile (10-kilometre) journey from Circular Quay to Manly in thirty-five minutes, but the new hydrofoil did the same trip in under fifteen minutes. Many of the Arup workers who had moved to Sydney lived at Manly. Whoever was at the top of the shell around knock-off time would yell out when they saw the ferry leave Manly. Those who lived at Manly would scurry off the worksite and usually make it to Circular Quay in time.

The new Liberal premier, Bob Askin—also a Manly resident and by this stage installed in his prestigious Bower Street water-side residence on what was sometimes referred to as Sydney's Riviera—was keen for commerce. He was transforming the city. Under the leadership of the state's first 'professional politician', Sydney was evolving quickly into a pro-development city— all in the name of progress.

'Slum clearance' became a hallmark of his government. Askin went to great lengths to convince the public he was a no-nonsense modernist. But he was unsympathetic to the idea of the Opera House largely because he thought it would shine like a beacon, honouring the legacy of Joe Cahill, who had been his long-time political rival.

That year entertainment impresario Harry Wren floated a novel idea to help the Askin government pay for the Opera House. Wren's 'gorge rose when he read the latest estimates of the Opera House costs', the *Mirror* reported, so he floated his idea of a Monte Carlo–style casino with five hundred poker machines, twenty-five roulette wheels and a TAB office with closed circuit television for punters. At this time, casinos were still not legal in NSW, but Askin was well known at Sydney's underground drinking and gambling venues. He had even worked as an illegal starting price (SP) bookmaker on the side before entering politics.

• • •

Until this time, the members of the Opera House Executive Committee had been the client Utzon, as architect, answered to; he liked the Executive Committee and it liked him. As the client, the committee gave Utzon great freedom and often let him do what he thought best, rather than the ideas offered by Ove Arup's engineers.

Utzon had had a long relationship with the committee members, most of whom he'd known since his 1957 competition win. They included committee chairman Stan Haviland; competition judges Henry Ingham Ashworth and Cobden Parkes; Sydney town clerk EW Adams; ABC manager Charles Moses; general manager of Hoyts Theatres, John Glass (Utzon's plans had provided for a large cinema); director of the state Conservatorium of Music, Bernard Heinze; the Elizabethan Theatre Trust's Hugh Hunt; Sydney Symphony Orchestra's musical director, Nicolai Malko; the secretary of the Trades and Labour Council, Jim Kenny; and the Director General of Education, Harold Wyndham. They had Utzon's back as long-term supporters of the project, but in 1960 a bill had passed through the state parliament that made the Opera House the responsibility of the minister for Public Works, who was at that time Norm Ryan. Ryan did not enforce the change and he continued to allow the committee to remain in charge. Hughes intended to change this arrangement.

At the very first Cabinet meeting of the new government, Askin insisted Utzon provide a final price and completion date for the Opera House. He gave Hughes free rein with Utzon, and the new minister for public works took control of the entire Opera House project in September 1965. He appointed himself Utzon's paymaster. It was control by chequebook.

When Hughes took command, he told the Opera House Executive Committee it was no longer needed. He claimed the committee was too unwieldy and not nimble enough to make quick decisions; it was hampered by too much process. He kneecapped it by taking over full control of all decision-making on the project.

He also made his presence known on site with frequent visits. The 1960s was an era of low unemployment and high union membership in Australia. During stage two, there were thirty-six work stoppages over ninety days. The unions on the site were becoming increasingly militant. This would only intensify as time went on with Askin wanting to take action against the Building Workers' Industrial Union and crack down on strikes.

All told, around ten thousand workers from more than ninety different nationalities worked at the site during the construction phase. Typical were Shorty the crane driver and Jimmy the dogman (the worker who directs crane operations while riding on the material being lifted), who both worked on the shells. One day they hoisted the beloved blue Morris Mini Cooper of their boss, Hornibrook project superintendent Bob Selby-Wood, to the crest of the Opera House's highest sail. It was a joke that entertained much of Sydney and even Selby-Wood, a car aficionado, saw the funny side of it. But minister for Public Works Davis Hughes did not. Subsequently, Selby-Wood was posted to another construction job.

Stan Haviland, considered by the new government to be a public servant darling of the old Labor regime, retired as president of the Water Board and was appointed to assist on the land valuation royal commission. The Askin government held Haviland, as the former administrative head of the Opera House project, at least partly responsible for its spiralling costs. NSW members of the Legislative Assembly on both sides were said to be shocked to learn many thousands of pounds had been paid to Utzon for travelling and special expenses. 'Utzon has been paid as much money as four Opera House lottery wins,' one newspaper proclaimed. That coupled with the 'secret office', as the press called his Palm Beach boatshed, meant the Dane was no longer the darling he once was.

● ● ●

By the second half of 1965, the tension between Utzon and Hughes was palpable. Not only that, but, as former premier and now Opposition leader Jack Renshaw pointed out in the NSW parliament in November 1965, costs had risen to £24.7 million—in the six months the Liberal–Country Party had been in power, there had been a huge increase of 42 per cent on previous Labor estimates. Renshaw left Hughes red-faced and exposed his ineptitude during his early days in office.

Sensing a story, the press pack began to stalk Utzon at his office at Bennelong Point, at his boathouse office at Palm Beach, at his home, anywhere.

Utzon's two loyal lieutenants, Australian Bill Wheatland and Mogens Prip-Buus, claim the minister simply started going behind their backs directly to Arup's for building solutions. Not only that, the minister also approached the Royal Australian Institute of Architects to ask whether it thought Utzon's team was capable of completing the drawings for stage three.

In letters home to his parents and in his own personal diaries, Prip-Buus documented the decline, when from the end of August, the minister began to hint he might put someone else in charge of the project. 'Utzon received a telephone call asking him to go to the gate, where a man in a green car would be waiting for him. The man turned out to be Norm Ryan, the former minister for Public Works,' Prip-Buus wrote on Thursday, 2 September. Obviously concerned at being recognised, Ryan said he knew the present government would try to make a scapegoat of Utzon, but he assured the architect that he and the Labor Party would

support him. He asked Utzon to ring him on Sunday at home—
Ryan was worried his work phone was tapped.

By late September, Prip-Buus's diary notes, at a meeting with
Minister Hughes, even the committee members agreed Utzon
could not have *everything* he wanted, and that he would have to
compromise, for instance on the use of plywood. On 1 October,
two letters arrived from the minister at Bennelong Point. Utzon,
in jest, threw them both into the wastepaper basket. Prip-Buus
fished them out: one enquired about their chances of getting
the drawings finished, the other asked about why they needed
50-foot panels of plywood.

At a lunch with Utzon on 6 October, Norm Ryan told him
the government already had two architects it wanted to associate
with the project. The 23 October funeral of Ron Thomson, the
former Secretary of the Opera House Executive Committee, was
an awkward gathering of many people involved in the project.
'Walter Bunning came across to Jørn—smiling and obsequious;
how can a man behave like that when at the same time he is
blackening our name in the newspapers?' Prip-Buus wrote in his
diary of the architect who still thought he should have won the
Opera House competition.

According to Prip-Buus, Michael Lewis, Arup's site manager,
was also emerging as an enemy. He was undermining Utzon's
team by going behind their back to the minister, the Dane wrote
in his diary. Lewis had visited Armidale, Hughes' electorate, he
told Utzon and Prip-Buus after the funeral, something both the
men found strange.

By late 1965, Utzon was facing serious financial problems.
The minister had stopped paying him, so he couldn't pay his
staff, and he'd just received a substantial tax bill from Australian
authorities that he couldn't afford to pay. He warned his secretary he would have to reach a settlement with the government

or leave the country. In October 1965 he informed the rest of his staff of this. The government was only going to pay for the work already done, which was why it refused to pay for the plywood models to test the mullions that Utzon wanted to source from the Symonds Homebush factory.

On 17 December 1965, Utzon had a meeting with Hughes, Ashworth and Haviland. Utzon had formed the opinion that Haviland was not far from a heart attack, so he kept himself in check. 'If I don't like plywood, I won't have plywood,' the minister repeated. Ralph Symonds' company had gone into receivership in February 1964. While this did not bother Utzon and his colleagues, it did bother the Askin government, which wanted nothing to do with a company that was failing financially.

The following day, Utzon left with his family for a six-week holiday in Hawaii and Japan. This did not win him fans in Australia; many felt he was always heading away on exotic holidays rather than completing the job.

In the new year, at a meeting on 24 February 1966, the ABC dropped a bombshell. Its acoustics engineer, Warwick Mehaffey, announced that the main hall would be unsuitable for concerts by the Sydney Symphony Orchestra, because it did not have enough seats to make this financially viable. There was also inadequate provision for television and recording cables, and the issue of the harbour noise had not yet been solved.

After many politely worded letters between the architect and his minister regarding the bitter stand-off over the £51,000 in outstanding fees and the suspension of progress payments, Utzon decided to speak with Hughes at his Phillip Street office. He would be accompanied by his Australian offsider, Bill Wheatland.

The agenda items were: mock-ups, mullions and money. The disagreement between Utzon and the NSW government was about to finally come to a head.

Chapter twenty-one

High noon at the Chief Secretary's Building

The year 1966 was an eventful one for Australia. It was book-ended by two dramatic events: on 26 January, Australia Day, the country's longest-serving prime minister, Sir Robert Menzies, resigned after eighteen years in the top job. It ended with the December arrival through Sydney Heads of solo around-the-world sailor Francis Chichester. In between those two events, decimal currency was introduced, the miniskirt arrived, war hero Sir Roden Cutler became NSW governor, and a young Prince Charles arrived at Mascot on his way to school at Geelong Grammar's Timbertop.

Nearly a million people lined the Sydney streets to catch a glimpse of Lyndon Baines Johnson, the first US president to visit Australia, on his way to a state reception at the Art Gallery of New South Wales. New prime minister Harold Holt vowed to go 'All the way with LBJ' and his war in Vietnam, but when anti-war protesters jumped in front of the president's motorcade, Premier Askin is said to have told his driver to 'run over the bastards'.

But the showdown that took place in the Chief Secretary's Building on the final day of February 1966 had a more lasting impact on the shape of modern Sydney than any of those events. What exactly happened during the momentous few minutes is uncertain; what is certain, however, is that it had been a long time coming and Hughes most likely had been hoping it would end the way it did.

On 6 February, after Utzon returned from his six-week Christmas holiday, Mogens Prip-Buus wrote in a letter home to his parents: 'the guns are in position, and we are ready for battle'.

But the battle had begun long before the Askin government had come to power. Utzon's relations with the government had begun to sour even when Labor's Norm Ryan was in control. Indeed, most of Utzon's office, and especially Prip-Buus, had been optimistic at first about Askin. In a letter home to Denmark just after the election on 17 May 1965 he wrote: 'The government lost the election, so now we are saddled with a new lot of idiots. I suppose we'll find peace some time, but first the new lot have to have it all explained to them, and then I think they will be better for us than the last crew was. That would be a relief.'

That optimism did not last long. By the next month, June, he wrote: 'The election threw the Labor Government out after it had been rooted there for 24 years, and there are now people in office who seem to have had a little more than 6 years education in elementary school. There is even a slight chance that some of them have heard that over on the other side of the globe there are countries where people have theatres, and something called operas, things that have nothing to do with football.'

Prip-Buus was not impressed with Australia's 'she'll be right' attitude; he felt it was holding the nation back. He was also not impressed with the White Australia Policy. Although it was starting to be dismantled in the 1960s, the old racist attitudes still lingered. In a letter home, he explained how his wife had tried to find an African doll for their daughters, but 'it seems the "White Australia policy" extends even to dolls'.

He called Arup's team 'swindlers' and dismissed Bill Wood, the government architect appointed by the Public Works Ministry to oversee their work, as 'senile'. He claimed Wood had 'only got his job because he rescued the previous minister from criminal proceedings, and who now wants to be able to say that he has produced the Opera House, a desire he shares with Arup's and the contractors, all of whom are scarcely capable of coping with even a small part of this complicated field and in the space of two years have raised the price of the shells from $1.8 to 5.1 million. But propaganda and a shared hatred of the architect can obviously achieve much.'

Prip-Buus had a point. It wasn't just Utzon's team causing the mounting costs. Arup's team and Hornibrook contributed too; but, as the public face of the project, Utzon bore the blame.

A story had been circulating in Sydney that during a dinner party to celebrate the Liberal–Country Party's election win, Hughes' daughter, Sue Burgoyne, made a boast that her father would sack the Danish architect once he took the reins at Public Works. There had been so much scuttlebutt that it was hard to know what was real and what was rumour.

Utzon had discussed how best to respond with his two most trusted employees, Prip-Buus and Wheatland. They had decided an ultimatum was the best way to deal with Hughes. They would also cut off relations with Arup's team, most notably with the site manager, Michael Lewis.

Prips-Buus noted in his diary: 'If it were an ordinary building and an ordinary situation, this wouldn't be of importance, but unfortunately it represents everything I believe in and hope for, and so the paradoxical situation has arisen that in order to carry through something known as humanistic architecture, it is necessary to behave in an inhuman way.' He was echoing a sentiment felt by many in Sydney: this was no ordinary building, and it was an extraordinary situation that led to the stand-off on 28 February 1966.

• • •

Jørn Utzon strode purposefully up the five steps under the sandstone bust of Queen Victoria that formed the portico labelled 'Secretary for Works' at the Phillip Street entrance of the Chief Secretary's Building. It was a vestige of times past designed by colonial architect James Barnet in the Venetian Renaissance style.

Utzon opened the heavy green door and took the lift up to the first floor. He walked down the marble corridor to the minister for Public Works' office, located in the north-west corner. Hughes' office 'was a chamber about 24 square feet with a ceiling 20 feet high, around which ran a cornice finished in gold paint. The elaborate marble fireplace had the date 1876 carved into it. Near it hung an oil painting of Queen Victoria's Diamond Jubilee procession.'

Utzon was prepared for a confrontation. Perhaps he was using his architectural hero, the Swede Gunnar Asplund, as a model. When progress on Asplund's most famous project, Sweden's Woodland Crematorium, was slow and when disagreements arose, he resigned. His Swedish clients eventually reinstated him and eventually Asplund had his way.

'Our ultimatum to the Minister runs out the 1st of March, when we shall give them a fortnight, during which time we prepare our packing,' Prip-Buus wrote in his diary. 'Everyone else believes the Minister will give in and that there is no danger.

Personally, I hardly know what to believe when politics comes into play. The amusing thing is we forced Arup's to withdraw their [adverse report on the plywood mock-ups] to the Minister. A great victory.' The meeting started well enough: Davis Hughes agreed to pay $20,000 per month (Australia converted to decimal currency on 14 February) as an advance on fees. Utzon then asked for payment of £51,626 ($103,252) for the work he had done on the stage machinery that had come from Austria. This fee was described as being for 'stage technique'— work that had largely been done in Denmark in the early 1960s. Hughes promised an answer 'this week'.

Utzon then asked about the plywood mock-ups. Hughes said he could not make a decision without a joint recommendation by the architect and the engineers. He drew attention to Arup's earlier adverse report.

Utzon replied that it had been withdrawn, but Hughes refused both to accept this and to investigate. He couldn't answer the question about the fees for the stage machinery until Friday, 4 March.

According to John Yeomans' book *The Other Taj Mahal*, Utzon said: 'You are always putting me off. I need the money.'

There was silence.

'Very well,' said the architect. 'I go. I resign.'

'You are always threatening to quit,' Hughes replied. 'This is no way to address a minister of the Crown.'

Utzon leapt to his feet in frustration while at the same time trying to contain his anger.

'Well, goodbye, Mr Minister,' said Utzon. 'That's it, I go.' Bill Wheatland now jumped to his feet, even though he didn't quite know how to interpret the scene that was playing out in front of him. Both architects turned and stormed out of the minister's office.

Hughes had forced Utzon into checkmate. It was all over in about fifteen minutes.

• • •

Utzon had contained himself and chosen his words with considerable care, but it was as if he had been ambushed by one of Ove Arup's beloved chess gambits. Arup would have been one of the first people he would have reported this dispute to when they were friends, but now they were foes.

Utzon stormed back down Macquarie Street to his Bennelong Point office. Cutting a familiar figure in the street, he was often approached by the public giving support and telling him how much they loved his white-sailed building. On this day, a car driver pulled over and offered him a lift down the road, but Utzon declined.

He was not unduly downcast: he half expected a phone call from Hughes, telling him to come back and talk things over quietly. Back at his office he wrote five drafts of his letter of withdrawal. Utzon refused to listen to Wheatland's suggestion that he get legal advice. Wheatland advised against sending the missive. The final version was typed up by his personal assistant Elsa Atkin, who delivered it by hand to architect Ron Devine who drove to the minister's office.

The Sydney Opera House Executive Committee's Henry Ingham Ashworth was in an emergency meeting with the minister when the letter arrived at around 3 p.m. It read:

In the meeting between yourself and Mr Wheatland and me today, you stated that you still could not accept my fee claim for £51,000 for stage technique which I have requested from you for the past several months and which is completely justified.

I have been forced to set the 15th February, 1966 as
the final date of the receipt of this payment, and as you
could not, at this date 28th February, 1966 satisfy me on
this, you have forced me to leave the job.

As I explained to you and as you know also from
meetings and discussions there has been no collaboration on the most vital items on the job in the last many
months from your department's side, and this also
forced me to leave the job as I see clearly that you do not
respect me as the architect. I have therefore today given
my staff notice of dismissal. I will notify the consultants
and contractors and I will have cleared the office of my
belongings and you will receive my final account before
14th March 1966.

Jørn Utzon

Importantly he did not write the word 'resign'.

The minister replied immediately:

Dear Mr Utzon,

I have received your letter of resignation which
I deeply regret.

I must point out that in the first place your opening
paragraph mis-states the position with respect to your
request for a payment of 51,000 pounds as fees for
Stage Technique. In our discussions this morning, I twice
informed you that a decision on the question of this
payment would be made this week.

You will also recall that I informed you that I had
approved the regular payment of fees at the rate of
$20,000 per month (note dollars not pounds), as you had
requested, subject to monthly review of progress.

I cannot concede that there has been any lack of
collaboration, indeed it has been my desire to see the
maximum co-operation with you between myself, the
Department and the contractors and consultants on the job,
and I believed that we had achieved this to a large degree at
our monthly meetings with yourself, representatives of the
Opera House Committee and myself.

I have referred your letter to my office to initiate
discussions as to the proper proceeding to follow your action.

Again, I am extremely sorry that this unhappy
position has risen.

Yours faithfully,

Davis Hughes

Hughes then called Premier Askin and told him about the
'letter of resignation'. He also spoke with the director of Public
Works public servant Colin Humphrey, Dundas Corbett Gore
at Hornibrook and Michael Lewis at Arup's. Gore and Lewis
both assured the minister of their support. They would continue
even if Utzon wouldn't.

The news of Utzon's 'resignation' leaked immediately. The
Herald's state political correspondent John O'Hara remembers he
learnt from political sources and not the minister. O'Hara knew
enough to write that night that Utzon had 'resigned verbally in
an angry interview'. His story was the front-page splash the next
day. It made the late-night ABC Radio news bulletin, and by
11.30 p.m. Ron Gilling, the president of the NSW chapter of
the Royal Australian Institute of Architects, was contacted for
comment by the *Telegraph*.

According to Wheatland, Utzon was 'stressed beyond imagination' and wrote 'straight from the heart'. Not a wise thing to
do with a politician like Hughes.

Early the next morning, the press descended on Utzon's Palm Beach home. He snuck out the rear gate through a neighbour's garden and into a waiting car and drove to the Paddington terrace where his oldest children lived.

• • •

Hughes took Utzon's letter to Cabinet, where it was voted unanimously that he should handle the matter as he saw fit. Later that day he rose to his feet in the Legislative Assembly and declared: 'Mr Utzon's resignation was neither sought nor expected by the Government. Let me say quite definitely that this was his own decision that he terminated his contract.' In a spirited defence of his actions, Hughes spoke for a full twenty minutes under the fire of Opposition interjections, assuring the parliament repeatedly that Utzon had resigned of his own free will.

Labor's former minister for Public Works Norm Ryan asked Hughes during Question Time: 'Is it a fact that probably the most important section of the work remaining to be done on the Opera House related to the acoustics of the major and minor halls? Are you aware that your predecessor, in view of the importance of this matter, instructed the architect to have special care in regard to these installations and the architect was directed to employ wood specialist consultants to assist him in the necessary investigations, quality of the project being the main consideration?'

Deputy leader of the Opposition, Pat Hills, asked the minister to inform the house whether Mr Utzon had resigned as a result of actions taken by the minister, and if a clash of personalities had occurred resulting in the architect's resignation. Would this result in an appreciable escalation of the cost of this multi-million-dollar project? Hills also asked for an assurance that the House would have the opportunity of an early debate on the Opera House.

'You're not fair dinkum,' Askin interjected. 'My last wish would be for a full debate on the whole history of the project. One cannot straighten out a big bungle overnight. My colleagues and I have been in office only nine months, and we are doing our best to straighten it out. But, after all, this was a bungle in the planning and the cost structure of the project.'

At Bennelong Point, the Opera House site was swarming with reporters and cameramen looking for Utzon, who by this stage had developed a nine-point plan with Wheatland and Prip-Buus as they walked around Centennial Park. They had decided to try for another meeting with the minister later that day.

At 5 p.m. the following day, Tuesday 1 March, an unsuccessful two-and-a-half-hour meeting took place at the Public Works Department. The deadlock remained.

On that same day, the 4-tonne erection arch on the main sail collapsed for the first and only time during the whole construction period. Breaking away from the main sail, it crashed 30 feet onto the smaller sail below. Six workmen scattered as it fell. Nobody was injured.

• • •

The news of Utzon's resignation ricocheted around the world.

Ove Arup in London tried frantically to get Utzon on the phone without success. But he did speak to the *Herald*'s London correspondent, Evan Williams. 'Mr Utzon has been very inaccessible lately,' Arup said. 'We have found it very hard to get any information from him. We have sent him a cable today at the Opera House site asking him to phone us without delay. Mr Utzon has been far too stubborn and unyielding on his part and the government is insisting on things which makes it difficult.'

The Danish daily, *Berlingske Tidende,* spoke to the grand old man of Danish architecture, Arne Jacobsen, who appealed to Utzon to 'stay in Sydney'. 'It is a very unhappy thing for Utzon and for all architects,' he said. 'An architect cannot withdraw from such a big task without very careful consideration. The remark that the building will be continued in Utzon's spirit is sheer nonsense—it just cannot be done.'

The *Herald*'s Gavin Souter wrote that this was the most disappointing development yet in the daunting history of the building of the Opera House. 'Stage three—literally the heart of the project—would be the responsibility of another.' He predicted that if it fell to the Government Architect to finish the project, there would be no lack of expertise. The NSW Government Architects, then under the leadership of Ted Farmer, had designed the Fisher Library at Sydney University and Goldstein Hall at the University of New South Wales (both of which won the Sir John Sulman Medal for architecture), plus the State Office Block and Mona Vale Hospital. Farmer led a team of enthusiastic young architects, including Peter Hall (the project architect on Goldstein Hall) and Ken Woolley (the project architect on the Fisher Library and the State Office Block).

In a feature for the *Telegraph* on 2 March, a day after the drama in parliament, Martin Long flagged potential acoustic problems in any new design not under Utzon's command. Given his lifelong interest in baroque and Elizabethan music (he had even made his own clavichord, a viola da gamba and several flutes), Long was well qualified to raise questions about the hall's acoustics. 'When the sculpture is finished, will it sing?' he asked. 'That is a question that will not be finally answered before the first performance and—since Opera Houses like other musical instruments must be played in—perhaps not even then.'

On Thursday 3 March, a group of protesters gathered at Bennelong Point. Architect Harry Seidler and the head of the Art Gallery of New South Wales, Hal Missingham, organised a march up Macquarie Street to Parliament House with signs that read 'Bring Utzon Back' and 'Griffin Now Utzon' (referring to the American architect Walter Burley Griffin, who had been removed from his role executing his grand design for Canberra after a dispute with then Prime Minister Billy Hughes). Among the protestors were many architects (and their wives, as the *Telegraph* reported!), university students, notable creative identities such as Patrick White and young artists Martin Sharp and Peter Kingston from *OZ* magazine, as well as the pioneering conservationist Milo Dunphy. A counter-demonstration by the Builders' Labourers' Federation demanded an Australian architect finish the job and that the workers get higher pay.

Police shut the gates to Parliament House. Around thirty parliamentarians and journalists gathered on the balcony to watch the marchers four abreast flanked by dozens of uniformed police. A petition containing 3000 signatures was presented to parliament.

John Weiley filmed the march and enjoyed one special advantage. His father Bill Weiley was the Country Party member for Clarence and was friendly with Hughes, who held the adjoining electorate of New England. Thanks to his father's position and the access this allowed to Parliament House, Weiley was able to film some of the best footage of the protesters as they chanted 'Bring Utzon Back'. Weiley's father was there that day on the balcony, scoffing at the chanting protestors. Like others in the government, he just wanted Utzon to get on a plane and get out of Australia.

Despite an editorial in the *Telegraph* the next day condemning the protest and declaring that the architects 'should not attempt pressure tactics like a group of disgruntled wharfies or bus drivers', Utzon was buoyed by the support he was receiving. From Rome, author Morris West had written to the *Herald* expressing his support for Utzon.

Later that week, on Friday 4 March, Utzon, who had been hiding out since that Monday, arrived in a Porsche for a meeting with Askin at the premier's office in the Treasury Building (now the Intercontinental Hotel) accompanied by Wheatland and Prip-Buus. It went for two hours, until 6.20 p.m.

He emerged from the premier's office through a side exit into a private parking lot. The *Herald*'s Tom McNeil was the first to spot him. Utzon tried to hide behind one of his companions, but within seconds he was surrounded by reporters, cameras and microphones.

Asked how his meeting with the premier had gone, Utzon replied 'We had a good and friendly meeting', while playfully straightening and stroking a reporter's tie. With each question, he appeared to step back until he was 'cornered' against a brick wall. The questions continued.

Utzon: 'We are in the middle of discussions to narrow the gap between us. Today's meeting was a good one, and there will be a final meeting on Monday.'

Reporter: 'Will the architects on your staff go back now?'

Utzon: 'You will get the answer to that on Monday. I am in the middle of a dispute, you must understand that. All of us are trying our best to narrow the gap.'

Reporter: 'Are there any personal differences between you and Mr Hughes?'

Utzon: 'I think this building is completely above personal differences. Everyone involved would say that. It has nothing to do with personal feelings.'

Reporter: 'What do you think of yesterday's demonstration?'

Utzon: 'The demonstration was marvellous for me. I am very glad people seem so enthusiastic for me. Above all, it shows there is a deep feeling in the community for the building.'

Reporter: 'Do you think the building could be finished if you do not go back?'

Utzon: 'I can say what I can do myself, but I can say nothing for anyone else.'

Reporter: 'Where have you been hiding out?'

Utzon: 'I won't tell you because I will still be hiding out. I will tell you on Monday.'

Reporter: 'Was the meeting with the premier helpful?'

Utzon: 'Mr Askin was very helpful. The political football, which it has been, should not exist any more.'

Reporter: 'There has been a lot of public discussion, as well as at a political level, about costs.'

Utzon: 'Yes, I admit that, but this has nothing to do with this situation. I have only one desire. That is to build an Opera House that you will enjoy. I look on the Opera House as a living room, or a lounge room, for you to enjoy.'

• • •

The media pack now staked out the Utzons' Palm Beach home. The family's Citroën station wagon was parked on the lawn. Utzon had long ago swapped his imported Jag for two Citroëns: one a green ID19, and an off-white ID station-car. At one point, Lis Utzon, sitting by the pool of her home dressed in a black and white–check swimming costume and deeply tanned, yelled to reporters across her back fence that 'the final decision will be made after the meeting on Monday. Until then my husband has gone away [probably on a sightseeing trip to the Blue Mountains with fellow Dane, Peer Abben] and he will make no comment.'

'Do you like Australia, Mrs Utzon? Do you want to stay?' one reporter asked.

'Of course, we all enjoyed it here, and we want to stay if we can. But we will not try to influence my husband's decision. That is his own responsibility, and we will not interfere.'

The week following the resignation, newspapers were over-whelmed by letters. 'The many letters we have received about Mr Utzon's resignation as architect of the Sydney Opera House reflect a fervent, even passionate, public reaction,' commented the *Herald* on its Letters page on Friday 4 March.

'Blame the judges (our Australian architects are just as good as anywhere in the world),' screamed one letter writer in the *Herald*.

David Moore, the photographer who was painstakingly documenting progress at the site, wrote: 'This resignation must surely rank as one of the greatest setbacks to the arts Australia has known. If [Utzon] does not return it may well be 50 years for such a high point in world standards of design.'

Another correspondent wrote, 'We are about to suffer the same fate as Barry's London Houses of Parliament, Le Corbusier's League of Nations building, Walter Burley Griffin's Canberra frustration. The politicians have inherited a hot potato and either way they stand to lose.'

'The plans for the Taj Mahal were prepared by a council of architects from India, Persia, Central Asia and beyond, and many of those were dead before the structure was completed,' commented AS Carter of Earlwood.

'Thirty years ago, it was Griffin and now it is Utzon. But no doubt in 20 years, when a lot of water will have washed past the Opera House and today's politicians will have been forgotten, we will make amends, and, as with Griffin, honour Utzon on one of our postage stamps. For such is the size of our visions,' wrote architectural writer Eva Buhrich of Castlecrag. She followed this up with another letter. 'Once again politi-cal power juggling, professional jealousy and narrow-minded bureaucracy are driving a man of genius from our midst.'

'Let's take a sane view of the Opera House imbroglio and the hysterical correspondence it has brought from certain quarters. If these pro-Utzon writers had their way they would not be content with anything less than the abdication of the State Government and the ceremonial handing over of the keys of the Treasury to Mr Utzon,' wrote R O'Neill of Lane Cove. 'From the turning of the first sod of soil . . . the whole scheme has been a colossal and disgraceful waste of public money . . . Surely now is the time to stop work on this monument to irresponsible Government spending and channel the money into essential public services,' suggested WW Warden from Boorowa. 'It is obvious by now that to start this Bennelong Point project was a mistake.'

'The Opera House has already cost millions—painlessly extracted from a willing public. Let it cost a bit more and be finished in the same inspired manner of high perfection in which it was conceived and begun,' said Mrs JS Horn of Bellevue Hill.

Andrew Young, on behalf of sixteen other architects, threw down the gauntlet: 'No worthwhile architect would be so devoid of professional integrity as to accept Utzon's vacated post.'

At the suggestion of the premier, Hughes had agreed to meet Utzon again on Monday 7 March. At the Bennelong Point office, a prankster—perhaps from Arup's team or one of the other onsite contractors—put a sign up on the door that suggested the Government Architect's team was about to move in. It simply read: 'E H Farmer & friends—coming soon.'

• • •

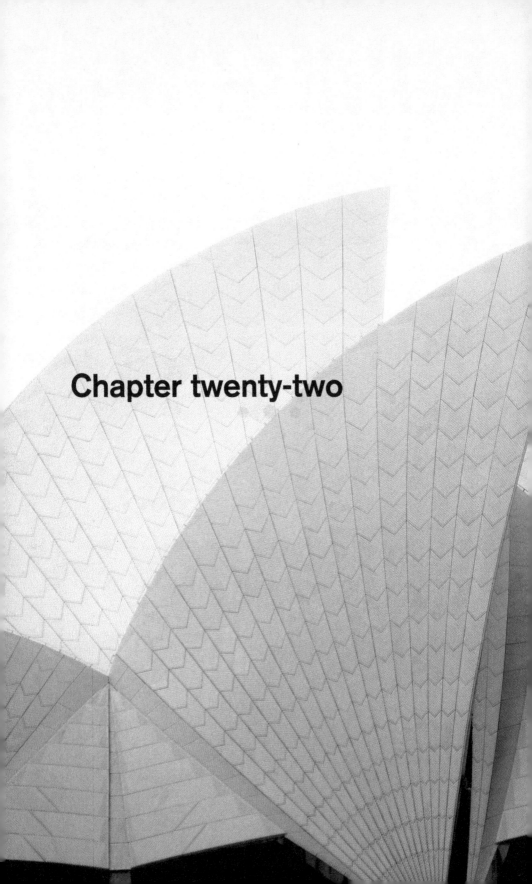

Chapter twenty-two

I am still available

Ted Farmer was the sixteenth Government Architect of NSW, a role that had existed since 1816 when convict Francis Greenway—the first Government Architect—started to design his distinctive early colonial buildings for Governor Macquarie. Through the office's ranks have passed the best and brightest in Sydney's architectural world, but it was usually only the most conservative who made a whole career here. At this time of high drama, seventy-five out of its eighty-five architects signed a petition to retain Utzon on the Opera House project.

Ted Farmer had always thought the problem with the Sydney Opera House competition was that there was no properly defined 'client'. Design by committee just didn't work. And that had been the problem with the unwieldy Sydney Opera House Executive Committee—too many voices. The problem wasn't being solved by having a government minister in charge, however. It may have been a different matter if the Government

Architect had been appointed as client from the start. But it was too late now for that—the Government Architect's Office was being called in to fix the whole sorry mess.

The wider architectural profession was split on the Utzon affair and the Askin government's dealings with the architect. It seemed like every Australian had an opinion as well. Walter Bunning used his platform as architecture critic in the *Herald* to call for a royal commission into the 'Opera House bungle'. 'A smoke screen has been thrown around the whole project for nine years,' he wrote. 'We need an inquiry into this appalling waste.'

Harry Seidler shot back that Bunning's rant was unfactual mudslinging and thoroughly unwarranted. 'Everyone seems to think Jørn has become a millionaire out of the Opera House job. That is ludicrous in face of the facts, which are that he is $80,000 in debt and hasn't been able to pay his staff in some weeks,' Seilder wrote. 'Utzon is broke.'

Utzon and Seidler had become firm friends, their two families spending a lot of time together. They bonded over design, but especially over their shared passion for Citroën cars. By 1961, Seidler had swapped his sensible Holden for a classier Citroën.

• • •

Monday 7 March—week two of the dispute—and the drama dragged on with another long meeting. It began at 3 p.m., and by 3.30 p.m. more than fifty mumbling and grumbling pressmen were waiting outside the minister's office with one elderly woman, who described herself as 'an Utzon fancier'. Cameramen outside the building passed word that they had seen Utzon and his team pacing up and down on the verandah.

At 6.30 p.m. the door opened and Utzon emerged, face flushed. He stormed past the waiting press, leaving via the

Bridge Street side door. Previously unpublished correspondence reveals it was at this meeting that Hughes invited Utzon to return to the Opera House, not as sole architect in charge but as the design member of an architectural team. Control was being taken away from him.

Utzon was furious. He raced across the road to the premier's office in the Treasury Building to ask Askin to intervene. He didn't wait for the ancient elevator but ran up the spiral marble staircase to Askin's second-floor office. He rang the doorbell and was ushered in only to emerge soon after. He had missed Askin by ten minutes.

The next day, Tuesday 8 March, Utzon told the *Herald*'s John O'Hara that his only hope of reinstatement lay with the opposition Labor Party and the people of Sydney. 'To kill the Opera House might take a long time, but it is dying and sick, on the bed now,' he said.

A few days later, on Thursday 10 March, Ron Gilling, the president of the NSW Chapter of the Royal Australian Institute of Architects, arranged a secret meeting between Utzon and Hughes at Lane Cove's Shore Motor Lodge in a desperate bid to patch up their differences.

Utzon left Bennelong Point with Bill Wheatland. Travelling in Wheatland's car, they tailed Gilling through the streets of North Sydney (comically, Gilling waved his hand out of the car window to get to the 'secret location' to ward off the press). Present at the meeting were Utzon, Hughes, the head of the Department of Public Works Colin Humphrey, the Government Architect Ted Farmer, Bill Wood from the Government Architect's Office, Ron Gilling, and Mogens Prip-Buus and Bill Wheatland. Too many cooks.

Hughes presented Utzon with an organisational flow chart that indicated where he stood in Hughes' management scheme.

This diagram was later to be lampooned in a cartoon as a noose around the Dane's neck.

'The main thing is the building,' Utzon said, exhausted and exasperated as the meeting wore on. 'You must have confidence, and only by having confidence can you help the architect, and that is what I ask for, confidence.'

The meeting continued into the night without resolution. The next day, 11 March, Peter Hall left his job after thirteen years in the Government Architect's Office. He wanted to go into private practice and test his professional capabilities. He'd given notice the previous month, but the claim was later made, led by the *Sun-Herald*'s Bob Johnson, that the timing of Hall's resignation was in order to make him available to take on Utzon's role.

• • •

On 14 March, on a day too hot for autumn, one thousand Sydneysiders gathered at the Town Hall for a protest meeting to keep 'Utzon in charge'. Harry Seidler had been a driving force behind the meeting. The letters pages that day continued to reflect the community tension about the treatment being dished out to the designer of their beloved Opera House.

Most architects were furious at Walter Bunning's crass comments and his call for a royal commission. From his Darling Point apartment, architect George Molnar wrote a condemnation of Bunning.

A *Mirror* vox pop revealed overwhelming support for Jørn Utzon. Reverend Ted Noffs, the Methodist minister who'd recently started the Wayside Chapel in Sydney's red-light district of Kings Cross, said: 'It is tragic that Mr Jørn Utzon should be made a scapegoat for the mounting expenditure when the government should have kept a watch on finances all along.'

Betty Archdale, the legendary headmistress of Abbotsleigh Private Girls School and former captain of the English women's cricket team, told the tabloid: 'We are making ourselves the laughing stock of the world and I don't like it.'

Archdale was asked to speak at the Town Hall meeting. And just as they had for the 'Bring Utzon Back' protest, the organising committee produced booklets, stickers and placards, presaging the anti-Vietnam War protests that would begin to rock the city later that year.

Standing on stage at the Town Hall, Seidler declared, 'Putting Jørn Utzon's Opera House sketches into the hands of a government committee is like putting dynamite into the hands of children.' Author Patrick White warned that 'the apostles of mediocrity are about to take over'. The president of the Society of Sculptors, Michael Nicholson, pledged to go on a hunger strike and wrote a 160-line poem in praise of Utzon.

> I therefor vow
> Before you all,
> To take no food for three days from now
> I am a fool who sees
> That those who can act should act
> And those who cannot might fast.

He was applauded enthusiastically.

On 16 March, the *Herald* was so inundated with letters that it could only publish extracts. Sixty-seven of the eighty-two members of the Sydney Symphony Orchestra also signed a petition pledging their support. But considerable interest was focused on a letter Utzon had written to Hughes. 'I am still available,' he wrote. 'It is not I but the Sydney Opera House that creates all the enormous difficulties.'

Chapter twenty-three

This chapter is over

And where was Premier Askin throughout all this drama? In parliament? At the Town Hall meeting? At Bennelong Point talking to Utzon? No. On 16 March 1966 he was at a toy trade fair, where he made a gnomic comment to the press on his dealings with Utzon: 'No matter how expensive toys become, they could not approach the expense of that toy of ours at Bennelong Point.' All guns were blazing now in the battle for Bennelong Point. And it was clear that the premier had withdrawn his support for the Danish architect.

The next day, 17 March, the legal fight began. Utzon sought an injunction to stop the state government from proceeding on the Opera House without him, and Harry Seidler retained his father-in-law Clive Evatt as senior counsel for the Dane. His legal team of JW (Jack) Smyth and Neville Wran, a barrister who would later become premier of NSW, advised him generally on his rights.

When it was reported that Utzon had sent in a bill to the government for unpaid fees of $1.2 million, a senior cabinet minister said: 'When I heard the amount, I reached for the port bottle.'

On 18 March, Utzon handed over his plans, drawings, documents, models and materials to the Government Architect Ted Farmer on the Opera House site. This formality took about 35 minutes. Utzon refused to be photographed or interviewed.

Stan Haviland was present but maintained his silence; no one knew whether he was supporting Utzon or not. All he said was: 'no comment'. John O'Hara, the *Herald*'s state rounds-man, revealed decades later that 'Silent Stan' was the man who 'dug the spadework for Utzon's grave'. And where was the rest of the once-supportive Opera House Executive Committee— now rebadged as the Opera House Trust—throughout all this? That was a good question. 'Where have all the trustees gone?' asked the city's newspapers.

On 19 March, Peter Hall wrote to Utzon from his North Sydney home: 'I have been asked by the Minister for Public Works to work with two other firms of architects at the Opera House. The Minister has assured me that your services on the project have been properly terminated.' Hall signed his name in orange pen. The letter was marked received at 9.50 a.m. on 20 April. A copy was sent to Utzon's legal team and filed away in his personal correspondence until his death.

On 21 March, fourteen senior architects at the Government Architect's Office who had signed the petition in support of Utzon were called in to see the director of the Public Works Department, Colin Humphrey. He waved the *Public Servant Act* under their noses and reminded them of their role as public servants. They refused to sign a counter-document or allow themselves to be intimidated.

But on 28 March—a month after his dispute with Hughes had reached its crescendo—Jørn Utzon finally declared he was officially done. The sense of loss and disappointment had set in when the government declared its negotiations were over. Utzon had been brought undone by his pursuit of perfection, his insistence on only the very best for this project, his unwillingness to compromise, and the greatness he aspired to for himself and the building.

Despite Arups declining all opportunities to speak with the press in Sydney, Utzon still felt betrayed, especially by Michael Lewis and his friend Ove Arup, who had presented themselves to the government as being in charge of the project, not him. Utzon was devastated that Arup had not resigned with him as a show of support, although he'd not asked him to do so. He refused to return Arup's phone calls and cables.

On 20 April, Arup penned a handwritten eight-page letter from the heart to Utzon in a last-ditch effort to keep him on the project. Although Danish was the first language for both of them, they always corresponded in English, which Arup did in this letter, but for the first word. The letter remained in Utzon's correspondence file until his death and only went into the Utzon archive in January 2018. Arup wrote:

Kaere Jørn,
I don't know whether this will reach you, or whether you will read it if it does. But I should like you to consider what I say in the following.
I realise that nothing I can say will alter your distrust of me or my motives. Lis's letter shattered me and showed me how completely you have misunderstood me. But forget about me.

It must be frightful for you to give up the job for which you have worked 10 years, and which has made you famous all over the world. You can of course easily get other work, and you are still young enough to create a body of work which will consolidate and extend your position as one of the world's leading architects. But how can you leave this child of yours to be messed up by other people? Can't you see this will hurt you immensely? It is a disservice to architecture and it will always be held against you. You will be known as the architect who didn't finish the Opera House. You will say that you were forced into this situation. I will not dispute this, but this is not the point. The question is whether something can not still be done to save the situation, or at least to make it better.

I feel that I am the man who is in the best position to bring about a compromise solution which will at least prevent, that the Opera House is spoilt by others, even if it does not satisfy you entirely. The chances of doing anything are perhaps small, but they depend very largely on your attitude.

It would of course be easier if you trusted me, but I am content to be judged by my actions. Distrust me if you must but consider my arguments.

Is it not the most important thing, that the Opera House is saved? Is it not more important than what happens to you and me? You used to say at the beginning of our collaboration, that architects should be anonymous, that it did not matter who did it, as long as it was done rightly. I realise, that you have moved a long way from this attitude—but there was something very fine in it. It is not given many to reach such as a state of humility. But a little humility is no barrier to the production of great art.

And I am afraid a little humility is needed on your part
in this case if there shall be any hope of moving the
government from their position.

I can almost feel your distrust of me rising in you, as
you read this. But what can I do? I am only stating a fact.
I do not want to humiliate you, but humility coming from
within, from respect for architecture, for your mission,
and from gratefulness for the divine spark in you—such
humility will do no harm.

I am of course not suggesting that you should
compromise on design or architectural matters—that
should not be necessary if you have good structural and
other advisors. I am coming to Sydney on the 27th of
April. Could you not see me then? I am staying at the
Belvedere. Even if you don't trust me—it couldn't do any
harm could it? The situation can't get any worse so why
not try?

Yours Ove

Utzon replied to Arup immediately that day, in a letter that
was not made public until 2018.

Dear Ove

You say in your letters several times, that the Opera
house will be destroyed without me.

Act accordingly:

Tell the Minister for Public Works that Utzon must
be in charge . . . I want you to sincerely understand that
I do not dare to take the enormous responsibilities of
being attached to the scheme without being in charge
as the sole architect. As little as you—as structural
engineer—would ever dare to take on the responsibility

for the structure of a bridge without being fully in charge
of all the phases of its construction.

The letter was typed with a handwritten signature. Reading
between the lines, Utzon considered Arup continuing to work
with the NSW government without him an act of betrayal. Even
his fellow Dane, he felt, was turning against him. Utzon longed,
no doubt, more than ever for Joe Cahill's steadfast support and
vision.

• • •

In the tightly knit community of Palm Beach, they were called
'the Lonesome Utzons'. As the battle between the state government and the architect intensified, Lis and Jørn started declining
social invitations, but they had begun a Saturday morning family
ritual: a swim at the pool at the south end of Palm Beach. There
they met *Woman's Day* cookery editor Margaret Fulton, her
husband and their children. The families became friends.

It was during this difficult time that Fulton made a heartfelt plea for people to respect the Utzons' privacy. Published in
Woman's Day on 21 March 1966, at the height of the drama,
she wrote: 'The Opera House, dream of his professional life,
has become the nightmare of his social life . . . a couple who
have almost been sacrificed in the cause of a great architectural achievement.' When a cab driver launched into a tirade
against them, 'They, being quiet and courteous people, said
little in reply . . . But the hurt was there. And it makes my
blood boil to think of such ignorant and malicious attacks
going unanswered.'

'We just sort of closed the doors and tried to be as support-
ive of him as possible,' Utzon's daughter Lin now recalls of those
dreadful days. During this period, a journalist asked Lin how

she felt about going back to Denmark. 'I suppose I have mixed feelings,' she replied. 'It will be good to see Copenhagen again, but there will be many things I miss about Australia. And, of course, I would have liked to see my father complete his work on the Opera House.'

'Maybe there's still a possibility?' the reporter suggested.

'I don't think so—I think it is all over,' she said sadly. The family had made many friends since they first arrived in Australia.

In order to pay his employees and his taxes, Utzon needed to sell all the family's assets: the land at Bayview, the house in Windsor Street, Paddington he was renovating for his children, the two Citroëns and the plywood yacht.

On 27 April, the same day Arup boarded the plane to Sydney to make the long trip from London, competition judge and decade-long friend Professor Harry Ingham Ashworth wrote a letter to Utzon addressed to his Palm Beach home. As with Arup, Utzon had not replied to any of Ingham Ashworth's phone calls. 'In my book, friends of ten years' standing should not be treated in this way without any explanation,' the architecture professor wrote. He continued:

> After all these years of working together and the
> continued support I have given the project, I find it
> difficult indeed to accept that you should in any way think
> that I have been remiss in supporting you recently—I have
> in fact, done everything possible to try and persuade the
> Government not to let you go in this way.
>
> Both Ella [Ingham Ashworth's wife] and I would
> be very sorry and disappointed if you have been
> contemplating leaving the country without meeting us
> for a drink or possibly joining us for dinner.

The letter also referred to the fact that Utzon had expressed a desire to meet with the Opera House Executive Committee and the Technical Advisory Panel before he left. Ingham Ashworth convened a special meeting, hurriedly calling members to invite them to drinks on the site, but Utzon did not show up. This letter from his former friend remained in Utzon's confidential files until a decade after his death.

On arriving in Sydney, Arup told the *Bulletin* the situation was a personal disaster. Echoing his handwritten letter to Utzon, he said, 'It is folly to expect that all that has to happen is for Utzon to come back in charge and everything will be all right . . . Why should I resign to force Utzon's return on his terms, if I think that would be wrong? It is the Opera House that is important, not people.'

• • •

As the sun rose on 28 April 1966 to a sparkling Sydney day, a deep melancholia descended on the Utzon's Palm Beach house. No one was in a good mood, least of all Lin. This was the day the family was due to leave Australia. Through her connections with Qantas, Martin Sharp's mother Jo had not only booked five tickets under a false name but had done so on the day of their departure so the press would not know the family was leaving. A few days before, Utzon had hosted a picnic at Palm Beach for his staff—Mogens Prip-Buus, Bill Wheatland, Richard Leplastrier and the other architects. He had kept the mood light and jovial, but they all knew it was a farewell party.

Utzon could see how distressed his daughter was at leaving. Lin had acquired not just a love of Australia and a circle of artistic friends, but also a boyfriend, Alex Popov. He was studying arts at university but wanted to be an architect. A keen surfer, Popov shared a house with fellow university student

Paul Witzig and his brother John at nearby Whale Beach. The three of them would ride their skateboards to the Utzons' place, where they would play surfing movies on a rickety old projector in the garage before having dinner with the family. They were often called upon to assist Utzon with English as he continued his communication with the state government. It had been a lovely life on Pittwater for them all.

On this glorious April day, father and daughter went to the beach and walked to the southern end for a last glimpse of the Barrenjoey Headland and its lighthouse. They sat on the beach and watched in silence as the tide rolled in. The waves were as clear as glass, the water looked divine.

'Well, you know,' Utzon said softly to his daughter. 'This chapter is finished.'

She looked him in the eyes but there were no tears. She knew, though, simply from the tone of his voice that he was aching inside.

They returned home, and the family then departed in their Citroëns for the airport. Lin was not to tell anyone she was leaving. Alex Popov knew, however, and waited with Paul Witzig to wave goodbye. They were in a milk bar in Avalon that served battered savs and milkshakes, the closest thing to a café in Avalon at the time.

As the family drove closer to the city the weather changed, and clouds started to roll in low. They crossed the Harbour Bridge, and Lin caught her father glimpsing left for one last look at Bennelong Point. And then the harbour fogged over, and the view to the Opera House was blocked by a cloud.

'There we were thinking we'd see the Opera House for one last time and there was a cloud sitting on it. Absolutely on it. It was amazing. I remember that so vividly. It was very strange,' Lin recalls.

Jo Sharp had not only arranged for the family's tickets to be issued to them on the day of their departure, but she had arranged permission for the Utzons to drive their Citroëns straight onto the tarmac. With only minutes to spare, they were then ushered out of their vehicles and hurried through customs and immigration onto the tarmac. 'Only prime ministers and dangerous prisoners usually get this VIP treatment,' one airline official joked. Utzon would often lament later that he left clandestinely, like a criminal.

Rushed up the stairs a few minutes before 5 p.m., they were the last passengers to board the Qantas QF 588 bound for San Francisco via Honolulu.

Exactly two months to the day after his contretemps with Hughes, Utzon left the country. The hasty departure took many by surprise.

'I had no knowledge of his going until after he had gone,' Hughes said in Sydney the next day. Later, he would say of Utzon: 'It was a great day when Utzon's design for the Opera House roof was accepted. Sadly, it was an even greater day when he resigned. He was out of his depth and could never have finished the job.'

Utzon refused to speak to the waiting reporters when the family arrived in Honolulu. They took refuge with their Danish friend, Peer Abben.

The family travelled on to Mexico. Utzon wanted to show his children Chichen Itza, the magnificent Mayan temples that had inspired him to build the podium as a base for the Opera House. He penned a postcard to his former assistant, Bill Wheatland, back in Sydney. 'Went to Yucatan,' he wrote. 'The ruins are wonderful. So why worry? Sydney Opera House becomes a ruin one day.'

Chapter twenty-four

• • •

Chapter twenty-four

The divine spark departs

John Weiley left Australia for the United Kingdom and a job with Granada Television on the same day as the Utzons: 28 April 1966. The two things he regretted leaving behind were his girlfriend Patricia Ludford and his filming of the Opera House. So, he handed the Opera House project to Ludford, who was one of the first female film directors at the ABC and like Weiley looked set to be on a trajectory for a promising career in film. In Europe, Weiley stayed in touch with the Utzons, sensing that their paths would cross again.

On the day he left Australia, Utzon wrote a letter to Labor's Norm Ryan, who had been entrusted by Joe Cahill to 'look after his baby'. This previously unpublished note was sent to Ryan's Marrickville home:

> I hope sincerely that it will be possible for you to get me back on the job. I see absolutely no possibility to deviate

from my position . . . Unfortunately I cannot stay here
longer and have to go quickly to Europe but it does not
matter really because you know the position and Mr
Wheatland represents me fully here, and I do not think
anything will happen in the near future anyhow.

I am looking forward very much to meeting you again
when I come back because I feel absolutely sure that I will
come back and I want to express my gratefulness for the
very stimulating years your job has given me and for
the very stimulating collaboration I have had with you.

It appears from his personal correspondence that Utzon
was convinced he could come back if there was a change of
government at the next state election.

He also wrote to the general manager of Ralph Symonds
saying he 'deeply regretted' the work they commenced together
several years ago was not allowed to come to fruition, and that
he valued their 'splendid co-operation'. 'What could have been
a remarkable project will never be realised. I would also like you
to know that the Minister for Public Works has never understood my position as architect for this project and has sought
my removal as architect in charge to an unimportant position
which would have made me responsible for sketch design
work only.'

Utzon did not want to be confined to the role of 'sketch
maker in the corner', as he put it so poignantly in a previously
unpublished letter to Sigfried Giedion in Switzerland. 'The new
minister for Public Works was the main enemy for the scheme
and he is a Country Party man and the Country Party is not
interested in the Sydney Opera House.'

'I write to you,' Utzon continued, 'because you have
dared again to support ideas in being and a building which is

unfinished, and I am deeply sorry if I have let you down by not being capable of mastering the situation and being able to remove enemies. I have done everything possible; I have explained and my supporters have done everything possible but we believe we are really victims of a political situation.'

'So dear Giedion,' he signed off, 'these are sad times.'

• • •

When Utzon departed, he had warned Hughes that anyone taking over from him would be starting from scratch and coming right back to him to ask for advice. Although he had left his plans with Government Architect Ted Farmer, Utzon had warned Hughes for over nine months that he would not have very advanced drawings and plans until he had tested the mock-ups at Symonds' factory.

In time, the messy months prior to and after Utzon's departure were dubbed 'Malice in Blunderland' by the local and foreign press, because so much was being mishandled.

The international architecture world wanted the Royal Australian Institute of Architects (RAIA) to recommend that its members boycott the project. But Ron Gilling, the conservative president of the NSW Chapter of the RAIA, refused to do this and thus angered the likes of Harry Seidler, who would later claim that Gilling had backstabbed Utzon and lied about it in the institute's public statement.

On 2 March 1966, just days after the initial dispute between Hughes and Utzon flared up, Seidler attended a select committee meeting of the RAIA at Miller Street, North Sydney, according to an affidavit he signed later that month provided by his daughter, Polly Seidler. According to the affidavit, at this meeting Gilling said: 'The Minister of Public Works wants our help to suggest a panel of architects to complete the Opera House. We must give him this. What I envisage is a man with Utzon's spirit of design—Mr B. Mortlock, someone to do the working drawings—Mr O. Jarvis, because he had worked on the Opera House plans in Denmark, some years ago, and a firm to do the general administration—Edwards, Madigan and Torzillo, because they get along well with the Government Architects.' At this time, Utzon was still the architect of the Opera House, which is why Seidler regarded the discussions between Minister Hughes and the RAIA as such an act of treachery. From Los Angeles, on 4 April 1966 Richard Neutra wrote to Utzon: 'I have been appalled to hear that you have been having difficulties in matters of the Sydney Opera House. When I heard about it, I immediately sent a wire to Sydney and especially appealed to Harry Seidler who you know is trying to support your case as best he can.'

Not everyone had been unhappy to see Utzon leave Australia. Chief among them was his wife, Lis, who's said to have told Gilling: 'Please do not try to keep Jørn here, he is not a well man.' She saw he was emotionally spent and, as she'd feared in her letter to her husband on his first visit to Australia in 1957, she felt the building had almost broken his heart. Not to mention his spirit.

Hughes left it to Farmer to appoint the new architect when Utzon withdrew. Farmer is supposed to have asked two others from the Government Architect's design room to take over from Utzon: Col Madigan (later renowned for his design of Canberra's National Gallery) and Ken Woolley (a leading proponent of the style of architecture known as the 'Sydney School' or 'nuts and berries'). They both turned down the offer. Hoping for a third-time lucky, he picked up the phone and spoke to Peter Hall. According to the account in Anne Watson's book, *The Poisoned Chalice: Peter Hall and the Sydney Opera House*, the following conversation ensued:

'You wouldn't like to withdraw your resignation, would you?' Farmer asked.

'What for?' Hall replied.

'Utzon is resigning from the Opera House and I'd like you to do the design work on it.'

'Nothing doing, that's Utzon's job,' was Hall's reply.

When the Director of Public Works, Colin Humphrey, asked Hall the same question a few weeks later, he got the same answer. 'Look, it's Utzon's job, in fact, I've signed the petition of architects and interested people seeking to influence the government to keep Utzon on the job,' he told Humphrey.

Hall was no doubt flattered by the request. His contemporaries, Peter Webber and Ken Woolley, who both later wrote biographies of Hall, considered him one of the best architects of his generation. He subsequently did some initial scouting around to find out what stage Utzon's drawings were at and the general lie of the land.

Hall then decided to simply phone Utzon, given that they had been acquaintances ever since he first visited Utzon in Denmark. They had a long conversation, part of which according to journalist John Yeomans went like this:

> Hall: Mr Utzon, my name is Peter Hall . . . I've been asked to take on the design part of the Opera House project.
> Utzon: You're a brave man but I don't think you can do it.
> Hall: I cannot do it as well as you. I would prefer you to do it.
> Utzon: No, it is best that I go away now. But I will always be ready to come back anytime the Government is willing to allow me sole charge.

Hall—an ambitious and talented yet loyal man—was faced with a dilemma. 'Taking on the design of something that was so individual was really a very worrying decision to have to make,' he later said. 'Without any false humility, I thought of myself as better than quite a lot of my co-practitioners in the city. I also realised the job would have to go on.'

He sought the advice of other colleagues, all of whom warned him of the dangers of taking on a project that was not his own work. He also sought the advice of his father-in-law Bowen Bryant, a successful civil engineer whom Hall respected enormously. Bryant was in favour of an Australian completing the project and encouraged his son-in-law to have a go, to have the courage to do what no one else would.

Hall's wife Libby never wanted her husband to take on the Opera House project but, after much soul-searching, the architect decided the show called the Sydney Opera House must go on. He signed on the dotted line.

• • •

On 19 April 1966, Ted Farmer announced the appointment of the consortium of Hall, Todd and Littlemore to take over from Jørn Utzon as architects on the project. David Littlemore was to manage construction; Lionel Todd was to oversee contracts; and Peter Hall would be the design architect.

Documentation architect Lionel Todd was said to be more at home in a hard hat than behind a desk, and preferred to sit back and let others do the talking. Like his two partners, he was said to be dumbfounded when he first discovered the enormity of the task before him. 'I believe Utzon constructed something rather like a conductor conducts an orchestra—on impulse and feeling,' he told The Australian.

David Littlemore, described by the same newspaper as a 'short moustachioed man', was called to the State Office Block in March 1966, a few days after Utzon's meeting with

Hughes had ended so badly. He was asked if he wanted to join the Opera House team. 'I knew nothing about it at the time . . . I passed it every day and thought it was a magnificent sculptural shape . . . But the offer to help finish it came like a bolt from the blue . . . I finally asked for 48 hours to think it over,' he said.

He did not need the 48 hours the newspaper reported. He had decided to accept the challenge by the time the lift reached the ground floor.

A few weeks after their appointment, the new team sat down to go through the working drawings for the interiors. They were shocked by what they found, or rather didn't find. There were no appropriate working drawings nor was there documentation that would allow them to immediately go forward with the project.

Hughes hadn't given Utzon the money to test the plywood mock-ups for the interiors, which had been one of the main issues in the dispute that ultimately led to the Dane's departure. Hughes had wanted Utzon to put the plywood job out to tender and to use a cheaper plywood provider than Symonds' factory and especially one that was not in receivership. A Danish industrialist had even offered to provide the plywood for free, when he heard one of the points of conflict between Utzon and the NSW government was the cost. The offer came too late—and with little understanding of the architect's loyalty to his supplier, Ralph Symonds' company.

For Utzon it was all about the relationship with the craftsmen he already had at the Symonds' factory, where the mock-ups had now been made up to full scale. He knew the precision of their work and he trusted them. He also knew that this was a world-class plant, manufacturing some of the longest strips of plywood in the world.

The local plywood industry was up in arms that there had not been a tender. In a letter in the *Financial Review* on 8 March 1966 WCL Badge, the manager of Hancock Bros., based at Mortlake—now Breakfast Point, in Sydney's inner west—claimed Ralph Symonds Ltd had not formally applied for membership of the Australian Plywood Board in recent years. 'Tenders have not yet been called and price comparisons therefore cannot be made,' he wrote. 'I am sure the plywood industry awaits with interest, but without anxiety, the matter of who secures the Opera House plywood contracts, but at this stage places some importance in the manner they are offered or taken up.'

Whatever the state of the plywood mock-ups and mullions, Hall had taken on the job in the belief that he would be simply following Utzon's plans. The trouble was that, if such plans existed, Hall didn't have them.

What did exist, however, were four Finecraft Scale Models of Utzon's interiors. Two 1:96 models had been commissioned by the state government for public display at the viewing pavilion atop the 53 steps of the Tarpeian Way. One was on display and the other was a back-up. But, after the Utzons left Australia, these two models were removed from the pavilion and stored in the basement of Alex Popov's parents' house in Castlecrag.

The other two were 1:128 scale models that showed the main hall in opera mode, as Utzon had intended. These had been commissioned by the federal government and completed in March 1966, with the intention that the Department of Trade take them overseas to promote both the Opera House and Australia. In April 1966 these models were taken to Tokyo for an 'Australia on Parade' promotion that was attended by tennis great Frank Sedgman, Dawn Fraser (fresh from her success at the 1964 Tokyo Olympics) and Miss Australia 1966,

Sue Gallie. The models were sent to New York with representatives from the Elizabethan Theatre Trust and then on to San
Francisco, where they were displayed at the San Francisco War
Memorial Opera House and Joan Sutherland was photographed
with them. They then travelled to London and Germany, before
returning to Sydney in 1967.

While the models did a world of good in promoting the
building abroad, they were not much use as guidance for Peter
Hall. He was left with a completely blank canvas.

Chapter twenty-five

SOS to London

Four days after his thirty-fifth birthday, Peter Hall sat down at his old portable typewriter in his North Sydney home, in a quiet cul-de-sac surrounded by tall gum trees, to pour his heart out on the page. It was 20 May 1966, three weeks after Utzon's departure, and already Hall was feeling overwhelmed by the task before him.

He took out some airmail paper to write an SOS to Jim Anderson, his old university friend in London. He felt isolated and intimidated and needed to open up to someone he could trust. He asked Anderson to return home to help him out on the biggest architectural commission of his life.

As students, they would get together on occasional Thursday nights with architect Stan Smith and fellow architect-in-training Tom Heath to practise drawing. Heath had gone to Cranbrook with Hall and was the dux of their year. Anderson went to nearby Scots College. At Sydney University, their cohort included George Molnar and Arthur Baldwinson as

lecturers, artist Lloyd Rees as a drawing teacher, and Ingham
Ashworth as the dean of their school.

Hall and Anderson hadn't seen each other for six years, but
Hall trusted his old uni pal. He wrote:

> You probably know of the recent happenings in Australia
> about the Opera House and these I am afraid are going
> to stop me writing you a decent letter for the time being.
> I don't know what sort of stories are filtering through to
> Europe, but I'm pretty sure they couldn't give any idea
> of how complicated and extraordinary the situation has
> become and still is. Utzon in fact resigned over a matter
> that certainly was not worthy of resignation and the
> Government showed itself not prepared to have him back
> without some control of cost, time and documentation.
>
> All sorts of rumours are circulating as to whether
> in fact he wanted to go on with the work or not. My
> investigations make me think just about anything is
> possible. Certainly he has not been able to work with his
> consultants, builder or client for some time, and there are
> a lot of things he didn't even tell his own staff.
>
> Something that may be regarded as typical of the job
> I experienced only yesterday when I went out to Moniers
> to look at sample panels of paving and cladding that
> they had erected. These are superb; but a count of major
> hall seats made on the same day shows numbers can be
> accommodated far below what the client has said are
> the minimum acceptable. This aspect seems not to have
> been important to Utzon, and is without doubt one of the
> reasons for the Government's desire to establish controls.
> The really remarkable thing about the seating is that
> nobody has known after all these years what the numbers

planned have been. This is only an isolated instance and
I mention it only to suggest to you that all you hear may
not necessarily be true.

The main point of my writing to you is to ask what
you plan to do when you return to Australia—also when
do you plan to return to Australia. Do you think you
might be interested in working on the Opera House?
Sandy Bishop [fellow uni friend] is working on it with me,
and finding it pretty interesting. The consultants involved
are first-class people—Ove Arup's staff are quite the
brightest engineers I have worked with. There seems to be
about three years of pretty intensive work in it.

In June 1966, one month after Hall wrote this letter, the
number of architects on the project rose from ten to twenty-
five. In the same month, Hall headed off on a three-month world
tour of opera houses. He planned to visit Utzon in Denmark.

Accompanied by Libby's sister Mary (who had been in
England for a wedding), Hall met with Ove Arup and his senior
staff in London. They were ambivalent about the young Australian, although impressed by his intellect. Hall also arranged
for Jim Anderson to meet Arup, who was by then a giant of
engineering. Meeting for morning tea, their interview continued
until 7 p.m.

Arup expressed concern about the legal case between Utzon
and the NSW government, and was worried he would be called
to give evidence. 'If I need to do that, it will crucify Utzon,' he
confided in Anderson. 'And I don't want to do that. The man is
a genius, I want to work with him again.'

'Hall is not a genius,' Arup said. 'And I'm not sure about
you yet.'

● ● ●

Former general manager of London's Royal Festival Hall, Ernest Bean, a bald bespectacled Yorkshireman, saw the shells of the emerging white building as he flew into Sydney on 22 December 1966. He arrived on the same day as Robert Vaughn, the suave star of the hit TV series *The Man from U.N.C.L.E.*, and became mixed up in the screaming melee greeting the American actor.

'Wearing a travel-worn grey suit, Mr Bean was slightly nonplussed by the fact that his arrival had been marked by airline officials as "VIP No Publicity". He wanted to talk about the Opera House. He even asked questions about it,' *Telegraph* columnist Leslie Wilson wrote. From his bird's eye view above the city, Bean recognised the shells as 'something to lift the spirits. A bit perhaps like a galleon about to stride the seas.' It's no surprise that many felt the form of the building resembled an up-ended Viking ship—slightly similar to the bow of the spids-gatter boats Aage Utzon had designed.

No stranger to controversy, Bean had managed the building of the permanent home for London's Symphony Orchestra, with Sydney Opera House competition judge Leslie Martin as architect. He had been selected by Premier Askin to examine whether the main hall should cater for both opera and ballet—as originally intended—or for symphony music as the ABC was now pushing, and to prepare a technical report.

A story in Britain's *Guardian* newspaper headlined 'The Importance of Bean, Ernest,' had convinced the NSW government of Bean's managerial credentials. Such was the cultural cringe at the time that Askin had looked to London for an arts consultant rather than in his own backyard. Similarly, when an international search for the Opera House's first general manager began, the NSW government would again look to London, eventually choosing Bean's confrere, Englishman Stuart Bacon, then deputy general manager at the Royal Festival Hall.

Before he left for Sydney, Bean visited Ove Arup's London office to read newspaper clippings for background. 'They brought me into the library and brought out the clippings . . . Well, it was like reading the *Decline and Fall of the Roman Empire*,' Bean joked, recalling how he'd pored over the stories that detailed a narrative already riddled with feuds and calamities.

On the day Bean arrived in Sydney, the news broke that two of the three Babcock-Weitz G 280 cranes, worth $100,000 each (a great deal of money at the time), would be put up for sale in the new year as they were no longer needed. 'Mr Festival Hall', as the management consultant was dubbed, was due to give his report to the state government three weeks later, on 16 January 1967.

In the wake of his departure, Utzon had left behind an issue over the seating, as Hall hinted in his letter to London. In the main hall, he had planned for seats behind the orchestra to be sold at a cheaper price to students. But symphony conductor Sir Bernard Heinze and ABC boss Charles Moses both told Utzon they did not think this was a good idea.

Utzon examined other ideas such as bringing the seat rows closer together to allow for 2800 seats. When Utzon's Stage 3 drawings were handed over to the Department of Public Works by his lawyers, the department dispatched men with tape measures to compare the row spacing at the Opera House with other theatres such as Her Majesty's. Even Stan Haviland broke his usual silence when Hughes declared the row spacing and seating numbers were inadequate, and the major hall would have to be redesigned. 'The news is very upsetting,' Haviland said. 'It is quite a jolt.'

The issue over the main hall was simple, wrote journalist John Yeomans. 'The major auditorium so little suited the needs of the Sydney Symphony Orchestra that the ABC saw no point in taking the orchestra away from the Town Hall. Such a decision would have deprived the Opera House of its main permanent big-scale customer and made nonsense of the whole idea of building a new performing arts centre.'

• • •

During the second weekend of December 1966, the ABC News Department chartered a helicopter to film the expected arrival of around-the-world solo sailor Francis Chichester. But the solo yachtsman was delayed by bad weather, so the documentary department used the chartered chopper to film the Opera House. Patricia Ludford went up in the helicopter with cameraman Frank Parnell and pilot James Reilly.

It was a quiet Saturday, ideal to film progress at Bennelong Point. Parnell's camera was mounted firmly on a tripod attached to the outside of the door sill of the chopper. They flew over the Opera House and captured the cranes and construction work on its shells. But as the helicopter approached Circular Quay and the AMP building, then the city's tallest, something went terribly wrong. A bolt securing the tail rotor suddenly sheared off and the rotor assembly dislodged. The helicopter began to gyrate on its own axis, spinning round and round in mid-air, totally out of control.

Parnell kept filming. The helicopter clipped the twenty-seven-storey Gold Fields House, at 1 Alfred Street, across the road from Circular Quay, before it plunged through the roof of the nearby three-storey Paul Building on Pitt Street. The three people on board were killed instantly.

The tragedy was captured on film by Mike Franklin, a cameraman with the Commonwealth Film Unit, who happened to be present that day in the street below. ABC staff were bereft at the death of their colleagues and many sobbed when they saw footage of their friends' final moment for the 7 p.m. news bulletin.

Like many of his colleagues, John Keenan didn't sleep well that night. It occurred to the young journalist that no one had thought about the film inside Parnell's camera, which had been retrieved from the wreckage. The next morning, he phoned the film processing company that developed all the ABC's films. 'Do you know what happened to the film out of the camera on the helicopter?' he asked.

The camera was on the bench, but it was empty. The film had been wrapped in newspaper and dumped in a rubbish bin.

'I don't suppose it's been developed?' Keenan asked hopefully. 'Can we salvage anything?'

Two hours later he threaded the developed film through a projector and was stunned by what he saw. He rang ABC news reader Ross Symonds at home, sensing he had a scoop. Symonds raced to work immediately.

The ABC interrupted its normal transmission that Sunday afternoon to show Parnell's dramatic footage of the Opera House from above, then his dizzying death dive into the city building. It remains one of the most gut-wrenching clips of an aviation disaster ever filmed.

It was a design fault in the helicopter that had caused the tragedy. After it a modified tail bolt was introduced in all helicopter assembly. But the poignant terrifying final moments on film haunted many Australians, even if they were nowhere near Sydney that day.

John Weiley, on the other side of the world, remembers seeing his beloved Opera House on his black and white TV set at home in London and then those disturbing freefall images. His former girlfriend, Patricia, had expected to be in London the next month; he felt a terrible pang for her and for the cameraman Frank Parnell, especially for his six children. He was in shock and plagued by the thought: *It should have been me.*

On seeing the vision of the harbour Weiley thought about going to Denmark to talk to Utzon—he wanted to see how comfortable the family were after returning to Europe and leaving the Sydney Opera House drama behind them. He'd remained in close contact with Lin. He knew she was upset at having to leave all her friends in Australia; they were in the prime of their lives in their late teens and early twenties, forging exciting careers in creative industries. Suddenly, they'd had to flee like fugitives.

Weiley had spent a lot of time with the family on the northern beaches. They'd sometimes buy a big box of fish and chips and sit on a large rock to eat, overlooking the site where the Utzons were planning to build their Bayview house. Jørn Utzon had been incredibly generous to Weiley. So, the film-maker decided to recommence his Opera House story, not really sure where the journey would take him.

Weiley contacted the Utzons from London. It was a very difficult time for Jørn. In Australia he was suing the NSW government to reclaim the fees owed to him and those of the people he'd employed. The court case—for which he continued to receive advice from the young barrister Neville Wran—was about to commence. Utzon's friend, architect Bill Wheatfield, was managing the case in Sydney on his behalf. Utzon was keen to take part in Weiley's film but pulled out when his lawyers told him the film could jeopardise his chances of getting a pay-out from the NSW government.

• • •

In Sydney Hughes was calling for submissions to rename the Opera House—yet again—and the contract for the pink granite podium paving and cladding was being put out to tender. But, essentially, construction work had stopped with Utzon's departure and it would remain at a standstill for two years.

John Weiley began to think the building was as cursed as
Tutankhamun's tomb in ancient Egypt, and that somewhere above
its shells should be engraved the words 'Beware all who enter
here'. Michelangelo had been fired during his work at St Peter's in
Rome. The Leaning Tower of Pisa was built on soft ground and
the Sagrada Familia remained an incomplete masterpiece when
its architect, Antoni Gaudi, died. Christopher Wren had had his
struggles with St Paul's in London, and there had been controversy
while both the Sydney Harbour Bridge and India's Taj Mahal were
being built. Perhaps that was this white monument's fate too?

Many thought Sydney's beautiful Opera House would
simply lie idle forever. Utzon himself said he felt the shell should
be knocked down, remain empty, or be used as an outdoor
concert venue, almost like Melbourne's Myer Music Bowl. It
could be left as an emblem to what might have been.

• • •

Great works require superhumans to hold them together. This
was the case at Bennelong Point as much as with any other
grand architectural work. The question was whether Peter Hall
was superhuman enough to hold the project together.

After Hall's extensive tour and consultation with experts
such as acoustics specialist Dr Vilhelm Jordan in Denmark (who
had been engaged by Utzon), he returned to Sydney in September with emerging ideas. His friend Jim Anderson arrived from
London not much later and joined the team working on the
glass walls. Hall's team now had to prepare an entirely new
brief for stage three; the 'Review of Programme' would officially go to the government in January 1967.

Those who dismissed Hall as not being up to the job under-
rated the intelligence of the man whose bedtime reading as a
boy was Virgil. Clearly, they did not comprehend this Latin
scholar's persistence.

Chapter twenty-six

New man at the Opera House

Peter Hall loved fast cars. One early summer day in 1967, he whipped across the Harbour Bridge at high speed in his hard-top blue XK 150 Jaguar. His fellow Cranbrook alumnus, the journalist Craig McGregor, was in the passenger seat. Looking suave in dark half-glasses, Hall put his foot on the accelerator and manoeuvred the car confidently into third gear.

'Peter's terribly involved in sport; he'd love to be a racing driver,' Libby Hall had told McGregor, who was writing a profile on the architect for the *Herald*'s weekend magazine. 'New Man at the Opera House' was one of the first in-depth stories written of the architect given one of the most difficult jobs Sydney had to offer.

Are you ambitious, McGregor asked.

'Ambitious? No, I don't think so—though I am selfish, which I suppose is one of the ingredients of ambition,' he answered thoughtfully. 'I'm not the sort of architect who sets out to build up business for himself. I've just taken situations as they've come—a sort of Scott Fitzgerald approach to life. It all shows a shocking lack of self-knowledge.'

Like most self-sufficient people, he puts himself first in most things, observed McGregor. He noted Hall's penchant for bow ties, his long hair that curled at the back, his mutton-chop sideburns, his short baggy-trousered legs, and that he smoked fat cigars, drank Campari and soda, had a self-assured manner and a good sense of humour. He captained the debating team at high school and university. 'I'm used to talking,' Hall told McGregor.

'He depends far more on reason than emotion and never really becomes involved with people; he has no really close friends, doesn't warm to people easily and doesn't see much of his parents although they have moved to Sydney,' McGregor wrote.

Hall's university friend, solicitor David de Carvalho, used a cricket analogy to describe the architect, who had worked himself up from playing fourth grade cricket to captain the first-grade team at university: 'He's not a natural cricketer, in fact he was pretty hopeless when he started out. He became good at it by intensive study and by practising hard. Peter likes to be good at everything he tackles. He won't do anything unless he can do it properly.'

Hall had respect for Utzon, he told McGregor, but he felt Utzon belonged to a 'dying race of prima donna architects who regard architecture as a form of artistic self-expression rather than the science of designing buildings that work'.

Like Utzon, Hall enjoyed rifle-shooting and was a good sportsman. In most other ways, however, he was almost the exact opposite of the Dane, but most notably in height at a mere 5 feet 7 inches tall. Utzon was a good craftsman; Hall was a fine draughtsman.

When McGregor's story was published on 18 February 1967, Bill Wheatland objected to many things about it. He wrote a letter to the *Herald* detailing his complaints and defending his former boss. He denied the claim that no working drawings for stage three had been left behind: 'In October 1965 Utzon had contracted in writing with Mr Hughes to complete most of his working drawings by October 1966. At the time of his withdrawal the work was well up to schedule.'

Since Utzon's departure, Wheatland had been working tirelessly to sort out the documents for the project and to secure adequate terms of severance, with the help of lawyers Bob Nicholls and Neville Wran. For Wheatland it was an exhausting and disheartening process.

Internationally, many architects remained horrified that Hall and Co. had taken on the job. A boycott to stop people taking on the project was almost worldwide, even though the Royal Australian Institute of Architects under Gilling refused to support it. Peter Hall was called a pariah, and many wondered if he had a suicidal streak, driving himself at work as fast and furiously as the sports cars he loved.

When McGregor asked, 'Why did you take this job?', Hall's reply was simple.

'It had to be someone,' he said. 'Why not me?'

• • •

In the year after Utzon's departure, there remained a faint hope he might still come back. The world-famous architecture critic Professor Sigfried Giedion spoke for many when he said, 'We would rather prefer that a bomb would destroy the whole building instead of fulfilling the unreasonable disfiguration which will disequilibrate one of the few masterpieces in Australia.'

When the anniversary of Utzon's disagreement with Hughes rolled around on 28 February 1967, the Sydney *Mirror* called it D-Day. 'D for decision, D for disaster and D for disgrace. Utzon wants to return' was the headline on a story.

Asked if he would return, Utzon had replied: 'As I have said often my greatest desire is to return to Sydney and complete the Opera House as I have planned it. I believe I have the answer to the outstanding problems including that of the major hall. When I left the project a year ago I was already well advanced towards a solution that would certainly satisfy all potential users ... I would love to come back to Sydney to contribute everything I have to this building and the place it could have in Australia and the world.'

Hall understood the disappointment and anger many people felt. In 1967 he wrote the epilogue for one of the first books about the building, *The Sydney Opera House Affair*, by Michael Baume, who was then the financial editor of the *Bulletin* and would later become a Liberal senator for NSW. Hall felt the 'tear it down' approach was understandable and explained how many problems he had inherited when he took on the project. Most notable was that the acoustics experts Utzon employed— Dr Vilhelm Jordan, and Professors Cremer and Gabler—did not agree. And Utzon had not decided whose advice he should trust. During Hall's fact-finding tour, he met theatre consultant Ben Schlanger in New York, who was brought on board as a 'consulting theatre architect'; but responsibility for acoustics remained with Dr Jordan.

The *Herald*'s editor, John Douglas (JD) Pringle, became a strong ally of Peter Hall's. They met often for dinner and drinks and spoke regularly on the phone. During the course of Pringle's second editorship of the paper, from 1965–70, he ran regular editorials in support of the Australian architect, writing many of them himself. JD Pringle was a Scotsman who had become an influential opinion-maker through his book, *Australian Accent*, published in 1958. He loved the Opera House project but had some sympathy for the dilemma in which Askin and Hughes found themselves. He could see it reaping benefits that would be far-reaching for the government, the city and, by extension, Australia's arts and media.

Rupert Murdoch's *Australian* and Frank Packer's *Telegraph* continued to push for Utzon's return. Even Hall thought—or perhaps hoped—there was a possibility he might come back. But an offer did not come from the government.

While the 'Utzonite-Jacobites', as they were called in some quarters, dreamt and even plotted his return, fifty architects from the Government Architect's Office, half of its total staff, wrote a letter to Peter Hall telling him Utzon was still willing to return. Hall neither replied nor abdicated. 'No comment,' he told the *Herald*'s Helen Frizell.

Grey clouds—both real and symbolic—hung over the Opera House when the Duke of Edinburgh made a squelching tour of the site on 8 March 1967.

• • •

In a vast dark warehouse in inner Sydney's Waterloo sat the stage machinery sent from Austria to be used for opera in the main hall. In February 1967 it had celebrated its second birthday on Australian soil. Manufactured by Waagner-Biro in Vienna for $1.5 million, storage charges were $70,000 and rising.

Between two to four thousand cast-iron parts for the stage machinery—including the counterweights that Utzon had intended to use in the main hall—were stored in their delivery pallets in the Waterloo yard of a family-run iron foundry, George Marr & Sons, whose name was in gutters all over

Sydney because they manufactured the iron grates for the Water Board. The counterweights were to be used for many purposes: some were to be sewn into the bottom of the stage curtains to weigh them down, or to be used as the counterweights to help lift them. The main stage curtain for the multi-purpose hall was intended to front Utzon's planned traditional proscenium arch and could be seen in his Finecraft plywood models.

Ernest Bean delivered his report on 16 January 1967. The next day, the last rib of the last shell was laid three years and two months after the perfection and placement of the first had brought tears to Utzon and his colleagues' eyes.

Debate continued on the best use of the main hall. The Sydney Opera House Trust recommended to the minister for public works that it be available for opera and ballet as well as for orchestral concerts. The ABC continued to argue that it should be used only for its concerts.

The *Herald* ran a full page of letters on the issue, leading with one from architect Walter Bunning, who declared: 'Going back to the original brief for this building—the conditions for this architectural competition—nothing could have been clearer than the requirements for the main hall. It had to seat 3000–3500 for the purposes in order of priority (a) symphony concerts including organ music and soloists (b) large scale opera (c) ballet and dance (d) choral and (e) pageants and mass meetings.' As an entrant in the competition, Bunning was very familiar with its conditions—and he knew that orchestral music should be a priority, in line with Goossens' original proposal to find a new home for the Sydney Symphony Orchestra. Illustrator/architect George Molnar also weighed into the debate: 'Since I cannot understand opera in any language,' he reiterated reverberation times were an important consideration in determining the main hall's use.

'Arts should live together,' wrote the principal of the opera school at the Conservatorium of Music, Ronal Jackson. 'Symphony, opera, ballet, drama should live together, sharing each other's problems, creating perfect harmony under one sail.'

The Elizabethan Theatre Trust, under the leadership of the Governor of the Reserve Bank, HC 'Nugget' Coombs, joined the debate, arguing the main hall should be kept for both concerts and opera. If the ABC had its way, Coombs and others felt, Sydney would not be able to stage grand operas such as *Aida* because the minor hall would not be big enough.

Undoubtedly, the heart of this debate was about acoustics. Philip Parsons, senior lecturer in drama at the University of New South Wales, wrote a three-part series in the *Australian* in Utzon's defence, arguing that the architect had been working with three of the world's best acousticians to resolve the issues for a mixed-use hall.

John O'Hara, the *Herald*'s state roundsman, wrote on 11 February 1967 that the government had reached a deadlock. However, on 15 March 1967, Minister Hughes made an announcement in the NSW Parliament. There would be a change of plans: the ABC's symphony orchestra would be given priority and the main hall would become a concert hall; opera and ballet would be housed in the minor hall. On 21 March, Premier Askin announced that this had been agreed to by state cabinet.

The existing stage machinery, which had been manufactured specifically for use in the main/multi-purpose hall, was now redundant. Utzon's original concept for the large hall had been for it to have a capacity of 2800 for concerts, and a reduced number of 1700 for operatic productions. According to Utzon's early plans the main hall would have been converted mechanically for opera, with a reduction in the audience area and a vast increase in the stage area. The smaller hall, with its original seating capacity of 1100, was conceived primarily for plays, intimate opera, recitals; every effort would be made, Utzon said, 'To capture the intimacy so essential to such uses.'

To augment these two large halls, Utzon planned for a small experimental theatre that would seat 430 and have its own foyer. Utzon hoped the experimental theatre would not only satisfy the needs of amateur theatrical societies, but house a School of Dramatic Art. Also detailed in Utzon's plans were another performance space for chamber music, a canteen and rehearsal rooms.

But now that the main purpose of the main hall had changed, the question remained of what to do with the stage machinery. On 31 October 1967, Hughes told the newspapers: 'The suggestion that the machinery will be scrapped is complete nonsense.'

In late 1967 the machinery was crated and moved to nearby Surry Hills. Negotiations began with the many different contractors to see if it could be used elsewhere, and an expert was sent to Europe to pursue this hope. However, despite Hughes' previous denials, the stage machinery was ultimately scrapped. It was not dumped into the harbour, as a rumour circulating in Sydney at the time claimed, but was transferred to a vacant paddock at Silverwater, near Homebush on the Parramatta River.

The cast-iron counterweights, too, were no longer needed. George Marr was able to purchase them 'very profitably' for scrap iron. Marr's son, journalist David Marr, remembers his father's response: 'He'd never profited from a job in and out like that so easily.'

By this stage there was incredulity that such a major change had taken place at such late notice. 'The whole grandiose Opera House project is studded with "whys",' a *Sun-Herald* editorial declared. 'Why was expenditure allowed to get so out of hand? Why was it not discovered earlier that the needs of opera and orchestral concerts could not be both met in a hall of sufficient seating? Why was opera given preference anyway when the Sydney Symphony Orchestra was going to be principal customer?' Why indeed still call it an Opera House?

Opera fans were outraged. The singer June Bronhill warned that Joan Sutherland would likely boycott the opening due to the downgrading of opera to the minor hall. Many joined 'Nugget' Coombs' lament that large-scale and complex operas, like Wagner's *Ring Cycle*, might not be able to be staged in the smaller hall. This was disputed by the *Telegraph*'s Martin Long, who by now had a music column. He claimed the second smaller hall would be quite adequate for all but a small handful of established repertoire operas.

Stan Haviland, the Sydney Opera House Executive Committee chairman, claimed that neither he nor the trust could be blamed for anything that had gone wrong between 1960–65 since the trust had not been consulted or even informed of developments, and was either gagged or ignored. Utzon dealt directly with Public Works Minister Norm Ryan, he said, washing his hands of any responsibility for the lack of direction given to Utzon. This was a convenient whitewash by the man they still called 'Silent Stan'.

Peter Hall was stumped about how to proceed. At work and at home, his life was becoming difficult.

Chapter twenty-seven

Autopsy on a dream

Gough Whitlam was a giant of a man—both physically (standing at 194 centimetres or six feet four inches tall) and politically. The Labor member for the south-western Sydney seat of Werriwa became federal opposition leader in 1967. From that moment, he was touted as a strong contender to win the next federal election. With a state election looming in New South Wales, he began working behind the scenes with his state colleagues in an attempt to bring Utzon back to Sydney. This was largely thanks to lobbying by the Irish journalist Francis Evers, who had worked as a Sydney theatre critic, notably for *The Australian* in its early days.

Evers had returned to Europe, where he worked as a correspondent covering the Vietnam peace negotiations in Paris, but he came to public prominence in Australia and abroad because of his spirited defence of Utzon's work. Writing to Whitlam from Paris, he outlined his reasons why the Danish architect should be returned to complete his controversial design.

Former lord mayor and NSW Labor leader Pat Hills lent his public support to this idea, and Whitlam sent a telegram to Evers on 15 February 1968. 'Pat Hills has announced Labor State Government would invite Utzon back to consult stop.' It was signed 'Gouth Whitlam'; his name was misspelt by the telegram operator. The telegram remained in Utzon's personal confidential correspondence until after his death. As did a letter from Evers to Whitlam, explaining he would pass on the cable to Utzon and that he may 'send you his own written thanks'.

On 19 February 1968 Utzon did write to Gough Whitlam at Parliament House in Canberra. 'I am deeply grateful for your kind interest,' he said. 'I am writing separately to the NSW Labor leaders. It is my sincere hope that I will be invited to return and complete this magnificent project.' He kept a copy of the letter in Denmark.

In the lead up to the second anniversary of his departure from Sydney, Utzon sent a cable to Askin indicating his willingness to return. With little progress on the site the world's Big Six in architecture—Sigfried Giedion, Alvar Aalto, Walter Gropius, Josep Lluís Sert, Steen Eiler Rasmussen and Kenzō Tange—sent a cable to Peter Hall begging him to support Utzon.

The move to bring Utzon back was spearheaded by a Double Bay divorcee, Elizabeth Price. She took out a full-page ad in the *Herald* as an open letter to the people of NSW calling for their support. A single mother and grandmother, she had few assets other than her car (a Morris 1100), two diamond rings, a flat in a red-brick building and $94.56 in savings, but she was steadfast in her support of Utzon. 'I love the Opera House, and have since I first saw it,' she said.

Price hired the Sydney Town Hall—which she partly paid for herself and partly with donations—to call a meeting to vote for Utzon's return. A tape-recorded message from the architect was played. She later phoned Utzon at 2 a.m. in Denmark to tell him of the overwhelming support he had received from the meeting.

But he did not have the support of the people who mattered: members of the Askin government, which was re-elected on 24 February 1968. Utzon, like the opposition Labor Party, once again conceded defeat.

The project continued to garner enormous interest, not just in Australia but around the world. Two books attempted to explain the imbroglio, but only added fuel to the fire. Architect Elias Duek-Cohen's *Utzon and the Sydney Opera House* was published in 1967 and journalist John Yeomans' *The Other Taj Mahal: What happened to the Sydney Opera House* was published in 1968. On 9 April 1968 Utzon turned fifty. The following day, 10 April, his Swiss hero and champion Siegfried Giedion died in Zurich.

• • •

In London in 1968, John Weiley went to see the new head of BBC2, another young documentary maker by the name of David Attenborough. The Australian could see a way of telling his story without Utzon's involvement. He pitched his idea to Attenborough, who told him to go back to Sydney and make the film. As was customary in these circumstances, the BBC sent a request to the ABC asking for the use of a camera crew and equipment. But, for the first time, the answer was 'no'.

Attenborough called Weiley to his office. He had received a long telex from Talbot Duckmanton, who had taken over as head of the ABC when Charles Moses retired in 1965. Duckmanton had taken time out from a conference he was attending in New Zealand to set down at length the ABC's objections.

'We are flatly told that we must not let you make this film,' Attenborough read out aloud to Weiley. And then, with that perfect articulation that would later become so familiar, he added: 'Well, they can get fucked.'

Weiley was provided with cash and given the authority to make his own film and to hire his own crew. He shot extraordinary images of Sydney and the construction of the building and interviewed most of the key players. Although Utzon didn't feature in the film, his towering spirit hung over it like the ghost of Hamlet's father.

In London, Weiley asked the Australian mate sleeping on the sofa in his flat to write and narrate the script. This was Bob Ellis, the friend he'd left Lismore with, who by then was beginning to establish himself as a writer.

'It's an object like no other object. Not so much a building as a thing, a thing like a pyramid or a Druid's altar, an object of almost ancient reverence, a gesture towards the infinite, like St Peter's. Yet its Gothic arches point up to no God, only to an ideal of functional excellence,' Ellis intones in his elegiac opening.

'And yet it's a failure, an appalling fiasco,' he continued, 'a 4½ acre, 220-foot-high scandal, an antipodean tower of Babel, the centre of a nation's debate of what art is worth and the greatest continuing local joke on record.'

The film's editor was their university friend and fellow north coast boy Ian Masters, the son of author Olga Masters and the brother of journalists Chris and Roy Masters and television producers Sue and Deb Masters.

Autopsy on a Dream, a beautiful homage to the building and those who made it, was first shown at a private screening of expat Australians in London, where it was met with loud applause and tears of homesickness. It was publicly aired on BBC2 in September 1968 and met with critical acclaim.

The film raised many questions because it not only criticised the NSW government for its role, but it also included interviews with some of the project's leading figures. Ove Arup's pain over the disintegration of his relationship with Utzon is evident; it clearly broke his heart, as much as it had broken Utzon's.

Peter Hall was also interviewed. In the transcript of that interview, filmed on 11 May 1968, Hall spoke frankly of the difficulties he'd faced and compared Utzon to Spanish architect Antoni Gaudí.

'Coming into this thing new, with all these added elements of political pressure and emotional crises in the community and things like that . . . and working with two architects that none of us had ever worked together before, [David] Littlemore or [Lionel] Todd or I, we had administrative problems of course and things like that because there was work going on, on the job, the shells were still being built, tile lids were still being placed, we had to find out what was to go inside the building. If we'd found out that the thing was resolved everywhere by Utzon to the client's satisfaction, we would have simply followed that; that's what we did with the paving and cladding. We have used Utzon's shapes and we've worked out fixings and engineering details and things like that. But it turned out there was a lot that had to be done, by us.

'Decisions have been made that don't necessarily make our job easier; in fact, you know people think that if the stage tier had remained in the A2 shell [the main shells were called the A1 and A2 shells] our job would have been much easier to have kept the stage tier and built a smaller multi-purpose hall. And, of course, there's the architectural question of taking the stage tier out of the A2 shell, and you know I couldn't possibly argue that that is not an artistic loss. That in a way the unity of the architecture suffers from that.

'You do feel in the building, when you go over there, that there is a pressure which the building itself puts on you to—to get it in use because the city needs it, there's also a pressure which the building puts on you to design it in a certain way.

'I think Utzon is an architect of such unusual and really consistent thinking as Gaudí, a Spanish architect who died in 1925, and you see his buildings are extraordinarily unified, even the ones with a lot of cement on them, for example you know—this wonderful house . . . I think Utzon is a bit of the same sort of man and that I couldn't deny that there is an architectural loss in not having him finish the building completely as he would want to . . . One of the things that's been said about Utzon is that he's a perfectionist, and it's been said as if that's something detrimental; well, I couldn't say it was detrimental because in a way I'm a perfectionist myself, but less developed in how I think perhaps than Utzon.'

Having worked tirelessly on the film for eighteen months, Weiley went to Greece for a well-earned holiday in late September 1968. He was expecting *Autopsy on a Dream* to be shown on prime time on the mainstream BBC1, as was often the case with documentaries commissioned by BBC2. On his return to London, he found it hadn't been aired and that the master had been destroyed: literally cut into pieces on the BBC chopping block.

Weiley has never been officially told why his film was destroyed, but he suspects Ove Arup or others in his team were upset by his portrayal. Arup was understood to have been furious about the film because he felt it was unfair. Weiley was surprised by this. He had liked Arup. He'd thought they had understood one another.

In 1965 Arup's company, on a commission from British composer Benjamin Britten, had converted an old malthouse in Suffolk into a concert hall. While working on the project, Zunz had become friendly with John Culshaw, who was head of music programs for BBC Television. Weiley believes someone complained to Culshaw about *Autopsy* and that Culshaw sent a memo demanding the film be destroyed. But no one at the BBC has ever officially explained why this happened. David Attenborough remains in the dark to this day.

Back home in Australia, the ABC had declined to screen the film. Weiley suspected his father Bill, a Country Party member of the Askin government, may have been involved in that decision because of the bad light in which his friend Hughes was portrayed.

At the ABC, General Manager Talbot Duckmanton was unhappy about Weiley's criticism of the organisation and the role it played in making sure its symphony had a home in the main hall. Weiley had filmed the removal of the stage machinery, a task the contractor likened to 'cutting up a live deer'.

Weiley was absolutely shattered. He'd spent years on this project and it vanished overnight. The film's disappearance confirmed his suspicion that the Sydney Opera House was cursed.

• • •

Peter Hall may have shared this thinking. The project was causing him anguish, not just professionally but personally as well.

The new architectural team had to juggle the need to provide the required seating capacity in the main hall in a reasonably comfortable configuration within the space under the existing shells, as well as achieve an acceptable acoustic balance. This was a hard task indeed.

As would be documented many years later by the Sydney Opera House: 'Hall's solution (effectively forced on him by the Askin government and the Australian Broadcasting Commission's requirements) was to abandon the proscenium arch configuration and associated backstage space and equipment, and to transfer opera to the intended Drama Theatre. Instead he proposed to design a concert hall with relevant acoustic properties and to extend the seating round the orchestra. His recommendation was accepted by NSW cabinet. It was the largest of the many upheavals in the design history of the Sydney Opera House.'

Despite Hall's outwardly confident appearance, overwork and criticism were beginning to take their toll. Architect Peter Webber, his friend and later business partner, documented this stress in his book on Hall, *The Phantom of the Opera House*. His wife Libby remembers him pacing up and down at home for days and nights on end. He barely saw his children, Becca and Willy, confirming Libby's earlier apprehension about him taking on the job in the first place.

And then one day Libby's sister Mary, who worked as an assistant at the Opera House, walked into Jim Anderson's office to tell him, 'Peter can't get out of bed, he's exhausted.' Hall's doctor insisted he seek treatment for nervous exhaustion.

* * *

Chapter twenty-eight

• • •

Chapter twenty-eight

'Hall's Balls'

Peter Hall's son, Willy, remembers being paid one cent for every nail he picked up on the Opera House construction site. The goal was to prevent punctures in the tyres of his father's beloved classic car, the XK 150 Jag.

Hall had become a complete workaholic, flogging himself professionally to prove he was capable of completing this major work. The only way Becca and Willy could see their father was to spend their weekends at Bennelong Point. His marriage had also fallen apart. With money gifted to Libby by her industrialist uncle George Bryant and the extra money Hall was receiving from his new job, the estranged couple bought the house next door to the family home in North Sydney.

Hall's former Cranbrook school friend, Tom Heath, by then a prominent architect and critic, wrote often about Hall in the global magazine *The Architectural Review*. The international design world remained fascinated by the drama at Bennelong

Point. Although still incomplete, the building had become Australia's most popular tourist attraction.

Hall found himself in demand from visiting VIPs intrigued to know how the new team was coping. He was a generous host and would often foot the bills for extravagant meals. Finnish film director Jörn Donner, a contemporary of Ingmar Bergman, was one such guest.

Donner had first come to Australia in 1967 as a guest of the Sydney Film Festival to promote his film *Adventure Starts Here* where he met a young woman, Penelope McDonnell, and was bewitched by her beauty. He wanted her to star in his movies. When Donner returned to Sydney the following year, McDonnell had every intention of returning to Scandinavia with him.

The director expressed a desire to visit the Opera House, so after calling Hall's office, he went down to the building site with McDonnell. She was wearing a 'Bring Utzon Back' T-shirt. 'Can you get one for me?' Peter Hall asked. Even though they were both involved with other people, there was an instant attraction between the two of them.

Libby had now taken up with another architect, David Turner, and she and Peter were both at peace with their separation. He was seeing other women.

Hall, the ever-charming host, invited Donner and McDonnell to dinner at his North Sydney home. She remembers Hall as being fun, smart, interesting and engaging.

McDonnell didn't travel to Scandinavia with Donner but stayed in Sydney. As a lark she called Hall's office a few weeks after their dinner to ask about a job as a model-maker and she learnt that Hall's secretary, Deidre, had been calling every McDonnell in the phone book on a mission from her boss to track her down.

When McDonnell was put through to the architect, he asked, 'Can you read plans?'

'Yes,' she lied.

'Let's meet for lunch then,' he suggested.

They did meet for lunch. Not only did she get the job, they also started a relationship. McDonnell was twenty-one; Hall was sixteen years her senior.

Jim Anderson, now working on the problem of the Opera House glass, felt his friend was looking for a distraction. Hall was under enormous pressure; many, it seemed, wanted him to fail. He was in a dark place not just because his marriage had failed but also because his relationship with Arup's team was faltering over the issue of the glass walls.

Hall and McDonnell moved into an apartment together on the fortieth floor of the Park Regis, the CBD's first high-rise residential building with one of Sydney's best views. To the north they could see straight out to the Opera House.

• • •

Despite Hughes' denials, by 1969 there had been a complete breakdown in communication between the Sydney Opera House Trust and the Department of Public Works. An editorial in the *Herald* asked why the trust had not protested about the breakdown sooner.

Technically the trust, which was effectively the rebranding of the Executive Committee after 1966, was not meant to come into existence until the building was completed, according to the act that established it. But to further diminish its power, the Askin government introduced a bill limiting the age of trust members to seventy and reducing their number to eight. University of New South Wales Vice Chancellor Philip Baxter was appointed chairman, and he was joined by luminaries that included Professor Zelman Cowen and Lady Macarthur-Onslow. None, however, was a performing arts practitioner, an essential requirement for such an advisory role.

Tours of the site, which had taken place most Sundays since construction began, ended in early 1970 as the work went into a fast gallop towards the finishing line. Hall was working himself senseless and driving his team hard to meet the demands of the government and the public.

When it was announced that jackhammers would be brought in to implement the structural changes necessitated by the repurposing of the halls, Hughes warned that 'the whole place will be jumping'. He was very much the public face of the Opera House construction.

In March 1969, in the interests of transparency, Hughes delivered a two-hour speech to the NSW parliament detailing the costs of the project. Stage one (the podium), completed in 1963, had cost $5.4 million. Stage two (the roof and tiles), completed in 1967, had cost $12.5 million. Stage three was a work in progress.

Hughes had gone on a three-month world tour of thirteen theatres in 1967, causing some fuss within political circles, but especially from the NSW Opposition. Compounding the political fallout, not long after Hughes' March speech to the parliament, fellow Country Party member Charles Cutler was sent on a three-month overseas fact-finding mission visiting New York's Lincoln Centre, Milan's La Scala and opera houses in Rome, Vienna and Berlin. The government explained that as minister for education, Cutler would be studying the administration of these theatres. The public whiffed a gravy train.

Then, on 13 July 1970, Kerry O'Brien reported in *The Sun* that provisional estimates on the cost of maintenance for the building showed it could never hope to pay its own way.

'Project engineers estimate that maintenance on the $85 million Opera House will cost well over $1 million a year. Insurance premiums alone would cost as high as $130,000 a year . . . Even by charging high rentals the trust would be unable to cover its staggering maintenance costs.'

• • •

When they had started working with Peter Hall in 1966, Jim Anderson and the Arup team had been set the task of filling the huge empty mouths of the shells with an acre and a half of glass, just as Utzon had envisaged. It took years of work to understand how to do this.

A panel of Australian and international glass manufacturers tendered for the job, which eventually went to the French group, Boussois-Souchon-Neuvesel. The glass walls that were to descend from the roof needed to resist gale-force winds and expansion and contraction due to the sun. They also needed to muffle harbour sounds such as ferry whistles and fog horns.

At the end of 1969 both Hughes and Hall flew to France, Hughes to discuss the supply of the tinted glass with Boussois-Souchon-Neuvesel, and Hall to talk with chemists about the final colour, which was to be a topaz unique to the Sydney Opera House. Utzon had originally wanted a whiskey colour. 'Once you get glass in thickness it starts to look very green. The warm colour takes the green out. It also removes glare and goes better with the general colour of the building,' Hall later explained.

About 2000 panes of glass in more than 700 different sizes were shipped from France. The individual panes ranged in size from 1.2 metres square to about 4 metres high by 2.5 metres wide, and were cut to size onsite using diamond-edged circular saws in a temporary factory built on the boardwalk at the harbour end of the Opera Theatre. Using two layers of glass,

one plain and one topaz, most of the panes were 18.8 milli-
metres thick. They were laminated together with such strength
that a low-velocity bullet would bounce off them. The inner layer
had important sound-excluding properties.

Tenders for the steel mullions, as per Arup's wishes, went
out in March 1970. Like Utzon, by this stage Hall found his
relationship with Arup's team fraught. His friend Jim Anderson
had been asked to leave the project due to a dispute with Arup's
engineers, and consensus on the best way to construct the glass
walls had been as difficult to reach as it had been for Utzon
and Arup. Finally, agreement was reached in 1970. It had taken
years of arguments, for Hall since 1966.

Work began on installing the northern glass walls in January
1971. They were supported by the mullions—which, under Hall
and Arup's direction, were made of specially shaped vertical
steel instead of plywood as conceived by Utzon. Bronze glazing
bars embedded in a silicone putty to allow for expansion and
contraction were attached to the mullions to carry the panes of
glass. The windows were the only elements of the entire Sydney
Opera House project that were assembled with the use of a
computer. Apart from a computer check of Joe Bertony's calculations for the roof shells, everything else at Bennelong Point was
designed with little more than old school geometry. Arup's team,
working with the architects, calculated mathematically the exact
size of each pane of glass.

Four leading Sydney glass companies (O'Brien, Vetro, Sandys
and Astor) undertook the glass cutting. A special machine that
used suction cups instead of hooks lifted each pane, and eight
men would direct it into the correct spot. Ferry commuters were
delighted to observe the daily activity.

• • •

Utzon's pursuit of the money he claimed the state government still owed to him had moved to the NSW Supreme Court. Late in 1970 the arts writer for the *Australian,* Katharine Brisbane, travelled to Denmark to interview Utzon, and found him surprisingly gracious and without rancour toward Hughes.

'I made the Opera House for the people of Sydney and they are very much like myself,' he told her. 'They are sporty, happy, healthy people who like exciting things. They are daring and said: "We can make such a thing as this." I could not make such a thing in Switzerland.'

On 13 August 1970, Peter Hall married Penelope McDonnell in the Wesley College chapel at Sydney University. Hall asked Jim Anderson to be his best man. The service was followed by a reception at the popular and chic Rive Gauche restaurant in Surry Hills. McDonnell wore a red dress: 'I was the scarlet woman, so I felt I may as well dress like one,' she recalls. In the same month, acclaimed violinist Yehudi Menuhin asked Hughes' permission to hold rehearsals at the Opera House. Menuhin was impressed by Hall's work.

Before they were married, the Halls had bought a house in Mosman, as well as a farm in the Hunter Valley for tax reasons. Hall loved to retreat to this place, especially with his children, both of whom called him Pete, not Dad. Hall sold his North Sydney home to his friend Jim Anderson and settled into the Mosman house. Hall's daughter Becca (who lived with her mother and new husband David Turner in Hunters Hill) recalls: 'They did it up very glamorously, put in a pool, a garage for the cars, painted the dining room jet black. I was regularly sent out from there by Penny to buy cigarettes when Pete was at work.'

By 1970 increased union militancy meant 48,000 working hours had been lost on site in industrial action, mainly by the Builders' Labourers' Federation. Minister Hughes called for a national moratorium on the strikes that were plaguing his pet project.

That same year the approaches to the Opera House were paved with 10 acres of reconstructed pink granite from Tarana, near the NSW country town of Bathurst. The cement for the 1.5 million tonnes of concrete came from Portland, west of the Blue Mountains.

• • •

On April Fool's Day 1971, Hughes led a group of journalists into the Concert Hall for their first sneak peek. They were eager to see Hall's work. Utzon's original idea—for a rippled ceiling that would fit inside the curves of the outer roof like a walnut—had been abandoned. Hall's version was more like a hollow raft suspended from the roof ribs. The focal point was a crown piece of white birch containing many light sources. The hollow space between the shells and the ceiling was used to hide wiring and air conditioning.

The contractor for the supply and installation of the white birch veneer was Cemac Brooks Pty Ltd. It tackled the job of building the ceiling on a firm-price basis, as the public works ministry wanted. Hughes had been frustrated that sub-contractors under Utzon had been unwilling to give firm prices and time scales for completion of their work.

To assure complete homogeneity of visual effect, the birch was treated with a white filler or pigment and sealed with a Wattyl spray application known as Uformel. Acres of timber from around the NSW country towns of Wauchope and Dungog had been used in the wood and plywood for the ceilings of the four auditoriums.

White birch had once been discarded as rubbish by local builders and furniture makers. The high starch content of this

European deciduous tree had made it a favourite of the Australian lyctus beetle, but CSIRO's Division of Forest Products had found a way to make it resistant to the borer. The plywood industry then fell in love with birchwood as its logs peeled well and its timber had a tight grain and an attractive colour.

As well as the white birch, 27,000 square feet of laminated brushbox was used on the floors and walls. The largest sawmilling company in NSW, Allen Taylor & Co. (now a subsidiary of Boral), was awarded the contract for manufacture and supply of the laminated brushbox for the main Concert Hall and Opera Theatre.

Hughes paraded the visitors around a hall that would accommodate 2690 people with good seating and viewing conditions and a large orchestra and choir and have a reverberation time in the middle frequencies of the order of two seconds. 'How do you like it?' the proud minister asked, waving towards the ceiling.

The building was amassing some other impressive boasts. In a small factory in Mortdale, a southern suburb of Sydney, work began on building the world's biggest organ for the Concert Hall. The Opera House would also be equipped with the most modern internal and external telephone system.

• • •

With the building now taking substantial shape, talk turned to a possible date for an opening night. The big question was whether Joan Sutherland would be available. It seemed unlikely that she would.

The main opera company in Australia was the Elizabethan Trust Opera Company under Stefan Haag (its name was later changed to Opera Australia). With its limited budget it simply could not afford the appearance fees that Sutherland was now commanding internationally. Moreover, it was expected that Peter Sculthorpe would be commissioned to write a contemporary Australian opera for the event, thus ruling out Sutherland, who refused to sing modern opera and usually only performed when her husband Richard Bonynge was conducting.

The first full theatrical performance at the still unfinished site took place in November 1971 when the Q Theatre group—which gave lunchtime performances in the AMP Theatrette at Circular Quay, and played to workers in factories, workshops and on building sites—performed the Australian play, Jim McNeil's *The Chocolate Frog*. The hard-hat wearing audience cordoned off the auditorium steps, and the actors went through their paces.

That year the contract of Stuart Bacon, the British general manager, was not renewed. The trust began scouting for a replacement. 'Whoever *he* is, *he* is going to have his work cut out for *him*,' one gossip columnist noted in September 1971.

In October, the NSW government settled its account with Utzon. He was paid $1.296 million, which included his legal fees. Not long afterwards, Utzon moved to Hawaii to take up a university professorship.

That same month it was finally acknowledged that no use could be found for the abandoned stage machinery, which had been sitting idle in a paddock near Silverwater jail for years. Arrangements were made to transfer it to the Department of Corrective Services, where it would be used for prisoner training programs in Long Bay and Silverwater jails. A loss of around $769,000 was sustained, a substantial amount of money for the time.

Penelope Hall gave birth to two children during the early heady days of their marriage. A girl, Hermione, was born in 1971 and a boy, Thomas, in 1972. Tragically, Thomas succumbed to cot death at eleven weeks of age. Hall sought refuge from this heartbreak the only way he knew: in his work, which he sustained at a frenzied pace.

Like Libby before her, Penelope quickly learnt that her husband was a workaholic. His drive, she felt, came from a good place. 'Mostly it was a vile time,' she recalls of those early days. 'He was criticised constantly, and it impacted our marriage. But Pete was just trying to do the best job he could.' It took some courage, she believed, to do what he was attempting.

As Hall's work continued, he began to focus on the total experience future theatregoers would have. Because the bulk of visitors would come at night, he decided to illuminate the structure externally, creating a cathedral-like atmosphere at a cost of $2.7 million. Lighting companies Philips and General Electric were called in to collaborate.

He also decided the boardwalk areas would be lit around the perimeter by a row of fifty-one clear spherical polycarbonate balls on numbered bronze poles developed specifically for the site. To reduce glare and make the spheres themselves look as unobtrusive as possible ('transparent by both day and night'), the light source was placed inside the pole and a sophisticated reflector system was installed inside the top of the sphere to maximise the spread of illumination. They became fondly known as 'Hall's Balls'.

These were the finishing touches and flounces. They signalled the time had finally come for the spotlight to shine on the Sydney Opera House itself.

Chapter twenty-nine

Not a job for boys

'Rump à la Rolf [Harris]' or a slice of '[Robert] Helpmann Ham' were touted as possible contenders on the menu at the Opera House's Bennelong Restaurant before it opened. The Australian entertainer Harris, who was very popular in Britain, especially with Queen Elizabeth II, promised to return to play his digeridoo for the gala opening celebrations. Robert Helpmann, the internationally acclaimed actor and dancer, who as a young man had danced with Anna Pavlova's company, vowed to return for the Australian Ballet's opening season despite being upset that the ballet had been downgraded to the minor hall.

While the city waited with breathless anticipation for news about the all-star line-up for the opening, potential patrons were more concerned with the sound of the performance space and what it would look like than the food that would be served at the restaurants. With two restaurants, six bars, a bar-restaurant, a staff canteen and reception centres for two thousand people, the catering requirements were considerable. The Harbour Restaurant would be self-service, but the Bennelong Restaurant, occupying the two smaller southern shells, was to be the jewel in the epicurean crown. 'Spaghetti Caruso' and 'Hors d'oeuvres Utzon', journalist Janet Hawley joked in *The Australian*, would help make the menu sing.

There were no surprises when restaurant entrepreneur and refugee from Hitler's Germany Oliver Shaul was awarded the catering concession for the whole building. At the time he ran the world's largest revolving restaurant, The Summit, perched atop Harry Seidler's Australia Square, then the country's tallest building. From its opening in 1968, The Summit was considered the height of dining elegance. It was so popular and became so profitable that Shaul once boasted he could buy a Mercedes each year from the sale of garlic bread alone in The Summit.

But at the Bennelong he promised there would be no pavlovas in the shape of the Opera House nor Peach Melbas. 'It will be first class with table service and will seat 130 people,' he said. Significantly, though, he also assured the hungry hordes, 'We will make our own pies.'

Shaul hoped the eating facilities would become as much a part of the Opera House as the productions. 'Eating out is a change of experience,' Shaul said, one he hoped Opera House–goers would enjoy. Although the $20 price tag for a couple to dine there horrified a number of commentators, not to mention the cost of a dozen oysters ($2.75), a roast beef salad ($4.50), $5.00 for beef Wellington, $1.90 for a bloody Mary and $1.50 for mandarin cheese cake. But the real outrage came when the *Mirror* revealed 'No Draught Beer'; only beer cans would be sold at intermission from the building's bars.

It wasn't just the performing arts that would be on display beneath the giant white sails. Italian immigrant Franco

Belgiorno-Nettis, who had founded the construction and engineering company Transfield, suggested that contemporary art be showcased in the building that was itself a work of modern art. He proposed a Biennale of Sydney, modelled on the Venice Biennale, to encourage creativity and change the attitude of Australians towards contemporary art. With the support of other arts patrons, he assembled the works of thirty-seven modern artists and planned for these to go on display when the building was complete, now expected to be sometime in 1973.

• • •

When three-time Archibald Portrait prize-winning artist William Dobell died in 1970, a foundation was set up in his honour 'for the benefit and promotion of art in NSW'. The foundation approached the Opera House Trust with the idea of sponsoring a mural for the northern foyer of the building. Sydney artist John Olsen was commissioned by the trust to create the work.

'There had been more drama in real life at the Opera House than anything it would ever accommodate on its stages,' Olsen said. And it wasn't even yet completed. He wanted to make a work that reflected all that colour and movement, so turned to the sea and to poetry for inspiration.

Joe Lynch had worked as an illustrator for *Smith's Weekly*, a popular larrikin magazine published from 1919 until 1950. On 14 May 1927, having finished work, Lynch put on his overcoat and walked down to Circular Quay to catch a ferry. He downed a few schooners of beer with colleagues at one of the many pubs in the area before catching his ferry with a couple of bottles as a chaser in his pockets.

A drunken Lynch fell overboard near Fort Denison and was dragged to the bottom of the harbour by the weight of the bottles of beer in his overcoat. His *Smith's Weekly* colleague, journalist Kenneth Slessor, had been on the ferry with him. Deeply moved by the drowning, eight years later he penned his famous poem, *Five Bells*, about the tragedy. It began:

> *Time that is moved by little fidget wheels*
> *Is not my Time, the flood that does not flow.*
> *Between the double and the single bell*
> *Of a ship's hour. Between a round of bells*
> *From the dark warship riding there below,*
> *I have lived many lives, and this one life*
> *Of Joe, long dead, who lives between five bells.*

Moved by Slessor's elegy, Olsen decided to paint a mural based on the poem. He began work on the commission in a warehouse in The Rocks in September 1972. Using the brawn of the men who had once been William Dobell's muscle-bound assistants—Bob 'Human Bomb' King, a former wrestler, and Bill 'The Bouncer' Jackson, a strongman turned picture-framer—he set up the giant work he described as being 'not a job for boys'. (This was also the name of the ABC documentary about the mural.) He used a cobalt blue—the colour of a Reckitt's Blue Bag, a popular washing whitener of an earlier era—as backdrop for what at the time was the largest ever mural created in Australia and painted what he called a 'kinky combination' of other colours: violets, blues and greens, the imagined underwater world of a drowning man.

Later that year, the five pieces of the massive mural were moved to Bennelong Point in a removalist truck to be completed in situ. But the painting was defaced with pencil and yellow spray paint. Olsen accused workmen on the site of this desecration, telling them to 'piss off'. The workers shot back that the painting was so 'out there' it was hard to tell what was art and what was graffiti.

Olsen's *My Salute to Five Bells* was one of the major decorative interior features of Peter Hall's Opera House. It was a 'nocturnal mural', Olsen told Margaret Jones in the *Sydney Morning Herald* at its 1973 unveiling. With his use of phosphorescent colours, it was an artwork designed to be seen to fullest advantage at night, an undersea kingdom of fish, plankton and dead men. If you look at it today, says Olsen, you will still see the drowning man's reflection in the glass walls of the Opera House.

Olsen's blue painting fitted boldly with the purple carpet of the northern foyer. Hall's colour palette was of its time and reflected the primary use and mood of each of the Opera House's venues: from the Concert Hall's magenta wool-covered seats, to the Drama Hall's vermilion seating, the red leather of the Opera Hall and the charcoal grey of the cinema's woollen seats.

Australian wool was to be showcased in the Drama Theatre and Opera Theatre tapestry curtains designed by the respected artist John Coburn, a former ABC set designer. The two $90,000 curtains took Coburn less than a day to design, but more than three years to complete. Woven in France by Pinton Freres, the world-famous tapestry workshop created under Louis XIV, Coburn moved his family to Aubusson for those three years to oversee the project. There were early problems; in particular, fire- and moth-proofing the Australian wool affected its colours. It took six months to devise a system that worked satisfactorily. 'On the whole, the weaving went pretty smoothly,' Coburn later said.

The Opera Theatre's 'Curtain of the Sun' was dominated by a glowing gold sun fringed by abstract shapes depicting the earth, fire, air and water. The Drama Theatre's 'Curtain of the Moon' was finished in deep blues, purple, greens and silver, highlighting a shimmering moon and plant forms. 'When I was being shown over the Opera Theatre in 1969 I immediately saw in my mind what I wanted to do,' Coburn said. 'I could see all the colours of the sun in the design as I stood there. The Drama Theatre posed a bit of a problem, but it seemed to follow to feature the moon.'

Shipped from Germany, the curtains arrived in Australia at the same time as Coburn, who was returning to head the art school at East Sydney Technical College. Each curtain, which took six men to carry, was intended to be a major centrepiece of the building.

• • •

By 1972, the Sydney Opera House stopped being a myth people scarcely believed in. It was on its way to completion, and the whole world could see that.

Apart from the carpark, the only thing unlikely to be completed in time for the opening was the pipe organ in the Concert Hall. Electronics technician Ron Sharp, who had only built a handful of small (but very good) instruments in Sydney, was still toiling away to build the largest mechanical action instrument in the world. Ron had been nicknamed 'Arp' Sharp, after the famous German organ builder Arp Schnitger (1648–1719), whose instruments can still be heard in Germany and the Netherlands.

The building of the carpark was caught up in what would become known as 'green bans'. The Builders' Labourers' Federation leader Jack Mundey sought to protect the ancient Moreton Bay figs in the Botanic Garden the government wanted removed for the carpark it intended to build under the Tarpeian Way. 'We're not going to desecrate this area now for the greedy sake of present day expediency,' proclaimed the union leader.

There was considerable interest when the minister for Public Works ceremoniously lowered himself into one of the Concert Hall's seats on 5 September 1972 to test it 'provided the total visual experience', as the *Herald* reported. Tenders had been put out in November 1970 and by 1972 the 2690 seats made of laminated white birch had been fixed in place. They were the only theatre seats in the world with their own seat hydraulic anti-noise device (a seat plunger hidden in the left leg of the chair). The hall design used 'continental' seating (no centre aisles), which worked well in Europe where the spacing of rows was generous.

As Hughes was testing the seat comfort, technicians above were winching into place twenty-one large, clear plastic, lifebuoy-shaped Perspex rings known as 'acoustic clouds' suspended in the airspace above the stage in the Concert Hall. These sound reflectors were installed to give musicians instant feedback and were immediately nicknamed 'donuts' and 'giant Lifesavers', names that stuck.

Sydney Morning Herald reporter Lenore Nicklin was there that day for what she called the 'ministerial sit-in and donut display'. She wrote he tested the 'wriggle proof seats' that were claimed to be 'anti-squirm and non-slouch' and had been previously tested by 'ergonomic mannequins' to ensure they gave plenty of room for 'long Australian legs'.

'As you can see,' Hughes told her, his grey suit contrasting nicely with the magenta seats, 'the Opera House is in its final stages of construction. We expect to be handing over to the trust in early January.' Hughes continued to defend Peter Hall's work: 'Practically no plans were left for the interiors and those which were left were sketchy to say the least,' he said.

This was one of Hughes' last official duties at Bennelong Point before the announcement was made that he would take up the plum role of NSW Agent-General in London in 1973, a political reward by the Askin government. Leon Punch would be appointed as the new minister for public works to replace him. Hughes promised to return for the opening in 1973. At NSW taxpayers' expense.

• • •

In December 1972, Labor's Gough Whitlam won the federal election and became the new Australian prime minister, in the same month Hughes carried out his final official duty as minister for public works.

On 17 December the Sydney Symphony Orchestra performed in the Concert Hall to test its acoustic qualities. The orchestra wanted to play for the construction workers to express its gratitude for its new home, but a few days before the concert the workers voted to boycott the performance because 115 of them had not been allocated seats. The dispute was resolved when the VIP seats—those of state parliamentarians—were reallocated and over 2000 workers, many casually dressed, and their wives filled the hall. The only VIPs there were Premier Bob Askin, Minister for Public Works Davis Hughes, the Minister for Cultural Activities George Freudenstein, the former Minister for Public Works Norm Ryan and Peter Hall and his wife.

Hall had worked well not only with the staff of the Government Architect and Public Works offices, but with the construction workers too. They were happy to see the architect in the audience for the test concert. He had been popular and approachable. Wilf Deck of Arup's explained that Hall had much more of a presence and a more common touch than Utzon. One worker paid Hall what he considered a veiled compliment: 'We always thought you were a poof, but we like you anyway . . . You're an okay bloke.'

In July that year, Hall contributed to a newsletter, *Progress at the Opera House,* produced by John Yeomans, who by then was working at the Opera House. Hall wrote: 'If you think realistically about it, Sydney had a far better chance of getting a building much more resembling a Leagues Club than a piece of monumental sculpture on Bennelong Point.'

• • •

The test concert was held on a gloriously sunny afternoon. 'I have ever since thought of that day, and not the great season of September and October 1973, as the true opening of the building,' John Yeomans wrote in his book about the Opera House.

Dr Vilhelm Jordan planned to fire six gun blasts into the hall to test the acoustics. The audience and the orchestra had been warned that blank bullets would be fired and told to ignore them; the orchestra would play on.

The concert began fifteen minutes late. Under the moulded plywood ceiling panels of white birch, and the laminated walls and balustrades of reddish brushbox, the workers (many of European background) were entertained with familiar tunes from *The Merry Wives of Windsor* and Mozart's *Eine Kleine Nachtmusik.*

After Jordan fired his pistol six times, he declared: 'This hall will be one of the best in the world,' although, 'It would be unwise to say the best.'

The *Sun-Herald*'s Lindsey Browne and the *Sydney Morning Herald*'s Roger Covell were also invited to this concert. Browne, as opera and music critic at the *Sun-Herald* from 1948 until 1960, had followed the saga of the Opera House from the time Eugene Goossens had floated the idea of a symphony hall for Sydney. Plans to make a music hall were considered something of a joke in 1940s and 1950s Sydney, he recalled. 'But it had turned into a transcending vision to Sydney's conscience and many sought to convert this vision into a reality.' The 'fiddle fuss of the interiors [is] quite at odds with the simplicity of the Utzon-conceived exterior'.

Conductor Bernard Heinze sang the praises of the Concert Hall. 'Delightful in its resonance,' he was reported to have said.

Sydney Morning Herald critic Roger Covell wrote its acoustics were already more satisfying than London's Festival Hall. 'It had more bite and attack than the muddy echoes of the Town Hall. We may have a first-class Concert Hall or something very close to it on our hands. It is already clear that the orchestral works and showpieces of Rachmaninov, Debussy, and Stravinsky will be effective as never before. Music will be helped instead of hindered . . . it will be even harder now to put up with the Town Hall for the ten months before the Opera House's official opening.'

In the end, the Sydney Opera House, as completed by Peter Hall, boasted a 2690-seat Concert Hall, a 1550-seat Opera Theatre (with its plywood stained black), a 550-seat Drama Theatre, a 420-seat Music Room, a Reception Hall for special dinners and intimate recitals, plus five rehearsal rooms, a recording hall, two restaurants, several offices and a library.

All that remained was the official ribbon cutting, and for the people of Sydney to step inside.

• • •

Chapter thirty

Opening daze

The joke in 1973 Sydney was that the Opera House would have more openings than Dame Nellie Melba's never-ending farewells. The *Daily Telegraph* estimated every man, woman and child in NSW had each contributed about $21 to the glory of the Sydney Opera House, which it called the 'Eighth Wonder of the World'.

In May 1973 the NSW Department of Education signed a contract for sixteen major school concerts, making it prospectively the second biggest hirer of the Opera House halls in 1974, its first full year of operation. The Opera and Drama theatres were booked out until 1976.

The plaque that had been donated by Utzon and put in place by Premier Cahill in March 1959 was moved to a more prominent place on the steps of the podium. General Manager Frank Barnes, who had replaced the Brit Stuart Bacon as general manager, copped a lot of criticism before the opening because of the steep podium steps. When work had begun on the interiors in 1969, escalators had been scrapped for aesthetic and structural reasons. Barnes was forced to concede that at least five people had already been injured on the front steps—one suffering a broken limb—before the building had even opened.

Critic WL Hoffmann, writing in the *Canberra Times,* said walking from the concourse—the taxi drop-off area—up the stairs into the entrance foyer was depressing: 'toiling up those steps like the approach to a Mayan tomb was about as exciting as an underground railway station . . . It's a tragedy after so much time and money to have ended with this.'

On 15 July, it was dentists who claimed the first official function at the Opera House when Governor-General Sir Paul Hasluck opened the 1973 International Dental Congress in the Concert Hall. On 18 July, the Sydney Symphony Orchestra performed a specially commissioned symphonic work for the occasion.

The following day, 19 July, the Australian Ballet's *Don Quixote* film, starring Rudolf Nureyev and Sir Robert Helpmann (Australia's most famous ballet dancer), had its premiere in the Concert Hall on a screen that was raised from beneath the stage. Before the film screening, man-about-town Stuart Wagstaff compered a fashion parade. Helpmann gave away the 'Opera House Bride'—model Di Ward wearing a white dress inspired by the white curves of the building.

'A Di and Bobby Dazzler' is how the event was described by the *Sunday Telegraph*'s Maria Prerauer, a former opera singer turned arts journalist. Rushcutters Bay couturier Leon Paule had designed the dress in French fabric made by Lalonde of Paris. It was capped with a 'roof' headdress—each little shell topped with a tulle veil of its own. The bride's bouquet was a single Peace Rose, especially designed by jeweller Kenneth Mansergh and made from 80 to 100 carat white and brown diamonds on a 2-foot-long gold stem. The brainchild of Lady Mary Fairfax, the president of the Friends of the Ballet committee and wife of newspaper proprietor Sir Warwick Fairfax, the Peace Rose was estimated to have cost $250,000. The only bridal attendants were armed guards.

NSW Governor Sir Roden Cutler and Lady Cutler arrived in an open carriage and were greeted by Premier Bob Askin, Lady Askin and the prime minister's wife, Margaret Whitlam. An elaborate supper was later served. The *Herald*'s Lenore Nicklin described it as the party of the year for the 1243 'minked, sequined, turbaned, tiaraed people' there.

From the trumpet fanfare to the event's conclusion seven hours later, when guests danced cheek to cheek on the plush purple pile of the northern foyer, it was deemed a huge success. So successful that the organising committee members 'began to chew their nails for fear they would steal too much of the Queen's official thunder later in the year', Prerauer reported. It was in every sense a fitting dress rehearsal for the official opening on 20 October, to be organised by Sir Asher Joel, the Country Party member of the Legislative Council who was regularly dubbed in the media as 'Mr Organisation'.

• • •

Asher Joel's superlative event management skills had first come to the attention of the Askin government when he organised the controversial visit of US President Lyndon B Johnson in 1966. He then enjoyed enormous success in 1970, organising both the tour of Pope Paul VI and the bicentenary of Captain Cook's arrival on Australian shores.

The Opera House should have been called the Sydney Entertainment Centre, Sir Asher told the *Mirror*'s columnist,

Ron Saw, as he prepared for this much-anticipated event. 'We don't want only stuffed shirts and diamond tiaras . . . If they want to see a strip-tease dance there, or a pop show, or professional wrestling, then they should see it.'

Early in 1973, Joel had declared to the press that the opening would go off with 'a bloody big bang' of fireworks, pigeons and balloons. So, in the lead-up to the event, a call went out for recruits for 'the Big Flap', the 1000 pigeons that would be released at the same time as 60,000 balloons.

Roy Ryan of the Federated Racing Pigeons was nervous—the pigeon racing season would end only two weeks before the opening and he was concerned there would not be enough birds for the event. White doves were enlisted for the official opening, which became part of what was dubbed the 'festival fortnight'. The Opera House opening festivities combined with Sydney's spring fair known as the Waratah Festival that traditionally began with a parade of floats through the city streets led by the Waratah Spring Festival princess.

Coloured plastic overhead canopies (much like Ralph Symonds' wooden ones for the Queen's 1954 visit) were placed above the streets to celebrate the combined festivities. Over 1300 banners and 780 flags lined streets and parks from Queen's Square to Taylor Square, from Wynyard Park to Kings Cross.

Around seven hundred volunteers assembled at Sydney's Kingsford Smith Airport from mid October, handing out city maps and festival programs to welcome arriving visitors. In a show of inter-city rivalry with Melbourne—which until then had been always billed as Australia's cultural capital—the Sydney festival promised to be 'Better than Moomba'.

Melbourne's Moomba had established itself as the most widely recognised city festival in Australia, and one of its popular features was the crowning of the 'King of Moomba'. British actor Robert Morley had been the very first King of Moomba in 1967, and he now weighed in on the rivalry by dismissing Sydney's brand-new building as looking like 'a cement works'. He said it was folly for Australians to build such a monument to culture if they had nothing to put inside it. 'This is a most extravagant gesture and has nothing to do with the arts. You need it as much as we need the Concorde.'

'It's hard to know when Mr Morley has his tongue in his very fat cheek,' the *Sunday Telegraph* sniped back. On a later tour of the Opera House, the actor was taken into a theatre storage cupboard by mistake. He said its interiors were like the 'lower deck of a troop ship'.

From July 1973, Sydneysiders lined up in their thousands to take guided tours through the much-talked-about interior. They were no doubt reassured by the fact the shiny new building had plenty of ashtrays, eight public phones, and was air conditioned. While Utzon's early plans did not accommodate air conditioning, he soon rectified this, enlisting Danish engineering firm Steensen Varming to cool the building using seawater taken directly from the harbour. The system circulated cold water through 35 kilometres of pipes to power both the heating and air conditioning in the building.

The lack of carparking continued to create problems. Members of the Sydney Symphony Orchestra threatened to boycott the opening unless parking was provided for its ninety-seven members. Bowral motel owner Fred Von Nida tried to buy HMAS *Sydney*, the former flagship of the Royal Australian Navy, as a floating carpark but this idea was vetoed by Canberra. A monorail from the Domain carpark was also suggested to solve the parking problem.

And then the orchestra members discovered that the temperature in the Concert Hall was interfering with the tone of their instruments. They also complained that there were not enough rehearsal and tuning rooms and that the canteen facilities were inadequate and went on strike.

A shortage of stagehands in the building also threatened to disrupt the opening production, meaning each set change might take an hour to complete. The opera preview full-dress performance was called off because of the lack of stagehands. Around sixty members of the Theatrical and Amusement Employees' Association went on strike in protest and Actors' Equity sent a telegram to Premier Askin threatening that the Opera House opening might not go ahead.

The Bennelong Restaurant's licensee, Oliver Shaul, was losing around $800 a day as these issues were being resolved. A $1 park-and-ride system from the Domain carpark appeased both the performers and the public.

• • •

On Friday, 28 September, the opening season of the Opera House began appropriately—with the Australian Opera's production of *War and Peace* by Prokofiev. The official opening on 20 October 1973 was being referred to as the 'second opening', as many believed this 'first opening' would position Australia on the world stage culturally. The world's most important music critics were assembled in Sydney for the opening season, representing the major newspapers including *The Times*, the *Sunday Times*, the *Financial Times* and *The Guardian*, the *Los Angeles Times* and *Music World of New York*.

War and Peace went off with a bang—literally—with volleys of cannon fire exploding before the audience that included Prime Minister Gough Whitlam and over 1500 opera lovers who had paid for the privilege of seeing this first performance.

On Saturday 29 September, Australian conductor Charles Mackerras led the Sydney Symphony Orchestra in a program that featured the world-renowned Swedish soprano Birgit Nilsson as soloist. Visiting orchestras from Cleveland and Moscow would also play during the festival.

The next day, Sunday 30 September, Australian entertainer Rolf Harris starred in a variety concert in the Concert Hall, the first of the 'Sunday Night with the Family' series of concerts. He'd been flown back from London for the occasion. Support acts that night included Barry Crocker, Lana Cantrell and Normie Rowe. Other performers in the Sunday night series were to include the American comedian Carol Burnett, Welsh Goon Harry Secombe, and other British favourites such as Des O'Connor, Petula Clark, David Frost, Reg Varney and comedy duo Morecambe and Wise, all supported by Australian entertainers. Ticket prices of around $15-$16 were considered outrageously expensive. 'It was a rip-off and I feel terrible about it,' Carol Burnett even apologised.

Outside in the foyer concert-goers drank champagne and cans of beers for sixty cents a pop—expensive for the era. Performers were furious about the cost of food and drink, Lenore Nicklin reported for the *Sydney Morning Herald*. 'Do they think we are made of money?' tenor Donald Smith harrumphed, vowing to bring his own sandwiches and avoid the hefty 20 cent cost of a cup of tea in the Harbour Restaurant. Even more shocking than the prices, Nicklin said, were the electric shocks built up by static electricity from the Green Room's metal balustrades.

Musica Viva, the chamber music organisation, provided eleven concerts during the first season, two of them for children. The Old Tote Theatre Company—which had begun as the theatre company of Australia's National Institute of Dramatic

Art and was the precursor of the Sydney Theatre Company—
opened the Drama Theatre with Shakespeare's *Richard II.*

In the lead-up to the official opening, the Opera House
was referred to as the 'Uproar House' in some of the commentary of the day. Sydney, *The Australian* said, was divided into
two groups of people: 'The first lot is easily identifiable as the
anti-culturalists who regard it as a monument to poofters [sic]
who never have and never will patronise a live performance
unless it happens also to be a football final . . . The second lot
of Bennelong knockers are those who produce, direct, conduct
or otherwise provide muscle in the theatrical and musical
activities.'

What the organisers feared most was that the official
opening would be a fizzer, 'a failure like the eastern suburbs
railway', the political controversy occupying many newspaper
column inches at the time. Impresario Harry M Miller was only
mildly amused when he first heard the story that the Opera
House could always be listed as an entrant in the America's
Cup yacht race if the opening was a flop. In a story penned for
The Australian, he wrote it was time to stop the jibes and jokes
about the building, it was time for a 'fair go'. 'For a while its
patrons will be among the most hypercritical on earth. There
will not be a seat, an ashtray, or a rest room hot water tap that
is not submitted to the most stern and demanding evaluation.
Scented water will be expected to flow from its cisterns and
honeyed grandeur from everything on its stages.'

In preparation for the opening, the eastern face of the Esso
building on Kent Street was especially lit with horizontal stripes.
On Macquarie Street, five of the state's grandest buildings
were illuminated with 25,000 light bulbs. There were Opera
House-themed window displays at David Jones, Farmers and
Mark Foy's, the city's major department stores. Woolworths at

Town Hall was wrapped with red and yellow flags and Waltons was festooned in bunting. Every household from Cremorne to Kirribilli—on the northern shore of the harbour, across the water from Bennelong Point—was asked to turn the lights on to light up the harbour. There would be extra train services and over 1600 police on duty for the twenty-minute fireworks display from Fort Denison that was to follow the grand opening by the Queen and the Duke of Edinburgh. And three days before the official opening, the Opera House featured on a commemorative 7 cent stamp from Australia Post.

While the official celebrations were all being paid for by the NSW government (there was no contribution from the federal government), some of Sydney's rich list had started to make generous contributions to the building in the lead-up to its opening. Polish-born Dennis Wolanski, a survivor of the Warsaw ghetto, had migrated to Australia in 1950, making a fortune as the inventor of the Lido clip-on tie and then in property development. He donated $10,000 to a public fund for an Opera House Library of Performing Art.

The 19 October Opera House Opening Ball was hosted by Lady Mary and Sir Warwick Fairfax at Fairwater, their harbour-front house with its lawns stretching down to Seven Shillings Beach. A thousand guests, a who's who of Australia, danced among the family's collection of sculptures by Rodin and Degas. The party lasted until the wee hours of 20 October, the big day code-named 'Operation O' by the event organisers.

• • •

Over at Bennelong Point, workers began placing 10,000 seats and 200 cushions on the forecourt, from 4.30 a.m. Cleaners had been brought in to ensure the windows, tiles and granite steps were spick and span. By mid-morning fifteen army and navy helicopters and nine F-111s, the first Sydney display of this new strike aircraft, were practising to fly past in formation.

It was a sunny but windy day. Asher Joel, who dreaded the possibility of a downpour on his parade, was relieved. The Queen and Prince Philip arrived at Sydney's Kingsford Smith airport at 11.15 a.m. and were driven via the Town Hall to Government House in the Royal Botanic Garden, not far from Bennelong Point, to prepare for their official duties.

The harbour was at its sparkling best. Water craft had been out from the early hours to snag the best vantage points. On the harbour foreshores, spectators—some clad in bikinis or shorts—scrambled for the best vantage points. The hungry hordes bought 96,000 meat pies, one tonne of hot dogs, 2000 gallons of fruit juice and 150,000 cups of coffee.

Wearing a duck-egg blue silk dress and matching hat, the Queen was greeted at the Opera House with a trumpet fanfare and formally met by Premier Bob Askin and Prime Minister Gough Whitlam and their wives. Hughes had returned from London especially for the occasion. The Governor-General, Sir Paul Hasluck, was not there. As the Queen's representative in Australia, the protocol was that he could not be seen with Her Majesty in public. Instead, Sir Paul and Lady Hasluck, both distinguished authors, hosted a small literary luncheon at Kirribilli House, their official residence in Sydney. Invited to the luncheon were her editor, the distinguished poet and former bohemian Douglas Stewart, and the head of Angus & Robertson, former OZ editor Richard Walsh, and their wives. The somewhat raffish guests took turns at viewing the formalities through a large telescope the Haslucks had installed on their upstairs verandah, while offering a fairly acerbic running commentary.

Just after 2.30 p.m. Aboriginal actor Ben Blakeney, best known for his roles in TV shows *Matlock Police* and *Homicide*, got to play what he called 'the most important two-minute part of his life'. He was Bennelong, the Aboriginal man whose name is given to the land where the Opera House now stands. He told *The Australian* in the weeks prior to the opening: 'I'll be putting everything I've got into this one because I consider it important to our race . . . it's definitely got significance for Aboriginals because that was the point where they used to have corroborees. I hope my people will realise the importance of this building. White people may have built it, but the spirit of the Aboriginal still lives on the point.'

As Blakeney began the official festivities, half a million people watched from on the harbour and the packed fore-shore parks. Many millions more watched the opening live on television around Australia and the world.

'I understand that its construction has not been totally without problems,' the Queen intoned as she clutched her skirt and her speech notes to stop them blowing away in the blustery conditions. 'But every great imaginative venture has had to be tempered by the fire of controversy. Controversy of the most extreme kind attended the building of the pyramids, yet they stand today—four thousand years later—acknowledged as one of the wonders of the world. So, I hope and believe it will be with the Sydney Opera House.'

Asher Joel gave the secret signal, 'Anchors aweigh', and four tugs linked to the two peaks of the two biggest shells by sixteen bright red ribbons pulled away into the harbour. The ribbons cascaded into the harbour, releasing 60,000 hydrogen-filled balloons and 1000 pigeons. Instead of floating gently upwards, they were snatched up by the gusts and streaked off down the harbour and past the Sydney Heads out to the Pacific Ocean.

Emergency workers at nearby Sydney Hospital were on high alert. Threats had been made by Black September—the terrorist group responsible for the massacre of Israeli athletes at the Munich Olympics the previous year. The whole hospital was on standby that entire day. The operating theatres were empty, two complete surgical teams were in place, and the pathology labs, including biochemistry, haematology and blood bank, were well staffed.

'Operation O' was a great success, albeit very noisy. After the ribbons were cut, everything in the harbour from ships to small boats to canoes and surfboards took part in a 'two-minute cockadoodle-doo', making as much noise as they could to signify the building really was opened. A flotilla of 500–1000 decorated tugs and power boats and fourteen warships bobbed on a choppy harbour, as buoyant as the mood of Sydney.

The harbour carnival continued until nightfall. Finally, after sixteen years of sweat and toil, Sydney had something to show the world.

• • •

Inside the building guests queued to meet the Queen and Prince Philip. Engineer Ove Arup, who by then was Sir Ove, and his wife Lady Arup were presented to the Queen first. Next came architect Peter Hall in a camel suit, and his wife Penelope, wearing a dotted Marimekko kaftan that was see-through in the light, although she didn't know it at the time. Much was made of the fact that she hadn't curtsied, and that she'd committed the royal faux pas of telling the Queen they had met twice before.

Also at the official opening were journalists from around the world—from Chinese reporters sporting Mao jackets to Robert Hughes, the Australian-born *TIME* magazine art critic. He described the day as a watershed in Australian cultural history, although he also likened the interiors to the set of a Buck Rogers movie. The verdict of *Newsweek*'s reporters was that asking three architects to finish Utzon's design had been like 'asking three people to finish a Rembrandt'. 'Happy and glorious!' read the *Sunday Telegraph*'s triumphant headline the next day, reflecting the mood of Sydney.

That night's gala concert in the Concert Hall was an invitation-only black-tie affair. Members of Sydney's mink-and-diamond set were again out in force. Charles Mackerras conducted the Sydney Symphony Orchestra and Birgit Nilsson sang two Wagner arias that were broadcast live on radio.

A young cartoonist, Michael Leunig, had attended the afternoon opening ceremony with journalist Bob Ellis for the icono-clastic weekly newspaper *Nation Review*. After the ceremony they went to Chinatown for a meal and a few ales. With the courage of alcohol, they decided to return for the black-tie gala opening dressed as they were and still wearing their press passes.

Ellis, carrying a clipboard under his arm, easily passed himself off as an official. They went straight to the Opera House concourse, where a Rolls-Royce delivered the Queen ten paces from where they stood. She flashed them a knowing glare, the only men in the crowd not dressed formally for the glittering occasion. Nobody thought to question why they were there. They walked straight up the stairs and made a bee-line for the free champagne.

The opening, which ended with a dramatic fireworks display, was universally declared to have been one of Sydney's finest moments. For a total cost of $102 million—not the £3.5 million the quantity surveyor had taken twenty minutes to calculate in 1957—Sydney finally had its Opera House.

• • •

Noticeably absent from this glittering occasion was the man who had made it all possible: Jørn Utzon. On the opening day, cartoonist George Molnar penned a black and white cartoon for the *Herald* of Utzon walking down the stairs of the Opera House. 'Yesterday, upon the stairs, I met a man who wasn't there,' the punch line read.

On the day he was reportedly driving in Spain, the *Mirror*'s London correspondent, Leigh Bottrell, reported from Denmark. Locals in his hometown told the reporter they thought the Opera House was one of 'the greatest things a Dane has ever done'.

From the end of 1972 there had been speculation that Utzon would be invited and would attend the official opening. The myth developed that he had not been invited.

On 1 August 1973, at his home in Hellebæk, Utzon responded to the personal invitation he had received from the NSW premier Bob Askin. He sent a copy of his letter to his friend and long-time supporter from the ABC, Charles Moses, saying he was sad he could not attend the opening of the Sydney Opera House with him and their wives.

> Dear Mr Premier,
> Thank you for your kind invitation to attend the official opening of the Sydney Opera House on Saturday 20th October.
> Your invitation to my wife and me pleases me, and also it pleases the many architects, who worked in my office on the Sydney Opera House, because it proves that the government of NSW appreciates that nine years of hard work in my office has resulted in something good for Sydney.
> I am under great pressure from the press and also from some institutions and have received several invitations to visit Sydney at the time of the opening of the Sydney Opera House with the purpose of comparing

my project for stage III with what has been built, after
I left Sydney, and commenting on the removal of me as
architect by your Minister of Public Works and on his
alterations and reductions of the program of the building.

Unfortunately I cannot see anything positive in either
the actions of Mr Davis Hughes or work done by his team
of architects and engineers, so if I were to go to Sydney,
it would not be possible for me to avoid making very
negative statements, and as I cannot be the guest of the
Government of NSW and at the same time criticise one
of its ministers. I am sorry to say, that I therefore have
to refrain from coming to the opening of the Sydney
Opera House.

I sincerely hope, that the Sydney Opera House will
support and inspire the theatrical and musical culture of
your fine city. That was the goal the previous government
and its Opera House committee set for me, and that was
the goal to which I devoted myself completely in the many
years I enjoyed being the architect of the Sydney Opera
House.

With best wishes,
Yours sincerely
Jørn Utzon

Chapter thirty-one

Rapprochement

While to the world it may have appeared that the construction of the twentieth century's most recognisable building had made Jørn Utzon's career, in Denmark it pretty much ruined it. Returning home was not simple. Utzon owed massive back taxes and the controversy surrounding his dramatic departure from Sydney made it difficult for him to secure commissions. The project had pretty much bankrupted him. His accountant suggested he officially reside abroad considering he owed Danish taxes. He went to work in Hawaii, but harboured hopes he would return to Sydney to complete his building. Among his personal files of confidential correspondence donated by his son to the Utzon Centre in January 2018 was evidence that he had paid his annual fee in 1969 to remain registered as an architect in NSW.

The Danish Association of Architects made it clear he would never get a Danish government project because it appeared he had 'run away' from his duties in Sydney. He became reliant on foreign and private commissions. Notable among these was the dramatic Kuwait National Assembly Building that was damaged during the first Gulf War but later restored, the Melli Bank in Tehran and private commissions in Denmark, including Paustian House, a furniture store on the Copenhagen waterfront, and the Bagsværd Church commissioned by Lutheran parishioners in northern Copenhagen. This work, which he completed with his whole family in 1976, is said to be the interior that most resembles his plans for the Sydney Opera House.

He also designed the Utzon Centre with his youngest son Kim. Opened in 2008 and located on the Limfjord waterfront, the very place he sailed as a young boy with his brother Leif, the centre's 18-metre curving roof was built specially to accommodate one of his father's Spidsgatter boats, which shares a room with another Danish invention, tubs full of Lego.

Many other projects he worked on were canned: Zurich's curvy concrete-roofed Schauspielhaus, which Utzon had won the competition to build in 1964 and spent eight years working on, and the Jeita Grotto in Lebanon, which was cancelled because of the civil war. Utzon, always wary of strangers, became reclusive; some said he was depressed. Not a day went by when he didn't think about the Sydney Opera House. 'I have the building in my head like a composer has his symphony,' he told Australian journalist Geraldine Brooks in a piece she wrote for the *New Yorker* in 2005. As his colleague Oktay Nayman, the Turkish architect whom Utzon referred to as 'the fastest drawer in the west', would say later, he had great luck to build the Sydney Opera House, but it was a curse as well.

Post-Sydney, the family lived something of a peripatetic life—in Hawaii and Mexico, and then finally settling in Majorca,

Spain in 1972, after Utzon's father's death in Denmark in 1970. There he designed and built Can Lis, a beautiful house sculpted into the coast and named for his wife. It was the dream home he had wanted to build at Bayview—all vast vistas of the sea and additive architecture. Another house, Can Feliz, was set lower on the coast. The moves never seemed to faze Utzon. 'Home is wherever Lis is,' he would say of his wife, who not only typed all of his letters and diaries, but whose warmth, kindness and levelheadedness was considered by many to be the guiding force of the family.

His three children all became designers: Kim and Jan architects and Lin a ceramics artist. Jan still lives in the open-plan home his father built and is well known for his architectural work, as is his son Jeppe, whose minimalist Electrolux barbecue and unique furniture is renowned in the design world. Lin married her Australian boyfriend, Alex Popov, and lived in Denmark. They had two children, but later divorced. Their daugher, Naja, a designer/artist, lives near Lin in Hellebæk. Their son Mika, also an artist, lives in the Sydney suburb of Avalon with his Australian wife and family. His young Australian-Danish son is named Eero Utzon, in memory of the man who had chosen Utzon's magnificent, lonely idea out of a pile of rejects.

• • •

It took ten years, from 1969 until 1979, for the neo-baroque organ to be completed. Austrian organ expert Gregor Hradetzky was called in to help Ronald Sharp. Its initial budget of $400,000 blew up to $1.2 million and it was completed in May 1979, nearly six years after the Opera House opened. George Fincham, a Melbourne organ builder, called it an 'absolute public scandal'. Today it is claimed to be the most beautiful organ in the world.

The carpark issue wasn't solved until the 1990s. The idea for the unique underground twelve-storey double helix spiral carpark was sparked by a couple of beers between an architect and some engineers. It is nicknamed 'the donut for divas' because of its spiral shape.

By the time of the 1973 opening, Peter Hall had received some rightful praise for the speed with which he had so elegantly completed the building. It soon became the most beloved building in the growing city. Like Hans Christian Andersen's *Ugly Duckling*, it shed its fluff for feathers and learnt to fly. Ruth Park, one of Sydney's most beloved authors, called it 'a white swan in a land of black swans'.

'Sydney was tapped on the shoulder by a rainbow when it got its amazing Opera House,' Prime Minister Paul Keating later said, echoing the sentiments of many Australians. However, arguments about the quality of the acoustics and interiors continue to this day.

• • •

Peter and Penelope Halls' son Henry was born in 1974; and then in 1979 came daughter Antigone. Their father's post–Opera House chapter proved difficult for all his children.

During the course of their marriage, Penelope and Hall went 'boom and bust' several times. They lost their house in Mosman to receivers and both had affairs. The financial and emotional stress led to their marriage breaking up in 1981. He moved into a rented studio in North Sydney, while she moved with the children into a rented house in Cremorne.

Hall's daughter Becca, from his first marriage to Libby Bryant, fled Australia for London decades ago. His son Willy, now a builder, lives in the Southern Highlands.

After the Opera House, Peter Hall went into private practice first with his friend Jim Anderson. These businesses—Hall & Anderson, later Hall & Bowe, then Hall, Bowe & Webber—all folded. Hall did receive significant commissions from the federal government and was working in Canberra, but he became an increasingly isolated figure.

Fast cars and women were his weaknesses and he squandered money. He also began to drink heavily. Hall's financial acumen left much to be desired, say those who knew him.

Hall and his former sister-in-law Mary were in a relationship in the 1980s, 'when Mary came to work part-time for Pete in his office at Milsons Point chasing non-payers', Hall's daughter Becca recalls. 'This wasn't a secret and lasted a couple of years.'

• • •

Utzon's court case seeking payment of the $1.2 million in fees he claimed he was owed by the NSW government had been settled in 1971. His plans, along with about 5000 sketches and drawings, had been placed in storage by Bill Wheatland, where they would remain, largely unseen, until they were donated to the Mitchell Library in the early 1980s. Because of Wheatland's long commitment to Utzon, many still regard him as one of the Opera House story's unsung heroes.

Wheatland placed a ten-year moratorium on Utzon's papers being released. In the early 1990s Philip Nobis, a mature-age architecture student at Sydney's University of Technology, uncovered drawings that formed the basis of an exhibition at the Sydney Opera House in 1994–95 called *Unseen Utzon*. The exhibition was the undoing of Peter Hall. There was renewed praise for the perfection of Utzon's plan, while Hall's contribution was neglected and criticised yet again.

In March 1995, Lin Utzon visited Sydney, staying with artist Martin Sharp at his stately home Wirian. She presented the Opera House Trust with a model that had been kept with her former husband's parents for nearly thirty years. It was front-page news.

Ken Woolley came out in Hall's defence, as did Professor Henry Cowan and David Messent in the *Bulletin* (he later wrote a book on the Opera House). Davis Hughes spoke out from his retirement home on the Central Coast in support of Hall.

Hall had planned a press conference to correct the record, but by then he was unemployed, financially and possibly personally bankrupt, and unwell. At one point his children found him drunk and living on the streets, which had shocked and saddened them all. Hall wrote to mentor and former boss Ted Farmer, who'd originally chosen him for the Opera House job: 'If only this confounded nonsense about what happened could be finally scotched. Bill [Davis Hughes] has been doing his best but I feel he's feeling his age [then eighty-five] and is sick of the fight.'

Hall too, it seems, was tired of the fight. On 19 May 1995 he died of a stroke at Royal North Shore Hospital. He was sixty-four.

• • •

In 2006, forty years after they had worked together, Richard Leplastrier went to visit his mentor in Denmark. By then Jørn and Lis were living in a retirement home not far from Hellebæk. Leplastrier brought along his then teenage son Aero (named in recognition of Eero Saarinen, although his name was spelt the way it is pronounced).

'He [Jørn] looked at Aero and he said, "Aero, nice to meet you",' Leplastrier recalled. 'I had my hands on the table and, if you look at my hands, they're not the hands of an architect. They're a worker's hands, you know, like I've been in the sun. Jørn said: "Look at your father's hands. Those hands have won many regattas you know." And we all laughed, remembering our time on Pittwater. I didn't know what to say. So I said, "Aero, look at Jørn's hands. They drew the Sydney Opera House." Jørn laughed, he loved that.'

'Utzon believed in the future of Australia; what it could and should be,' the eighty-five-year-old Mogens Prip-Buus recalled in a long emotional interview from his home in southern France. 'I see the whole thing now—what happened between us and Davis Hughes—as a misunderstanding. We had a dream about the Sydney Opera House. Jørn was at least happy it was being used and that people loved it. But, honestly, I wouldn't be unhappy if there was a big earthquake that knocked it all down.'

• • •

Author of an Opera House book, long-time *Sydney Morning Herald* letter-writer and architecture lecturer at the University of New South Wales, Elias Duek-Cohen, had been campaigning for a 'rapprochement' with Utzon since the late 1960s. There may have been an opportunity for a reconciliation when Utzon's former legal counsel, Neville Wran, was premier from 1976 until 1986, although it was probably too soon. In 1985, Utzon had been recognised with an honorary Companion of the Order of Australia, but that had been about it.

But by the time Labor premier Bob Carr appointed businessman Joe Skrzynski to head the Sydney Opera House Trust in 1995, the same year Hall had died, the ground had shifted. Skrzynski believed a suitable grieving period had elapsed and he began talking to Leplastrier and Peter Myers, who had also worked for Utzon, about the most appropriate course of action. Skrzynski was invited to meet Lin Utzon in 1998 at Wirian.

This, he understood, would be a golden opportunity to explore how the trust and the NSW government might re-establish a relationship with Jørn Utzon. 'Like with the great cathedrals of the world, which have stood for 500–600 years, we wanted to ask his views on the design principles for anyone stepping into his shoes over the next 100 years,' Skrzynski said. The trust didn't want to leave anyone in the same position Hall had been left in in 1966.

Former journalist Evan Williams, who had attended the original sod-turning ceremony, now worked at the NSW Ministry for Arts. In 1998 he travelled to Denmark bearing letters from Bob Carr and NSW Governor Gordon Samuels offering to fly the elderly architect to Sydney first class—accompanied by a doctor, if necessary.

Williams remembers landing in Copenhagen and being driven to Hellebæk by Jan and meeting his father: 'Utzon sketched the Opera House for me. It was on the back of an envelope. "I'll frame this," I told him ... Utzon was eighty years old. He was totally with it. He was very genial and co-operative. But I knew he wouldn't come to Sydney—that it was a waste of time,' Williams said in an oral history recorded by the Sydney Opera House.

The following year, 1999, Skrzynski travelled to Europe accompanied by architect Richard Johnson, who had been appointed as supervising architect to oversee a project to conserve the Opera House. On his third attempt, Johnson met Utzon at his Majorca home and convinced the great architect, then aged eighty-one, to reconnect with the legacy of his greatest work. Utzon said he was too frail to travel to Sydney, so he sent Jan to oversee the development of the design principles.

In March 2001, in Sydney, Premier Carr greeted Jan Utzon, who was wearing the same linen summer suit his father wore to meet NSW Premier Joe Cahill on that first trip to Sydney in 1957. 'There I am, the political heir to Joe Cahill, in my office, and there he is, in his father's suit,' Carr recalled of this deeply moving replay of history.

In 2002, it was announced Jan Utzon would oversee the refurbishment of the Opera House under a set of design principles he would develop with his father. Architect Richard Johnson worked with the Utzons on the design of the Utzon Room, with its curved doors and sleek lines resembling the *sisu* roof Utzon had intended, and the refurbished toilet design. Carr, who calls Jørn Utzon the 'Einstein of Architecture', considers this reconciliation with the Dane his proudest achievement as premier. For years a handwritten letter from Utzon delivered in person by his son remained in a frame on Carr's office wall. Utzon wrote, 'To me it is a great joy to know how much the building is loved, by Australians in general, but Sydneysiders in particular.'

Not everyone was happy about this turn of events, however. Hughes confronted Carr about the re-engagement with Utzon. Skrzynski was also harangued in a 45-minute phone call. 'I did Utzon a favour,' Hughes told Skrzynski. 'He was like a dog you have to take out the back and shoot to take him out of his misery.'

Despite their differences, when Utzon heard of Hughes' death, aged ninety-three, he immediately wrote a moving message to his widow Philippa. His tone of forgiveness brought tears to her eyes.

• • •

Just as there was a rapprochement between the Utzons and the NSW government, so too there was a reconciliation for filmmaker John Weiley. He went on to have an illustrious film-making career. His film *Antarctica* grossed in excess of $100 million at the box office and he became a member of the Academy of Motion Picture Arts and Sciences. But still, there seemed to be little chance he would ever see his Opera House film again.

Then, in February 2012, an email popped into Weiley's inbox. 'Are you the man who made the Opera House film?' he was asked.

Sam Doust, a producer working on a joint ABC and Opera House-backed online documentary, was collating footage for the fortieth anniversary of the Opera House opening when he found a reject copy of the film in a BBC vault.

'It really was like recovering a lost child,' Weiley recalls. There it was, every frame, but without the soundtrack. He'd kept the original recorded sound-tapes in an old suitcase and spent hundreds of hours re-synching and updating the film.

Autopsy on a Dream, updated with its compelling back-story, screened for the first time, fittingly in the Concert Hall, for the Opera House's fortieth birthday celebrations. Weiley's friend and former housemate, Lin Utzon, was in the audience. It was broadcast on ABC-TV on 20 October 2013.

• • •

'He's an enigma,' Ove Arup said of Utzon in 1966. After their spectacular falling out, the two Danes never reconciled. Years after they had all worked together on the Sydney Opera House, Danish structural engineer Povl Ahm, who was an Arup partner and a mutual friend of both men, took Arup to Hellebæk hoping for a reconciliation. Leaving Arup in his hotel room, Ahm went alone to see Utzon at his home. Utzon refused to meet Arup. They saw each other just once, in 1978, at an awards ceremony in London where Utzon was being honoured for the Opera House by the Royal Institute of British Architects. The two exchanged pleasantries in public, but that was it.

Architects Walter Bunning and Harry Seidler never really reconciled either, continuing their professional dispute over Utzon until the end. Even at the Opera House opening, Bunning said because of Utzon's miscalculations, 'Sydney would have to build a real opera house in the next 100 years.'

In 1994 Prime Minister Paul Keating announced that the Sydney Symphony Orchestra and the other state orchestras would be taken out of the hands of the ABC. 'I wanted a world-ranking symphony,' he later explained, 'not a sheltered workshop of public servants.' He granted the Sydney Symphony Orchestra additional funding to increase its player strength, maintained its members' superannuation entitlements and supported international touring opportunities for them as a 'cultural export'. This cut the formal ties between the ABC, the Sydney Symphony Orchestra and the Sydney Opera House.

Keating was sixteen in 1960 when he attended Paul Robeson's performance at Bennelong Point. Decades later, he recalled that he had been studying Labor history at the time in the same library in the Queen Victoria Building where Cahill had called the first public meeting on the Opera House. Nearly sixty years later, Keating recounted enthusiastically his memory of the day: Robeson's deep *basso profundo* voice, his herringbone coat, the singer swiping away flies on his face as he sang for the crowd.

When Keating spoke at the 2006 launch of the book *Building a Masterpiece: The Sydney Opera House* by Anne Watson in the Opera House's newly restored Utzon Room, he declared: 'Somewhere in the Utzon head, there was inspiration for this. For his building is, without doubt, more art than architecture. Some creativity in that brain of his, inspired by nature, perhaps music or some set of passions, brought this conception into being ... Utzon's building, like all great art, never weakens. No matter how often you see it or from what angle you look at it or in what light it is cast, it always hits you in the heart because it is simply so great. It is without any shadow of a doubt, the greatest building of the twentieth century and one of the greatest of all history.'

When the book was first published, Anne Watson couldn't have agreed more with Keating. But then a mutual friend arranged for her to meet Peter Hall's son Willy, who suggested she look at his father's private papers. Kept in a shed on Willy's property in the NSW Southern Highlands, they hadn't been touched since his father's death. His mother had cautioned him against raking up the past.

These documents and diaries went on to form the basis of Watson's doctoral thesis and her 2017 book about Peter Hall, *The Poisoned Chalice*. They also led to an episode of *Australian Story* aired on ABC TV in 2016 that ended with a reconciliation between Jan Utzon and Willy Hall, sons of the men who had created the Sydney Opera House.

Like the Utzon and Hall families, the people of Denmark and Australia are in a way reconciled too. Denmark gave Sydney the idea for its most beautiful building, and Australia gave Denmark a princess, Mary, who will one day be its queen. Surely that's a happy ending worthy of a Hans Christian Andersen fairy tale.

And the people of Sydney and the Opera House? Well, that's a love affair that knows no end. As the country's number-one tourist attraction, it welcomes more than 8.2 million guests a year and hosts 1800 performances annually attended by 1.45 million people. Today the Opera House contributes $775 million annually to the national economy and is a more recognisable brand than Australia itself.

The people of Australia paid for it not with taxes, but out of their pockets through lottery tickets, which may explain the sense of ownership some feel toward the building. Three barrels were used for the lotteries. The first one disintegrated. The second is part of the Sydney Opera House archive held in the inner west suburb of St Peters. The third is kept in the permanent collection of the Powerhouse Museum.

While state politicians of the time kept up a constant complaint about the mounting costs, the country's most famous building had actually been paid for by the proceeds of gambling. Why worry about the cost, the *Daily Mirror* once asked, 'this is worth a nation'. And although $102 million was an enormous figure at the time, the consulting firm Deloitte has estimated its total social asset to be at last count $4.6 billion. The Opera House has paid its way many times over.

Although not technically an 'Opera House', Australia's 'Great Dane' retains the name. The minor hall used for opera has been renamed the Joan Sutherland Theatre. Recently refurbished, it still has only a seating capacity of 1500 people. In a twist that is 'oh so Sydney', a growing number of opera lovers are attending the opera outside the Opera House with the building as backdrop. In 2017 about 100,000 attended the opera at the Sydney Opera House, but another 50,000 attended the outdoor Handa Opera in the Royal Botanic Garden's temporary opera theatre on the harbour. It can seat 2900, almost the same seating capacity as laid out in the competition requirements.

• • •

Les Dés Sont Jetés (The Dice Are Cast), Le Corbusier's 6.5-square-metre wool tapestry, remained on the wall of the Utzon family home for decades. Jørn Utzon's personal correspondence with Le Corbusier shows he intended it for his home, but it is an example of the sort of work he would have commissioned for the interior of the Opera House. In 2016, the Opera House paid $415,000 to secure the tapestry at auction. Opera House CEO Louise Herron's excitement at the news reminded her 'of the feeling when my first son was born'. But the John Coburn showpiece tapestries, the Curtains of the Sun and Moon, have remained in storage since their removal in 1974. Their colours and patterns were considered 'too distracting' by theatre and opera directors. There are plans underway to bring back the curtains in the future. A test hang of the curtains took place in March 2018, with some members of Hall's family present. The family was moved.

The plaque Utzon brought from Denmark and gave to Premier Cahill for the 1959 'sod turning' is still at the bottom of the podium stairs. When the building opened, there was no mention of Utzon. The only commemorative plaque proclaimed the Queen had opened the Sydney Opera House in 1973 'in the presence of her husband'.

It took twenty years for a plaque to be laid acknowledging Utzon and how he arrived at the spherical solution. The plaque at the top of the podium outside the entry to the box office uses Utzon's words to describe the monument to architectural creativity and engineering skills. 'If you imagine a big ball,' he said, '. . . the ball could be divided like pieces of an orange,' thus ensuring the idea of the orange remained part of Opera House mythology.

On 10 March 2011, a plaque honouring Premier Joseph Cahill was unveiled at Bennelong Point. Journalist Evan Williams, who had been there at the sod turning, attended the plaque's unveiling with forty members of Cahill's family.

To date, Hall and his team's role in the creation of the Opera House has not been credited on the site, but an acknowledgement of his role is currently being planned. In August 2017, Anne Watson's book *The Poisoned Chalice* was launched in the Northern Foyer that his team designed. Watson's book was published by OpusSOH, a non-profit association established to acknowledge the contributions of Hall and the many others involved in the successful completion of the Opera House without diminishing Utzon's role.

In launching the book Louise Herron, who in 2012 was appointed the building's seventh (and first female) CEO, said the 2007 UNESCO World Heritage listing of the building refers to a collective creativity of architects, engineers and builders who contributed to the Sydney Opera House. 'The combination of talents, the great and nuanced and very individual contributions of so many people that allowed this incredible building to be built and some of whom are contributing to its renewal. And among the most important of these people was Peter Hall.'

From the other side of the harbour, the Luna Park face smiled benevolently on proceedings. Here was an attempt to give Peter Hall his rightful place in the narrative of the Sydney Opera House. Against the odds, he finished a building that had won praise the world over. A European idea completed by an Australian—much like modern Australia itself.

Epilogue

On 9 April 2018, on what would have been Utzon's 100th birthday, Denmark's Crown Prince Frederik visited Aalborg, Utzon's childhood home. He officially opened an exhibition at the Utzon Center as part of the architect's centenary celebrations. The centre's director Lasse Andersson promised that Prince Frederik would be 'Utzonised' by the end of the day.

The shipyards where Aage Utzon worked in this former industrial city 400 kilometres north of Copenhagen have long closed. As have the tobacco and aquavit factories that once made this northern city famous. It is now Jørn Utzon who makes this place famous. The Limfjord waterfront where he and his brother Leif used to sail, and where their father Aage created his wooden boats, is now home to a host of outstanding examples of modernist architecture. The Utzon Center is but one of them. Another is the Musikkens Hus where, on the birthday of the city's most famous son, a Danish documentary, *Utzon100*, was screened to a packed home crowd.

At the Utzon Center, surrounded by his family and royalty, Jørn Utzon's son Jan spoke movingly about his father. The mayor of Aalborg, Thomas Kastrup-Larsen, described Utzon as the most important Danish architect in history, who 'today defines a continent'.

A specially commissioned piece of classical music was played while the room came alive with Super 8 film of Utzon's travels and stop-overs on his many journeys from Denmark to Australia. There beneath the vaulted ceiling that took its inspiration from a Bedouin tent, I realised I had never been in an interior designed by Utzon; I'd never experienced the acoustics and the aesthetics. Later that night at a celebratory dinner, I was asked if Utzon would be as lionised if he had completed the Sydney Opera House as he had intended? Or was part of the reason for his enduring legacy the fact that he was a sort of 'James Dean' of architecture, whose idea died before his time? What if he had completed the building and had been criticised and condemned in the way Peter Hall had? What if the Sydney Opera House still wasn't complete? These questions took me longer to digest than the meal we ate of foraged food of the kind the Utzon family would have collected in their years living in Aalborg.

Later that week I visited the family's Hellebæk home. I felt I was walking on hallowed ground. I rode a bike through Hellebæk's forest, just as Lin had done as a small child on her way to find her father to tell him about the phone call from Sydney that would change their lives. I rode along the bike path on the North Strandvej from Hamlet's Helsingør castle to the tiny town where Utzon had his office. A bevy of mute white swans landed on the sea that stretched out to Sweden from this point. The wings of Denmark's national bird arced majestically

l gt 69

in a perfect curve as they skimmed the water. In that instant, I understood the inspiration for Utzon's Opera House's white curves.

At the Bagsværd Church in Copenhagen, said to be the Utzon interior that most resembles his plans for the Sydney Opera House, I recognised the *sisu* roof, the prototype of which had been created at Ralph Symonds' workshop. The stark white interior was so bright in natural light I needed sunglasses. I wondered how this very Scandinavian style would have sat in Sydney? The glare was the very thing I had just read about in the Utzon Aalborg archive. Sydney drivers were concerned the reflection of the building's white tiles would distract drivers on the Cahill Expressway. It was never a problem. Of course, Utzon had probably thought of this. Just as he had done as he built his house at Hellebæk in the middle of the forest, he no doubt watched how the sun rose and set at Bennelong Point.

And in that moment I tried to imagine the Sydney Opera House without the Peter Hall touches: the brilliant purple carpets of the northern foyer, the unmistakable Australianness of John Olsen's *Five Bells*, the Australian boxbrush woods, the magenta wool seats, even the donuts. I had my own reconciliation. I realised I loved the Sydney Opera House both inside and out. I used to think the story of the Sydney Opera House was a love story gone wrong. Now I see it as equal parts tragedy, equal parts triumph, with a cast of characters to rival any opera or Shakespearean play.

Coda

Long before Jørn Utzon even dreamt of his white sails gracing the shores of Sydney Harbour and Peter Hall was set the task to complete them, Bennelong Point had been a significant gathering place for Aboriginal Australians. Like the Coquilles St-Jacques, the iconic scallop shell that marks the route of the Camino de Santiago, the pilgrim route to Spain's Santiago de Compostela, shells have brought people to this place for centuries. Not only for food, but for drama, too.

Woollarawarre Bennelong, a tribesman of the Aboriginal Eora nation, was one of the traditional owners of the land that is now named after him. Dubbagullee, the small tidal area with a beach and rocks at the tip of the eastern arm of Sydney Cove, was probably separated from the mainland at high tide, but at low tide it formed a little peninsula.

In modern Sydney parlance, Bennelong was a 'westie'—a Wangal man from around Homebush—and his second wife,

Barangaroo, was from Cammeraygal land around Cammeray and North Sydney. Both had gravitated to Gadigal land, on the southern shore of the harbour where Circular Quay now stands. Barangaroo and Bennelong were the original power couple of Sydney when the First Fleet arrived in 1788. As respected Aboriginal leaders they were often invited to sit down and eat and drink with the Europeans.

In November 1789, under the orders of King George III, Bennelong was kidnapped to assist the colonisers to better understand the language and customs of the local people. He escaped from Governor Phillip's house on 3 May 1790, but subsequently returned peacefully after Phillip was speared in the shoulder by an Aboriginal warrior thought to be punishing the invaders for depriving Bennelong of his liberty. Phillip is said to have built Bennelong a brick hut on what became known as Bennelong Point. It was here, in 1791, that a group of convicts put on George Farquhar's *The Recruiting Officer*, the first play performed in the colony.

Thomas Keneally told the story of this performance in his novel *The Playmaker*, which was adapted by the English playwright Timberlake Wertenbaker as *Our Country's Good*. It was also referred to in the Queen's speech at the Opera House opening: 'This site was not only the birthplace of the nation, but also where the first European dramatic performance ever to take place in Australia was staged in a mud hut.'

Barangaroo died in 1791, the same year the hut was built, shortly after giving birth to a daughter Dilbong (which meant bellbird), who died in infancy. Barangaroo was cremated in a traditional ceremony with her fishing gear, and Bennelong spread her ashes in Governor Phillip's garden, which is now Circular Quay. A harbourside park and casino now take her name; while Bennelong Point, the land where the Opera House stands, takes his.

Aboriginal elders of the Eora nation believe a magical energy was released at Bennelong Point because it is where the saltwater of the harbour meets the freshwater of the Paramatta River. A confluence, just as Europe meets Australia, in the design of the building that stands there today.

Cast of characters

Arup, Ove: Engineer. Founded the global engineering company Arup in 1946 and the Arup Chess Company in 1975, both of which still operate today. After nine years of working together, then a major falling out, he and Utzon met by accident only once post-Sydney. He died in 1988, aged ninety-two.

Askin, Robin/Robert: His government is considered one of the most corrupt state governments in Australian political history. On the day of his funeral, allegations of corruption were published, detailing his long involvement with illegal bookmaking and organised crime.

Bertony, Joe: After the Opera House, he continued to work on a host of engineering projects, including the construction of Sydney's Roseville Bridge and the Pheasants Nest Bridge across the Nepean River. He turned ninety-six in 2018, and still lived in Hornsby. Sydney's Museum of Applied Arts and Sciences holds the copyright to the papers on which original mathematical equations for the erection arch were written. In 2018 he was honoured as a special guest at the Good Design Awards at the Sydney Opera House.

Blakeney, Ben: After starring as Bennelong's ghost at the Opera House opening in 1973, in 1977 he became the first Aboriginal Australian to join the Commonwealth Police. He was selected for the Cyprus peacekeeping force in 1979. He received a medal of honour for bravery in the line of duty and an Order of Australia for boomerang making, which he carried out from his home in Queanbeyan.

Cahill, Joseph: Premier of NSW from 1952–59 whose name is given to the expressway that visually garrottes Circular Quay. His eldest son was elected to his father's vacated seat of Cooks River and served as its member until 1983. His second son and namesake, John Joseph Cahill, served as a judge of the Industrial Relations Commission. Other than a plaque at the Opera House (which was often jokingly called the 'Taj Cahill'), a park at Wolli Creek and a Blue Mountains lookout are named for him.

Coburn, John: In 1974 the Australian Opera and the Old Tote Theatre Company pronounced Coburn's curtains of the Sun and Moon as too dominant for the Opera and Drama theatres. Coburn dismissed their views as quite absurd, but the curtains were removed and placed in storage in 1974, where they remained until 2018. A test hang took

place in March 2018, with the intention of a return to the building.
Davis Hughes, William: Without doubt, he was the most significant
political figure in the story of the Opera House. His press secretary
Tom Muir—who was ninety-three years old in 2018—believes that if
Hughes had been somewhat less combative with Utzon, there may
well have been a different outcome. After his resignation from
the NSW parliament in January 1973, Hughes served as NSW
Agent-General in London. He died on the NSW Central Coast in
2003 aged ninety-two.
Deck, Wilf: In 2017, at the age of eighty-two, the former Arup's
engineer embarked on a new career as a life coach. He swims most
days with Manly's Bold and Beautiful swim club.
Dusseldorp, Dick: After building the podium at the Opera House,
the Dutch builder went from strength to strength. As founder of
Civil & Civic, he turned building construction financing on its
head and created one of Australia's largest companies, Lendlease.
Grandfather of actor Marta, he died in 2000 aged eighty-two.
Farmer, Ted: The man who nominated Peter Hall, Lionel Todd
and David Littlemore (father of well-known silk Stuart Littlemore)
to complete the Opera House. Under his helm, the Government
Architect's Office won six Sulman Awards, two Blackett Awards and
countless merit awards for excellent architecture. He died in his sleep
in 2001, regretful to the end about the role he was forced to play in
this story.
Goossens, Eugene: When former student Richard Bonynge visited the
conductor near the end of his life, he found him 'absolutely destroyed.
It seemed he'd become half his size. He was also destroyed physically.
I believe that Australia destroyed him . . . He was pilloried by a very
insular society.' Goossens died in 1962 and left his estate, including
copyrights and royalties, 'to my faithful companion and assistant Miss
Pamela Main'. The ABC's Eugene Goossens Hall in Ultimo is named
for him.
Hall, Libby: Died in 2016. She was cremated with the school satchel
of her younger brother, Colin, who tragically drowned as a child. She
continued her love of colours and tapestries and stayed weaving at the
Sturt Craft Centre.
Hall, Penelope: Lives in Chang Mai, Thailand. She was present for
the March 2018 rehanging of the Coburn curtains at the Sydney
Opera House.

Hall, Peter: On his protégé's death in 1995, Ted Farmer wrote: 'The death of this man is a grievous blow to me . . . He was one of those most wonderful first group of men, who under the scheme originated by [Cobden] Parkes and Harry Rembert, were admitted to traineeships in architecture . . . Eventually, as all the trainees did, he resigned to enter private practice and began what would have been a fine career in that direction . . . Then the wretched Opera House affair came up and I had to choose a design architect who could replace Utzon. I then asked Peter if he would do this but warned him that the project would always be mixed up with politics. That it could lead to fame for him or the reverse, but without his ability I doubted if I could finish the place properly . . . After a great deal of thought he accepted. He succeeded beyond doubt . . .'

Haviland, Stan: Highly regarded in public service circles, with hindsight it was a significant misjudgement that his committee was allowed to continue running the Opera House project for as long as it did and with such lack of accountability. Having overseen the fluoridation of Sydney's water for the Water Board, he died in 1972, just a year before the Opera House opened.

Humphrey, Colin: As director of public works, his influence over Davis Hughes has been likened to that of Sir Humphrey Appleby in *Yes, Minister*. He had a low public profile but was considered the power behind the Hughes' throne.

Long, Martin: The journalist turned novelist and composer co-wrote with his film-maker wife, Joan, a book based on her film *The Picture Show Man*.

Molnar, George: He continued to work as the editorial cartoonist at the *Sydney Morning Herald* until his retirement in 1984. In 1968 he illustrated the bestselling book, *Sydney Observed*, written by *Herald* writer Gavin Souter.

Moses, Charles: The ABC general manager remained friends with Utzon up until his death in 1988. He enthusiastically took up wood-chopping in retirement and became vice-president of the Royal Agricultural Society of NSW.

O'Hara, John: *Sydney Morning Herald* state roundsman for twenty years, from 1957–77. He was mentor to many young *Herald* journalists, including Ross Gittins, who in 2018 was the *Herald*'s longest serving columnist. Gittins was introduced to his wife, Claudia, by O'Hara. He died in June 2018, aged ninety-one.

Parkes, Cobden: When he died in 1978, he was described as a man of character, charm, dignity, understanding and humanity, who had inspired 'affection in all who knew him'.

Robeson, Paul: Remembered forever in Sydney as the first performer at the Sydney Opera House.

Ryan, Norm: Served in the NSW parliament for over twenty years, most significantly as minister for Public Works. When he died in 1997, he was living on the Central Coast not far from his political nemesis, Hughes.

Saarinen, Aline: The former *New York Times* reporter and wife of Eero Saarinen went on to become an early pioneer for women in American morning television. In 1971 she was made head of NBC's Paris News Bureau, holding this position until her death from a brain tumour on 13 July 1972.

Saarinen, Eero: Died in 1961, aged fifty, of a brain tumour. He was a great architect but not the best of fathers. His son Eric came to forgive him, thanks in part to the role he played in the Sydney Opera House. Eric directed and co-produced a documentary about his father's work for the PBS series, *American Masters*.

Seidler, Harry: Died in 2006. His wife Penelope remained working as an architect in 2018 in the North Sydney office building Harry designed. The practice of Utzon's former son-in-law, the architect Alex Popov, is in the same building.

Souter, Gavin: The journalist who was there the first day Utzon saw Bennelong Point was eighty-nine and still living in Sydney in 2018. He has written several books on the history of the *Herald*.

Sutherland, Joan: 'La Stupenda' died in 2010. In 2012 the Opera Hall was named after this world-renowned opera singer. She donated the money for the statue of Eugene Goossens at the Opera House.

Thorne family: After the tragedy of their son's murder they moved to Rose Bay. Freda Thorne died in 2012 aged eighty-six, and was buried next to her son Graeme in Macquarie Park Cemetery and Crematorium. In his beautiful book on the tragedy, *Kidnapped*, barrister Mark Tedeschi says Graeme's father Bazil died of a broken heart in 1978.

Utzon, Jørn: Awarded the international Pritzker Architecture Prize, the world's highest honour for architecture, in 2003. He died of a heart attack in his sleep in Denmark aged ninety in 2008. He never returned to Australia to see the finished Sydney Opera House.

Acknowledgements

A month after Jørn Utzon's death in 2008 I emailed my old boss from *The Bulletin*, publisher Richard Walsh, to ask him if he thought it might be time for a narrative non-fiction book about the Utzon drama for a new generation. As always he brimmed with enthusiasm.

If I am the Utzon of authorship (over time, over budget) then he was my Joe Cahill, the NSW premier who always believed in the 'idea'. I know many times I got some serious Davis Hughes–style talkings to about deadlines and delivery dates, but Richard helped me more than anyone to understand the true meaning of the Finnish word 'sisu': to pull something out of yourself you didn't think possible. In my case it was writing a book while working as the *Sydney Morning Herald* opinion and letters editor and also while raising my son Liam on my own.

I thank Richard for entertaining me while editing my words, as well as for getting me in touch with Lin Utzon in 2009. 'It is too soon for me,' she told me when I approached her then. I thank her and her brothers Jan and Kim for all the ridiculous questions I asked, and for the generosity of their time. I hope this book helps them understand the depth of feeling I and most Australians have for their father . . . still. Mange tak.

I am indebted to Anne Watson, formerly curator of the Powerhouse Museum, who is largely responsible for restoring Peter Hall into the Opera House narrative as well as the non-profit opusSOH. I thank Anne for her introduction to Willy Hall, Peter Hall's son. His sister Becca, who lives in London, generously shared so much with me—most especially the fact that they were both for many years ashamed to say they were the son of the man who completed the Sydney Opera House. I would hope this is a point of pride for them now. Also thanks to their aunt, Helen Lo, stepbrother Henry and Henry's mother Penelope for their generous recollections of a difficult era.

In Denmark I thank the Utzon Center's Line Nørskov Eriksen, Lasse Anderson, Flemming Nielsen and Morten Byvald Pedersen, the man who helped me photocopy some of the documents in the eight-metre-long Utzon section in the Aalborg City Archives. At Nordisk Film Lene Borch and Anna von Lozlow for so much help, Prince Frederik for the invitation to see him launch the Aalborg Utzon exhibition, and last but not least and world famous in Denmark, my friend Jens Olaf Jersild.

In Sweden the Wiklunds, my exchange student family back in 1985 who were the first to tell me the Opera House tiles came from Sweden. Thanks to Lisen for the book about the Stockholm Exhibition 1930, and Kina for bringing it to Copenhagen.

In America thanks to my cousin-in-law Janet Frahm, an engineer at Michigan's General Motors Technical Center, who had all I needed to know about Saarinen's floating staircase; Eric Saarinen, who answered many questions about his father and the friends of Eliel Saarinen's Facebook group; Adrienne Harling, from the San Francisco Symphony Orchestra, and Teresa Conception, from the War Memorial Opera House. My American family: Gail Wilson, daughter of industrial designer Henry Dreyfus, who was an inspiration to Utzon, Evelyn Shaeffer and Peter Perez for minding my son while I wrote.

In Australia: the list is long but must begin with the Sydney Opera House staff, the ever-patient archivist Karen Stitt, Opera House CEO Louise Herron, Melanie Wellington, Brooke Turner and early advice from Matthew Moore. Janet Glover at Opera Australia and Caitlin Benatatos, formerly at the Sydney Symphony.

My Sydney sleuthing involved trying to track down anyone who was still alive who had been involved with the building at Bennelong Point. I had a strong sense that time was running out to tell their stories, that I may be the last person to get a first-hand account from these people who I knew were in their eighties and nineties. Two of them—John O'Hara and Waler Gibian—died the week this book went to the printers. I am so glad I got to tell their stories, as well as the stories of Joe Bertony and Wilf Deck.

Thanks to Bob Carr, Paul Keating, Joe Skrzynski and David Clune, for many years the manager of the NSW parliament's Research Service and the parliament's historian; they were all helpful in piecing together the politics of the era. All sorts of technical advice in their areas of expertise came from David Bidwell, Mark Abel, Hannah Merchant, Polly and Penelope Seidler, Rachel Browne, Cranbrook archivist Dominique Novak d'Hennin, former Cranbrook student David Richardson, Philip Drew, Peter McCallum, Caitlin Benatatos, Rayanne Tabet, Roger Covell, Ron McEvoy and Roger Szmitt. Thanks to the staff of the State Library of NSW, State Archives and the archives of the Art Gallery of NSW (formerly the National Art Gallery). Special thanks to Peter Kingston and his organising of the *Autopsy on a Dream* film night at his place and the introduction to John Weiley; Richard Leplastrier for a moving morning in his home in Lovett Bay.

I owe a huge debt of gratitude to the nameless hacks who wrote the non-bylined stories I spent weeks trawling my way through. So many times I laughed out loud at the headlines and the copy. Then when the bylines started to appear in the 1960s, many who covered the Opera House saga emerged as some of this city's finest writers—namely Gavin Souter, Evan Williams, George Richards, Peter Allen and John O'Hara. Special thanks to Tony Stephens, my mentor for many decades, for his recollections of covering the Sydney Opera House Lottery draws and gifting me his Opera House opening day souvenir liftouts. David Marr for his family story, David Salter for his extraordinary Eugene Goossens' reporting, Craig McGregor for his Peter Hall memories and Michael Leunig for making me laugh at his opening day antics. Richard Coleman, former Fairfax lawyer, for his George Molnar memories; and Damien Murphy, surfing consultant and the benefactor of some of the best stories in this book: the Peter Bowers upgrading letter and the exact location of the public phone used to make the ransom call in the Graham Thorne case. To my female journalistic forebears, Sandra Hall, Lenore Nicklin and Janet Hawley, and many others for forging the way: thanks. A posthumous thanks to Adele Horin, who I remember telling me about Dick Dusseldorp's good deeds. A newsroom is a repository of stories behind the stories, so to all my Fairfax colleagues past and present: thanks for sharing them with me.

The Fairfax librarians—Lyn Maccallum, Harry Hollinsworth, Stephanie Bull and Brian Yatman—who endured my jokes about the 'news from old codgerville', deserve a huge thanks, not just for this project but for the many years of behind-the-scenes help.

I used the Fairfax Sydney Opera House file, both personal and personnel, and kept asking my friends over at News Limited if I could borrow their old clippings files. No one seemed to know where they were until we discovered two cardboard boxes in the bowels of the Bauer building, formerly the Packers' Australian Consolidated Press Holdings, at 54 Park Street, Sydney. Inside were old photos and the newspaper clippings files; I even recognised librarian Kevin Schluter's handwriting. I felt like I had won the Sydney Opera House Lottery when I opened these treasure chests.

Thanks to my friends Rachel Knepfer for helping me sort through all the photos, photographer Louise Kennerley for helping me with the top 40, and Rosy Mobbs for always being available for coffee.

Thanks to *Herald* letter writers, in no particular order: Stewart Smith, Marie Del Monte, John Mann, Kevin Karp, Chris Johnson, Joe Campbell, Joy Jobbins, Peter Ryall, Peter Smith, Colin Booth, George Aungle, Brian McKeown, Fay Blight, Philip Cooney, Kersi Meher-Homji, Barbara Betts, Kevin Harris, Dave Horsfall, Michael Hayes, Jeff Coleman, Gordon Chirgwin, June Love, John Miller, Janice Creenaune, John Frith, Joan Croll, Daphne Roper, Paul Goard, Sandra Sullivan, Donald Hawes, Grey Fingleton, Allan Gibson, Anthony Healy, Lee Borkman, James Prior, Craig Lilienthal, Evelyn Klopfer, Thomas Muir and Diana Neale.

Long may you buy and love newpapers like you love the Sydney Opera House. As my very own 93-year-old deep throat Thomas Muir, previous press secretary to three public works ministers—Norm Ryan, Davis Hughes and Leon Punch—asked me once of the Sydney Opera House story: 'Of all the personalities: who is the one that remains most firmly in your mind?'

Please write to me at hpitt@smh.com.au and tell me who it is for you. Or at least tell me your own Sydney Opera House love story, now that you've read mine.

Yours, as that old Sydneysider Arthur Stace would say, in *eternity*.

Helen Pitt

Notes

Chapter 1   A phone call from half a world away

The opening scene was reconstructed from: interviews with Jørn
    Utzon's children Lin on 24.1.2017 and Jan on 9.10.2017 and
    subsequent emails; and the author's visit to the property in April
    2018. The Danish Weather Bureau confirmed it did not snow in
    Hellebæk on 29 January 1957.

The description of the interiors of the Utzon house came from: 'The
    Great Dane and his opera house', *Woman's Day with Woman*,
    18.2.1957; a radio interview with the Utzons by Karen Preben-
    Hansen; 'The perfect house', Patricia Scholer, *Woman's Day with
    Woman*, 9.9.1957; 'Jørn Utzon designs his home', *Sydney Morning
    Herald*, 1.8.1957.

The description of the Jones Street Broadway news room is from
    interviews with former Fairfax journalists including Gavin Souter,
    Evan Williams, John O'Hara and Peter Allen. For the details of
    radio telephone technology at Fairfax I am indebted to Peter Allen.
    There were no bylines in the *Sydney Morning Herald* in 1957, but
    journalists present remember that Martin Long made the phone
    call. Details regarding Fairfax employees in this book have been
    confirmed from their personnel files.

The interviews with Utzon in both the *Sydney Morning Herald* and the
    Daily Telegraph appeared on 30.1.1957.

The fact of Utzon's dyslexia came from an interview with Lin Utzon.

'I was the second dumbest boy in my class at school, only surpassed by a
    pure lunatic' is from Flemming Bo Andersen's website Utzon Photos.

Books
The Masterpiece: Jørn Utzon, a Secret Life, Philip Drew, Hardie
    Grant, 1999

Online resources
www.utzonphotos.com/about-utzon/about-Jørn-utzon/

Chapter 2   The young Jørn

The scene recreated from the Utzon Center in Aalborg is based on
    interviews with Line Nørskov Eriksen, 21.7.2017 and subsequent

emails. The boat-building research came from Thomas Arvid
   Jaeger, architect and professor at Aalborg University.
Information was taken from an interview with Philip Drew on
   23.1.2017.

Books
The Masterpiece: Jørn Utzon, a Secret Life, Philip Drew, Hardie
   Grant, 1999
Reconstructing the Stockholm Exhibition 1930, Atli Magnus
   Hubertsson Seelow, Arkitektur Förlag, 2016, courtesy of Lisen
   Wiklund
The Year of Living Danishly, Helen Russell, Icon Books Ltd, 2016

Online resources
https://utzoncenter.dk/en
https://utzon.dk/Jørn-utzons-maritime-origins-aage-and-Jørn-utzon/

Chapter 3   Scandi-style
The descriptions of Copenhagen are from the author's visit.
Information on how his parents met and the couple's wartime
   recollections are from Jan Utzon.
The Danny Kay anecdote is from an interview with Danish journalist
   Jens Olaf Jersild in July 2017.
The importance of Stockholm to Utzon is from an interview with Line
   Nørskov Eriksen on 21.7.2017.
The descriptions of Gamla Stan, Stockholm are from the author's
   diaries of 1985 and 1986.

Books
The Masterpiece: Jørn Utzon, a Secret Life, Philip Drew, Hardie
   Grant, 1999

Online resources
Guide to Utzon: www.utzonphotos.com/about-utzon/prolog/
https://utzoncenter.dk/en

Chapter 4   The mastermind
Eugene Goossens' United Nations performance was pieced together
   using records from the *San Francisco Chronicle* and the archives
   at the Civic Center and War Memorial Opera House, both in San
   Francisco.

Books
The Strange Case of Eugene Goossens and Other Tales from the Opera House, Ava Hubble, Collins Publishers Australia, 1988.
The Saga of Sydney Opera House, Peter Murray, Spon Press, 2004
Belonging: A memoir, Renee Goosens, ABC Books, 2003

Online resources
Opera House project, http://theoperahouseproject.com/#!/
    concept-design-architecture/chapter-1
Google cultural institute, https://artsandculture.google.com/partner/
    sydney-opera-house
http://adb.anu.edu.au/biography/goossens-sir-eugene-aynsley-10329

Chapter 5   The ordinary Joe who gave Sydney its Opera House
For their Tivoli reminiscences I am indebted to both Richard Walsh
    and Andrew Andersons.
Assorted reports on Goossens' spat with the government were accessed
    in Fairfax newspaper clips from the Fairfax files.
Peter Hall's recollections of his boarding school, Cranbrook, are from
    a letter sent to his grandmother that was written in 1942 (courtesy
    of Willy Hall).
Information on Utzon's travels to Morocco is from an interview with
    Line Nørskov Eriksen on 21.7.2017.
Information on Utzon's travels to the United States (notably the
    Studebaker story) is from interviews with Jan Utzon.
Information on Utzon's visit to Frank Lloyd Wright is from Rayyane
    Tabet's performance of *Dear Mr Utzon* in the Sydney Opera House
    as part of the 2018 Biennale.
Descriptions of Oaxaca are from a visit there in January 2001,
    recorded in the author's diary.
Utzon's travel diaries of the trip were reprinted in *RUM* magazine,
    Denmark, April 2018.
The background on Joe Cahill is from an interview with former New
    South Wales parliament historian David Clune.
The meeting between Goossens and Cahill is described in Murray's
    book.Details on the five-member government committee are from
    Sydney Morning Herald files and were confirmed by Tom Muir,
    former press secretary to William Davis Hughes.

Books

The Strange Case of Eugene Goossens and Other Tales from the Opera House, Ava Hubble, Collins Publishers Australia, 1988, p. 56

The Saga of Sydney Opera House, Peter Murray, Spon Press, 2004

Jørn Utzon: Drawings and Buildings, Michael Asgaard Andersen, Princeton Architectural Press, 2013

The Premiers of New South Wales, David Clune, the Cahill chapter, vols 1 and 2, The Federation Press, 2006

Online resources
https://www.sydneysymphony.com/about-us/history/our-history

Chapter 6   The magnificent lonely idea

Information on illustrator George Molnar is from Fairfax's personnel file and Richard Coleman, 2017.

Tram information is from Demolished Sydney, Museum of Sydney exhibit 2017.

Information on Joe Cahill is from David Clune, former NSW parliament librarian. Also thanks to interviews with Bob Carr, John Wilkinson and Rod Cavalier.

Information on speakers at the 1954 library meeting is from Messent's book. It was confirmed by *Sydney Morning Herald* newspaper clippings.

Information on the first committee meeting is from the Art Gallery of New South Wales archives and the Messent book.

The Ingham Ashworth information is from an interview with Philip Drew.

The international versus national debate is from the *Sydney Morning Herald,* 1955 and the Watson, Murray and Messent books.

Books

Building a Masterpiece: The Sydney Opera House, ed. Anne Watson, Powerhouse Publishing, 2006

They Called Him Old Smoothy: John Joseph Cahill, Peter Golding, Australian Scholarly Publishing, 2009

Opera House Act One, David Messent, David Messent Photography, 1997

The Saga of Sydney Opera House, Peter Murray, Spon Press, 2004

Chapter 7   Sex, magic and the maestro

For this chapter I am indebted to: the research of journalist David
    Salter and his article 'The Conservatorium director and the witch',
    Good Weekend, 3.7.99; Detective Bert Trevenar, who kept his
    1956 record of interview in his Ashfield garage until Mr Salter
    tracked him down over 40 years later; journalist Damien Murphy
    for his insights into the era; and Adam Shand for his insights into
    his grandfather, Goossens' counsel Jack Shand.

'"It is difficult to imagine a worse case," Mr JD Holmes QC said'
    comes from details of the day in court recorded in 'Goossens'
    "Guilty Plea" to customs charge: fined', *Sydney Morning Herald*,
    23.3.56. The list of obscene material is also from this story.

Information about Lady Marjorie in France was reported in the *Daily
    Mirror* in 1956.

Information was taken from the letters page of the *Sydney Morning
    Herald*, March 1956.

There are conflicting accounts about the number of entries received for
    the Sydney Opera House competition. The Opera House usually
    says over 230.

Notes were taken from the 'Brown Book', a booklet published by the
    New South Wales government, 1956.

Books
Building a Masterpiece: The Sydney Opera House, ed. Anne Watson,
    Powerhouse Publishing, 2006.

Online resources
https://www.smh.com.au/lifestyle/the-conservatorium-director-and-the-
    witch-20150702-gi3h8y.html

Chapter 8   Gentlemen, here is your opera house

The portrait of Aline Louchheim is from various sources including the
    New York Times and *TIME* magazine, 1954.

The background to Eliel Saarinen is from a 1948 profile Aline
    Louchheim wrote for the *New York Times* magazine, in the Fairfax
    library.

Information was taken from an interview with Eero Saarinen's film-
    maker son Eric in March 2017.

A conversation between *The Sun* journalist John Yeomans and
    Cobden Parkes not long after the judging is recorded in Yeoman's

book. The account of their walk through the Royal Botanic Garden comes from Yeomans.

According to Philip Drew, Saarinen was a master of the late arrival, letting others do the difficult work of culling while he took all the glory in the decision. He also did this in the decision-making process for the Toronto City Hall.

Information on Saarinen's stutter came from ABC recordist Warwick Macaffrey, as told to journalist John Yeomans.

Books

The Other Taj Mahal: What happened to the Sydney Opera House, John Yeomans, Longmans Australia, 1968

Online resources

http://theoperahouseproject.com/ie/transcripts/The-Year-Of-Competition.html

On the Saarinens, https://www.youtube.com/watch?v=Jd3PS-CO6l4

https://www.pbs.org/video/american-masters-aline-louchheim-and-eero-saarinen/

Eric Saarinen's movie *Eero Saarinen: The Architect Who Saw the Future,* https://www.imdb.com/title/tt5657112/plotsummary?ref_=tt_ov_pl

Henry Ingham Ashworth's movie *Design 218,* https://www.imdb.com/title/tt6892516/?ref_=nm_knf_t1

Daryl Dellora's *The Edge of the Possible,* https://www.imdb.com/title/tt1529339/

Chapter 9   And the winner is . . .

The description of the Art Gallery is by the author. Information on the preparation for the competition comes from the Art Gallery of New South Wales archives and correspondence from director Hal Messingham.

Information was gathered from newspapers in the days after 29.1.1957. Weather information comes from newspapers of that week.

Information on Kronborg Castle came from a visit by the author in July 2017.

Books

Opera House Act One, David Messent, David Messent Photography, 1997

The Other Taj Mahal: What happened to the Sydney Opera House,
   John Yeomans, Longmans Australia, 1968

Online resources
https://pidgeondigital.wordpress.com/2016/03/06/
   Jørn-utzon-louis-kahn-sydney-opera-house/

Chapter 10   Poetry or pastry?

The Harry Seidler information is from: his personal file in the Fairfax
   Library and the Seidler/Utzon archive; interviews with his wife
   Penelope and former business partner Colin Griffiths; and extensive
   emails from his daughter Polly Seidler.
The response from Walter Bunning was reported in the *Sydney
   Morning Herald*, 29.1.1957.
Reflections of the party in Denmark are from an interview with
   Ronald McKie about Utzon's first visit to Sydney in August 1957
   published in the *Women's Weekly,* and from the Utzon family.
Charles Moses' reflections are from his oral history, which is kept at
   the Sydney Opera House.
The reactions from readers to Utzon's design are from the letters page
   in the *Sydney Morning Herald* from 30.1.1957 to 2.2.1957.
The debate between Bunning and Utzon is recorded in the Seidler/
   Utzon archive.
Potential Opera House names come from both the *Sydney Morning
   Herald* and the *Women's Weekly*.
The Ove Arup information is from the Michael Moy book and an
   interview with long-time Column 8 editor and journalist George
   Richards in 2017.
The information on Joe Cahill is from Troy Bramston's story on Joe
   Cahill, *The Australian*, 13.10.2013.
Information on Utzon is from the Messent and Watson books.
Information on the ALP conference has been pieced together from
   extensive research of newspaper reports from May to September
   1957.

Books
The Poisoned Chalice: Peter Hall and the Sydney Opera House, Anne
   Watson, opusSOH, 2017
Sydney Opera House: Idea to icon, Michael Moy, Alpha Orion Press,
   2012

Opera House Act One, David Messent, David Messent Photography, 1997

Building a Masterpiece: The Sydney Opera House, ed. Anne Watson, Powerhouse Publishing, 2006

Online resources
Interview with Charles Moses on Radio National, http://www. abc.net.au/radionational/programs/archived/verbatim/ sir-charles-moses/2997606

Chapter 11   Bennelong pointers
The descriptions of Utzon's first visit to Australia came from the *Sydney Morning Herald*, *Daily Telegraph*, *Women's Weekly* and *Woman's Day* from July/August 1957, as well as extensive interviews with former *Herald* journalist Gavin Souter in 2017 and 2018.

For the anecdote about Utzon's first meeting with Cahill I thank Richard Leplastrier, interview at Lovett Bay on 29.11.2017.

Chapter 12   Kiss and sell
For the anecdote about Cahill I am indebted to David Clune and his interviews with Harry Jensen, 27.10.1987 and 23.6.1992.

For the account of the activity in the Sydney Town Hall on 7 August I have relied on two *Sydney Morning Herald* stories: '235,000 raised for Opera House in one hour after launching of Appeal' and 'Kisses earn 295 pounds for Opera House', both 8.8.1957.

The letter from Lis Utzon sent to her husband in Sydney in 1957 is in the Utzon Center in Aalborg.

Information on the lotteries is from NSW Lotteries. The story of the first winner of the Opera House Lottery was published in the *Sydney Morning Herald* on 11.1.1958.

Online resources
The letters between Utzon and Le Corbusier, http:// www.fondationlecorbusier.fr/corbuweb/morpheus. aspx?sysName=home&sysLanguage=fr-fr&sysInfos=1; https://www.pidgeondigital.com/talks/sydney-opera-house/

Lottery information, https://www.lottoland.com.au/magazine/history-of-the-australian-lotteries.html

Chapter 13   With a little bit of bloomin' luck

Ove Arup information compiled from his Fairfax library file.

For information about the relationship between Le Corbusier and Utzon I thank journalist Luke Slattery and his excellent piece published in the *Financial Review Magazine*, 'Le Corbusier tapestry The Dice Are Cast comes home to Sydney Opera House', 25.2.2016.

The report of the signing of the contract with Dick Dusseldorf appeared in both the *Sydney Morning Herald* and the *Daily Telegraph*.

In describing the sod turning I am indebted to Evan Williams' report 'Parties united over opera, says Cahill', *Sydney Morning Herald*, 3.3.1959 and his oral report. Details about the police band music and general tone of the event have come from Column 8 and the article 'Women envied Mrs Utzon's cool comfortable feet', both 3.3.1959.

Messages from politicians were recorded in the commemorative book for the 1959 opening, kept in the Fairfax library files.

Online resources

http://www.afr.com/brand/afr-magazine/le-corbusier-tapestry-the-dice-are-cast-comes-home-to-sydney-opera-house-20160112-gm46rm

http://www.fondationlecorbusier.fr/corbuweb/morpheus.aspx?sysName=home&sysLanguage=fr-fr&sysInfos=1

Chapter 14   A mini Greek tragedy

The Peter Hall information is from records of the University of Sydney (he graduated in May 1957 and 1958).

The Libby Bryant information is from interviews with her sister Helen, daughter Becca and son Willy.

The letter from Libby Bryant was published thanks to Becca Hall. Information on their time in Greece comes from Watson's book.

The account of Cahill's death has been pieced together from newspaper stories, notably the *Sun-Herald*, 25.10.1959, as well as interviews with David Clune and Bob Carr and Golding's book.

The Arup information is from *The Australian Dictionary of Biography* and the Opera House project.

Books

The Prince and the Premier, David Hickie, Angus & Robertson 1985

The Poisoned Chalice: Peter Hall and the Sydney Opera House, Anne
   Watson, opusSOH, 2017
They Called Him Old Smoothy: John Joseph Cahill, Peter Golding,
   Australian Scholarly Publishing, 2009
The Australian Dictionary of Biography, Australian National
   University, various years and online
The Masterpiece: Jørn Utzon, a Secret Life, Philip Drew, Hardie
   Grant, 1999
The Saga of Sydney Opera House, Peter Murray, Spon Press, 2004,
   pp. 32-3

Chapter 15   Rising up to the Aztec gods
The information on Dick Dusseldorf is from Adele Horin, Lend Lease
   and Wikipedia.
Paul Robeson's the 'Cosmic belch quote' is from the *Sydney Morning
   Herald* review of his performance at Paddington Town Hall in
   November 1960.
Details of the day are from an interview with former prime minister
   Paul Keating in 2017 and recollections of a *Sydney Morning Herald*
   letter writer, Brian McKeown, then a 15 year old from Forbes.

Books
Kidnapped: The Crime that Shocked the Nation, Mark Tedeschi,
   Simon and Schuster, 2016

Online resources
Robeson singing at the Sydney Opera House, https://www.youtube.
   com/watch?v=Eg7bPgrosAE
'Builder's vision saw Sydney grow and fortune shared', Adele Horin,
   Sydney Morning Herald, 23.10.02, https://www.smh.com.au/article
   s/2002/10/22/1034561495736.html

Chapter 16   The spherical solution
The Yuzo Mikami and Jon Lundberg information is from Line
   Nørskov Eriksen. THe Oktay Nieman quote is from the movie
   Utzon100, which will premiere in Sydney in October 2018.
The pre-stressed concrete information is from an interview with Arup's
   civil engineer Wilf Deck in 2016.
The Mulberry Harbours information is from http://www.engineering-
   timelines.com/timelines.asp.

All three Utzon children, Jan, Lin and Kim, and his grandson Mika
    confirm the orange idea was a way to explain the geometry
    underpinning the design, not an inspiration. Sigfried Giedeon,
    writing in *Architectural Digest*, is one of the first to confirm Utzon
    came up with the spherical solution.
Jan Utzon remembers burning the Sydney Opera House models in a
    bonfire before leaving for Sydney.
Information was taken from a paper by John Cochrane from the
    Faculty of Architecture at the University of Newcastle.

Books
The Saga of Sydney Opera House, Peter Murray, Spon Press, 2004,
    pp. 28-9
*Utzon's Sphere: Sydney Opera House – How it was designed and
    built*, Yuzo Mikami, Shokokusha Tokyo, 2001
Building a Masterpiece: The Sydney Opera House, ed. Anne Watson,
    Powerhouse Publishing, 2006

Online resources
Ralph Symonds, http://anzasca.net/wp-content/uploads/2014/08/
    ANZASCA-1998-Cochrane-SydneyOperaHouse.pdf

Chapter 17   The end of a romance
The opening scene is from 'I'm crazy to build it', interview with
    Graham Gambie published in *The Sun*, 4.11.1962.
Information was gathered during several interviews with David Marr
    in 2017 and from his book *Patrick White Letters*.
The flight to Sydney was constructed thanks to *Sydney Morning
    Herald* reports and recollections of Jan Utzon. Recollections of her
    early days in Sydney are from interviews with Lin and Lin's opinion
    piece published in the *Sydney Morning Herald*, 20.10.2013.
    Information also came from the catalogue introduction for the
    exhibition, 'Utzon's Opera House: Australian artists inspired by
    Sydney's architectural icon'.
The *Sydney Morning Herald* story was published 7.3.1963 and
    described as an example of 'outstanding reporting'.
Information was taken from 'Boom in Bayview Heights', *Sydney
    Morning Herald*, 13.1.1963.
Lin Uzton's 'white elephant quote' came from an article by Peter Grose
    in the *Daily Mirror*, 2.5.1963.

Barry Brennan's story on his 1964 interview was reprinted in *The Sun* in March 1966.
The family life information on Utzon is from an interview with Philip Drew, 23.1.2017.
The letter from Michael Lewis to Jack Zunz was published courtesy of his estate and Arups.

Books
Patrick White Letters, ed. David Marr, The University of Chicago Press, 1996
Patrick White: A life, David Marr, Vintage, 1992
Utzon's Sphere: Sydney Opera House – How it was designed and built, Yuzo Mikami, Shokokusha Tokyo, 2001

Online resources
http://theoperahouseproject.com

Chapter 18 The arch that changed the world
Information was taken from 'Dress rehearsals for the sail erection', Margaret Jones, *Sun-Herald*, 24.3.63.
The Jack Zunz story came from the Opera House Project and newspaper reports of 1963.
Peter Meyer's recollection of when the plywood forms were removed from the concrete are from Geraldine Brooks' article 'Unfinished Business', *New Yorker*, 9.10.2005.
Construction information came from various interviews in 2016/17 with Wilf Deck, Joe Bertony and Walter Gibeon, and a booklet in the SOH archives, 'A Guide to the Sydney Opera House', Government Printers, 1971, 1972, 1973.
The information on Symonds, Peter Miller and floating barges is from interviews with Richard Leplastrier, 19.11.2017 and with Mogens Prip-Buus in the south of France in 2017; also from Prip-Buus' book.
The information on the business name Utzon and Lis used to purchase their land in Bayview is from the Utzon archive.
The story and pictures of Joanna Collard and Lin Utzon quoting Libby Hall are from *The Sun*, 25.10.1965.
The quote 'Utzon's fate was sealed . . .' is from his assistant, Bill Wheatland.

Books

The Other Taj Mahal: What happened to the Sydney Opera House,
John Yeomans, Longmans Australia, 1968

*Letters from Sydney: The Sydney Opera House saga seen through the
eyes of Utzon's chief assistant Mogens Prip-Buus*, Mogens Prip-
Buus, Edition Bløndal, 2000

Additive Architecture – Jørn Utzon (a collection of articles), ed. L.
Davidseb, SS Kirkefeldt, 1988

Jørn Utzon: The architect's universe, ed. Michael Juul Holm,
Louisiana Museum of Modern Art, 2004

The Poisoned Chalice: Peter Hall and the Sydney Opera House, Anne
Watson, opusSOH, 2017

Online resources

Winifred Atwell's performance, https://www.youtube.com/
watch?v=mT-E1jKT2QQ

Chapter 19   Plain sailing

Information was taken from interviews with Lin and Jan Utzon and
with John Weiley in 2016, and from a film night at Peter Kingston's
house in 2016.

Information about: the site tour is from Gavin Souter; Jillian
Robertson's party is from various newspaper sources as noted as
well as an interview with Patricia Amphlett in 2017; the Sutherland
Australian tour is from interviews with Evelyn Knopfer.

Information was taken from an interview with Richard Leplastrier,
19.11.2017

Chapter 20   Millions and mullions

Information was taken from the Davis Hughes oral history, with
thanks to the Sydney Opera House for permission to publish.

The University of Newcastle citation on 24.5.1996, presenting
Sir Davis Hughes with his Doctorate of Education, provided
information, along with Hansard, the *Sydney Morning Herald*
throughout 1950, and the article 'The man who clashed with
Utzon' by Tony Stephens, *Sydney Morning Herald*, 26.3.2003.

The Bob Selby Wood information is from *Sydney Morning Herald*
letter writer George Aungle, with thanks.

Books

Building a Masterpiece: The Sydney Opera House, ed. Anne Watson,
    Powerhouse Publishing, 2006
*Letters from Sydney: The Sydney Opera House saga seen through the
    eyes of Utzon's chief assistant Mogens Prip-Buus*, Mogens Prip-
    Buus, Edition Bløndal, 2000

Chapter 21   High noon at the Chief Secretary's Building

The chapter heading references Utzon's obituary 'High noon at
    Bennelong Point', Elizabeth Farrelly, *Sydney Morning Herald*,
    1.12.2008.

The first paragraph is from the 1966 memories of *Sydney Morning
    Herald* reporters Craig McGregor and Gavin Souter. More
    information came from Prip-Buus' book.

The recreation of this scene is pieced together from visits to the
    building and extemporary reporting, most notably by *Daily Mirror*
    columnist Ron Saw, 8.3.1966.

While there is much dispute about the actual exchange, I have trusted
    accounts from both John Yeomans and Philip Drew's books.

Information was taken from copies of letters from the *Sydney Morning
    Herald* and Utzon archives and various interviews with John
    O'Hara.

The information about parliamentary proceedings outlines was taken
    from Hansard, March 1966 and about the march up Macquarie
    Street from interviews with John Weiley.

Tom McNeil's account was published in the *Sydney Morning Herald*
    on 5.3.1966 and referred to in various letters published in the
    Sydney Morning Herald. The information about the sign on the
    door comes from an account in Column 8 on 7.3.1966.

Books

*Letters from Sydney: The Sydney Opera House saga seen through the
    eyes of Utzon's chief assistant Mogens Prip-Buus*, Mogens Prip-
    Buus, Edition Bløndal, 2000
The Other Taj Mahal: What happened to the Sydney Opera House,
    John Yeomans, Longmans Australia, 1968
The Masterpiece: Jørn Utzon, a Secret Life, Philip Drew, Hardie
    Grant, 1999

Chapter 22   I am still available

The Ted Farmer information is from *The Dictionary of Biography* and the Government Architect's Office.

Information was taken from various *Sydney Morning Herald* reports by Walter Bunning, Gavin Souter, John O'Hara and George Molnar and from letters published on 16.3.1966.

Books

The Australian Dictionary of Biography, Australian National University, various years and online

Chapter 23   This chapter is over

The toy trade fair report was in the *Sydney Morning Herald* on 16.3.1966. The 19 March letter from Peter Hall was found in the Utzon Center in 2018.

Thanks to the estate of Ove Arup for permission to publish this letter, which was donated to the Utzon Center in January 2018.

Lin Utzon's recollections of her last days in Australia are from interviews in January 2018 and an interview when she returned to Copenhagen published in the *Daily Mirror*, March 1966.

The interview with Arup was in *The Bulletin*, April 1966.

The last day details are from Paul and John Witzig and an interview with Alex Popov in November 2017.

Books

Martin Sharp: His life and times, Joyce Morgan, Allen & Unwin, 2017.

Chapter 24   The divine spark departs

Information was taken from: an interview with John Weiley in 2016; letters from Utzon to Norm Ryan; Ralph Symonds' office; Sigfried Giedion; and an affidavit from the Seidler Archive, courtesy of Polly Seidler.

Richard Neutra supplied information that is kept in the Utzon Center in Aalborg.

The background to Hall is from various interviews with Helen Lo (nee Bryant), Libby's sister, in 2017.

The letter from W.C.L. Badge, the manager of Hancock Bros, was published in the *Financial Review* on 8.3.1966.

Books

Peter Hall Architect: The phantom of the Opera House, Peter Webber, Watermark Press, 2012

Reviewing the Performance: The design of the Sydney Opera House, Ken Woolley, Watermark Press, 2010

The Poisoned Chalice: Peter Hall and the Sydney Opera House, Anne Watson, opusSOH, 2017

Online resources

Finecraft models in the MAAS Powerhouse Museum, https://collection.maas.museum/object/211598

Chapter 25   SOS to London

The letter from Peter Hall to Jim Anderson is published thanks to the Peter Hall estate and Jim Anderson.

Information was taken from an Interview with Jim Anderson in 2017.

The Earnest Bean information is from the article 'Importance to us of Bean Ernest', Leslie Wilson, *Daily Telegraph*, 23.12.1966.

Information was taken from the article 'Behind the Scenes', John Keenan, *Courier Mail*, 17.3.2009 and from the 2013 documentary *Autopsy on A Dream*.

Online resources

Peter Luck interview with Utzon in 1973, https://artsandculture.google.com/asset/j%C3%B8rn-utzon-in-1973-interview-part-3/eQEJuBSzugLIXA

Chapter 26   New man at the Opera House

Information was taken from the article 'New man at the Opera House', *Sydney Morning Herald*, 18.2.1967 and from a letter to the editor by Bill Wheatland published later that week.

The Pringle information is from an interview with Penelope Hall in 2017.

The information on George Marr & Sons is from interviews with journalist David Marr and former sales manager Ron McEvoy.

Reports on the change of purpose of the halls come from various newspapers of 1966.

Books

The Sydney Opera House Affair, Michael Baume, Nelson, 1967

Chapter 27 Autopsy on a dream

Gough Whitlam's telegram and letter from Utzon to him are in the Utzon Center in Aalborg.

Francis Evers' obituary was in the *Irish Times*, 18.9.1996.

Articles about bringing Utzon back were published in the *Sydney Morning Herald.*

Information was taken during interviews with John Weiley and Jim Anderson in 2017, and from the article 'Destroyed film renewed for 40th', Tim Douglas, *The Australian,* 17.10.2013.

Books

Utzon and the Sydney Opera House: Statement in the public interest, Elias Duek-Cohen, Morgan Publications, 1967

Online resources

Autopsy resurrected, posted 31.10.2013, http://about.abc.net.au/2013/10/autopsy-resurrected/

Chapter 28 'Hall's Balls'

Information was taken from various interviews with Willy Hall, Becca Grey, Penelope Hall (nee McDonnell), Andrew Anderson and Jim Anderson in 2017 and from various newspaper reports on Hughes.

The information on the glass windows and lights known as 'Hall's Balls' is from the *Sydney Morning Herald* and from the 'Sydney Opera House Guide', State Archives & Records.

Chapter 29 Not a job for boys

Information was taken from reports in the *Daily Mirror, The Australian* and the *Sydney Morning Herald* in 1972.

The information about 'rump à la Rolf' was reported in the *Daily Mirror* by Norm Lipson in 1972 and about 'Spaghetti Caruso' by Janet Hawley in *The Australian.*

Information was taken from the Oliver Shaul obituary 'Summit pioneer fled persecution to reach the top of city dining', *Sydney Morning Herald,* 27.4.2010 and from an interview with John Olsen in 2017 at Tim Olsen's studio.

Online resources

Not a job for boys, ABC documentary 1973

Chapter 30 Opening daze
Information was taken from various reports in the *Daily Telegraph*
during 1973.
The opening day account is from interviews with Michael Leunig
in November 2017 and Lenore Nicklin in October 2017. Other
accounts of the opening day were given by various sources
including: Tony Stephens, Phil Cornford and Maria Prerauer; Ron
Saw's column in the *Daily Mirror*; various newspaper reports
from both the Fairfax and Australian Consolidated Press files; and
numerous letters sent to me containing opening day reminiscences.
Thanks to Richard Walsh for his first-hand account of the opening
from Kirribilli House.
The letter from Utzon to Askin is kept in the Sydney Opera House
archive.

Chapter 31 Rapprochement
Information was taken from interviews with Lene Borch and Anna
von Lozlow, makers of the *Utzon100* documentary by Nordisk
Film being released in October 2018.
This chapter was drawn together from interviews with various Utzon
family members, including grandson Mika, and with Paul Keating,
Bob Carr, Henry Hall, Becca Hall, Willy Hall, Richard Leplastrier,
Mogens Prip-Buus, Joe Skrzynski, Evan Williams, John Fink, John
Weiley, Polly Seidler, Anne Watson and Louise Herron over the
course of 2016-18.

Online resources
http://theoperahouseproject.com/

Coda/Cast of characters
The information about Bennelong came from various Aboriginal
sources, and about Denmark from the author's visits there in July
2017 and April 2018.

Index